EVOLVING ON PURPOSE

CO-CREATING WITH THE DIVINE

KATIE CAREY – AMBER BRIDEWELL
AMMA VENTELÄ – CELIA LOUISE – CHERISE GRESKI
DAVID KNIGHT – ERICA MARTIN – FIONA BLACK
GISELLE LORENA HURTADO –
JENNIFER ELIZABETH MOORE
JOS POUNE FAE –JULES IMPICCINI
KARL OLSON – KARLA KOPP
KATI LUDWIG – LALITHA DONATELLA RIBACK
LIDIA KULESHNYK – MICHELLE GRANT
SARAH BRIGID BROWN – STEPH DARMANIN
SUSANNE KURZ – TAMI ROACH

SOULFUL VALLEY PUBLISHING

Disclaimer

The publisher and the authors are providing this book on an "as is" basis and make no representations or warranties of any kind with respect to the book or its contents. The publisher and the authors disclaim all such representations and warranties of healthcare for a particular purpose. In addition, the publisher and the authors assume no responsibility for errors, inaccuracies, omissions, or any other consistencies herein.

The content of this book is for informational purposes only and is not intended to diagnose, treat, cure, or prevent any condition or disease. You understand that this book is not intended as a substitute for consultation with a licensed practitioner. Please consult with your own physician or healthcare specialist regarding the suggestions and recommendations made in this book. The use of this book implies your acceptance of this disclaimer.

The publisher and the authors make no guarantees concerning the level of success you may experience by following the advice and strategies contained in this book, and you accept the risk that results will differ for each individual. The testimonials and examples provided in this book show exceptional results which may not apply to the average reader and are not intended to represent or guarantee that you will achieve the same or similar results.

This is a work of creative nonfiction. The events portrayed have been done so to the best of each author's memory. While all the stories in this book are true, some names and identifying details have been changed to protect the privacy of the people involved.

FOREWORD

When I think of the magic, shifts, and even mountains that have been moved in order for you to hold this book in your hands today, it is mind-blowing!

I feel so honoured to be invited to write this foreword for many reasons. Katie Carey of Soulful Valley Publishing came into my world in 2020. Since then, I have had a front-row seat to watch her evolve on purpose, and what a journey it has been.

However, my own journey with the energies of *'Evolving on Purpose'* and *'Co-Creating with the Divine'* started long before my journey intersected with Katie's, and I became one of her mentors.

I have been a metaphysical teacher since 2000 and a law of attraction teacher since 2006. I teach metaphysical concepts, spiritual insights, and divine feminine energy alignment. I am an author, medium, and channel for a collective consciousness called Skylar.

Although back then, my life was improving bit by bit with some major roadblocks thrown in for good measure, it wasn't until I made a super solid decision to change my life that life really started to shift.

Please allow me to introduce myself. I am Joanna Hunter. I'm a mama of 3, plus a fabulous stepdaughter. I've been happily married for 26+ years, and I am a metaphysical teacher, and a spiritual life and business coach. I live in the magical Highlands of Scotland where I'm the founder of JoannaHunter.com and the Woo Woo Academy and am the proud owner of a nutty Jack Russell named Daisy.

I was born with my spiritual gifts firmly in the 'on' position, which led to not only a character-building childhood but also an awareness of the co-creative energies of the universe from an early age.

At the age of 23, I started my first business, by the age of 26 I had founded and created 4 separate 6-figure and multiple 6-figure companies from scratch, and I worked in them all, it didn't take long before the strain and pressure of working 72-hour weeks never taking holidays and constantly worried about business, family or a mix of them all took its toll.

Life as I knew it came to a screeching halt, in the form of being hospitalised with stress-induced multiple organ failure. I was told to write my letters to my young children and prepare my family for my passing. It was in that hospital bed, I realised that I had been living against my own spiritual nature and it was in that moment of need I turned inward and began once more co-creating with the divine determined to survive.

The recovery from multiple organ failure was complex and difficult, the road was long.

Just as I was getting back on my feet having sold all my businesses bar one in 2015, my family and I found ourselves homeless for a month, living with my mum in her cramped two-bedroom apartment. All six of us.

This was one of those major roadblocks, along with the multiple organ failure I mentioned earlier. There and then, surrounded by the chaos that was my life, I decided to 'Be My Own Rescue™.' This is where my own journey with evolving on purpose really started to take shape in miraculous ways.

Have you ever felt sick and tired of being so sick and tired? If that's a yes, then you'll know intimately the place I was in. I was so sick of being ill all the time. I was tired of having my light trapped inside me, feeling like I had the potential but never quite getting to it. Amid the chaos, hurt, and disappointment of life, I made a true and clear decision that this would not be the whole of my story.

Any journey of evolving on purpose and co-creating with

the divine has to start with a decision. A decision that you want more for yourself. A decision to change. A decision that your current reality will not be the whole of your story.

Scared that I would fail, terrified that my life would languish in mediocrity, and I would never know success, I went all in on myself. I showed up for myself like never before. I bet on myself. I invested in myself. I bought courses and spent hours reading and educating myself in healing myself and forging a better life, even when there was not one shred of evidence to back me up, I believed in myself. There were days it was hard and days where I felt like I was in a waking dream, but I stuck with being all in on myself, being my own rescue.

Within two years, I had retired my hubby from his day job, and in that same year, our eldest daughter also joined our company and quit her day job. I started to live my dreams out loud, bringing my message to the world and co-creating my reality with the Divine.

In 2021, I ran the world's largest metaphysical experiment which Katie joined. Using the commission payments that she earned from sharing that experiment with her friends, family, and clients, Katie was able to pay for her first entry into a multi-author book and became an Amazon best-selling author.

In that same year, my company made one million dollars in sales, a result of evolving on purpose and co-creating with the divine. Both Katie's life and my own life shifted before my very eyes.

Katie joined more of my programs and her determination always inspired me. You see, everyone has excuses for why they can't do something. When I started this journey in 2015, I had years of ill health and chronic illnesses and was in recovery from stress-induced multiple organ failure - and yes, I could have let all those valid reasons (excuses) stop me.

When Katie joined my world, she was registered as disabled and suffering from chronic illness. Due to the pandemic, her eBay business was falling apart around her. All those could have been valid reasons or excuses for Katie not getting off the starting blocks of life. However, she didn't let those things stop her.

As a direct result of our many interactions, Katie birthed her top-rated podcast and international publishing house. A world of opportunities opened and will continue to open for Katie and people like her that choose to take action and co-create with the Divine.

During one of my classes, Katie channelled the names and concepts of her first books. Those books have gone on to become Amazon best-sellers and have helped others create epicness in their own lives. She began channelling *Soulful Poems* and even created a best-selling poetry book. This is the ripple effect that happens when you choose to 'evolve on purpose' and 'co-create with the divine.'

I share all of this because I want you to see and understand the many intricately designed and moving parts that have had to come together and continue to come together so I could be writing this foreword in one of Katie's books. Now, I want you to think about all the transformations that have happened to the women in my world and the transformations that ripple out and happen to the people in Katie's world.

It can only be described as *magical,* and now I want you to appreciate that this is also open and available to you, dear reader!

The Magic.

The Co-creation.

The Evolution.

In your hands, you hold a masterpiece of magic. You can approach this magic in one of two ways:

1. You read this book like it's just a bunch of really nice chapters that may or may not connect with you somehow and you miss the magic entirely, or

2. You treat every chapter in this book like a quantum portal which has the potential to help you evolve on purpose and create the life of your wildest dreams, connect you to Source, and co-create with the Divine - a cosmic map, if you will.

My dream for you is that this book gives voice to the longings of your soul and lays out a road map to unfolding your light in this world. I hope that you feel inspired, uplifted, and open to the possibility that creating an amazing life is for *you,* too.

Joanna Hunter

Table of Contents

INTRODUCTION

I am delighted to bring to life the second book in the *Evolving on Purpose* series: *Co-creating with the Divine.* I have discovered that these book collaborations are certainly more than just the writing of a chapter in a book; they are a spiritual growth journey.

Since the series title *Evolving on Purpose* was channelled through me, I've been called to lead the way on the *Evolving on Purpose* path. My personal and business life has changed dramatically since the first *Evolving on Purpose* book.

If you read the first *Evolving on Purpose* book, you will recognise that several of the Authors have returned:

- *Sarah Brigid Brown* (who has written in all three of our collaborations)
- *Kati Ludwig*
- *Celia Louise,* and
- *Lidia Kuleshnyk*

INTRODUCTION

I've watched these authors all *Evolving on Purpose* since we first connected, and I am delighted to present their most recent chapters to you within the pages of this book.

And if you know me, *Katie Carey*, then you have probably heard me share that reading *David Knight's* books was the catalyst that started my own spiritual journey. David is one of the best-kept secrets in the world of spiritual authors, and I wanted to change that! I am deeply honoured that he has joined us in this collaboration.

Each author has written an incredible chapter – sharing vulnerably from various "chapters" of their own life story. I am so grateful for each and every one of them and for the support of our editor, *Angela Harders*, who co-authored and edited *Entangled No More*.

I know these chapters will light the way for you, giving yourself permission to be your true authentic Self. I know that this book will guide you to reconnect and tap into your own divinity and inspire you to *Co-create with the Divine,* whilst inspiring others and raising your frequency. There is some incredible wisdom in this book. So many coaching tips and healing tools, to help you on your healing journey. Feel free to share your thoughts and emotions about the book by leaving a review on Amazon. We would love to hear your feedback and how the book resonated with you. Your review will not only help others in their decision to read the book but also provide valuable insights for the authors and potential readers.

And now, dear reader, it is my honour to Co-create with *you.*

Katie Carey
Soulful Valley Publishing

AMBER BRIDEWELL

Finding the Light

I grew up way too fast. At 8 years old, I had to wake myself up, get ready for school on my own, and then make my way to the bus. Perhaps I wanted to portray that I was more mature than my age, or perhaps I just knew that if I missed the bus, then I would have to wake up my mother. I would have rather woken up a grizzly bear! Okay, maybe that was a tad dramatic, but in my 8-year-old eyes I felt if I showed my parents that I was mature and independent then they would somehow love me more and tell me how proud they were of me. Didn't quite work that way though. It seemed as though it was just expected of me.

I was an only child born in 1986 and raised by my mother with a lot of help from the babysitter and my mom's parents. My biological father wasn't in the picture. However, my mom married a man who adopted me at 9 years old. I didn't really understand what was happening, all I knew was that my last name changed. I was always led to believe that he was my biological father. You can imagine my surprise when at 14 years old, I was told by my mother that he wasn't my real dad, but he took on that role of "dad." Growing up I remembered big holidays and birthdays only because my grandmother had her VHS recording everything. But when I was home with my parents, I never remembered interacting with either of them much.

I always played alone because my parents would be locked in their own corners of the house dealing with things a child couldn't comprehend. Or if their friends came over, I was sent to my room. It was always a stressful vibe at home for me if I am being honest. My "dad" had PTSD from being in the Vietnam War and suffered from severe anxiety and bouts of depression. He was always on a different medication, and he swore Veterans Affair (VA) was trying to kill him. His reactions to loud noises around the house or outside would send him into fits of anger. My mother had her own addictions to pills. They both did a good job at hiding it.

My cousins were all much older than I and lived hours away, so I was always doted on by my maternal grandparents. My grandmotherr and I were like two peas in a pod. She graduated from the University of Kentucky with a bachelor's in secondary education in the 1940s. She loved music and playing the piano, so being a music teacher was right up her alley. She always told me, 'Amber, make sure you get your education, so you can be independent and not rely on a man to take care of you!'- My mom had more of a "find a man to take care of you" mentality.

I always competed in softball and cheerleading in school. None of my family ever came to my practices or games. My grandmother was elderly, it was hard on her to climb the bleachers without falling. My mom and dad? My dad said he couldn't handle the crowds. My mom just never made the effort, I can only assume it was because she was using.

Most of the time, my mom would forget to pick me up from practice or games. I'd always be the last kid standing there. "Can I give you a ride home?" my coach would ask. "Sure," I shrugged my shoulders and dragged my feet to his truck. I can't believe she forgot me - again! I had zero clue that both of my parents were struggling with addiction. I didn't get to have a lot of friends over because all the pre-teen girls laughing and squealing wreaked havoc on my dad's nerves. I remember wishing and praying to have a sibling, so I could have someone to talk to and so I wouldn't feel so alone.

At the young age of 14, I came home from school to find my dad's car packed with his belongings. "I'm moving out,

Amber. I'm heading back to Newport, so I guess I'll see you later."
As the front door slammed behind him, I stood there in
shock…completely alone. My mother wasn't even there, because
she was too busy hooking up with another man at my
grandmother's house.

2 weeks had passed before my mother came home. The
man my mother had started dating had just gotten out of a 12- year
prison sentence for burglary. He smoked weed and drank beer,
while my mom would pop her pain pills without being monitored.
My dad always kept the pills locked away in his safe and would
set out a daily pill count for my mother to abide by, so she wasn't
too messed up. But she would sneak and buy them on the side.

At 8 years old, I was in the passenger seat on her drug
quests- and it was quite the quest!! First, we would stop by
grandma's house, so she could get money to buy the drugs. I can't
even tell you how much of my grandparents' money that my mom
wasted on her pills. One time, my grandmother had to sell off 50
acres of land to someone. She got $160,000 for it. That money was
gone within a year. Next, we would go to the dope house. My mom
always made me wait in the car - even in the middle of summer
with 90-degree heat! The heat was bad, but the worst part was that
I couldn't understand why she would leave me behind. As a
teenager I understood that my mom was an addict, but as a
confused child cooking in a car, I couldn't understand.

EVOLVING ON PURPOSE

After my mom and my "dad" divorced, she got with the parolee. I went from being totally sheltered, not allowed to go anywhere, or have people over to my house, to throwing parties every day of the week. I would have all the beer and the weed that I wanted. My mom and the parolee partied with me and my friends. Drug use at 14 stunted my emotional and mental growth. I soon went from drinking and smoking pot to snorting pain pills. No one could tell me "No." Not only did I have no one to tell me no, but my own mother encouraged me. By the time I was a junior in high school, I was a full-blown junkie, so I dropped out. Thankfully I got my GED shortly after, only because my grandmother stayed on my ass about it (and I am so grateful she did) However, becoming an addict so young ripped away the last, most precious years that I could have had with my grandma.

Eventually, my mom got busted for doing drugs and was sentenced to almost 3 years in prison. My aunts decided to come and get my grandmother, so she moved two hours away. I was left all alone at 16, so my boyfriend's family took me in. The next time I saw my grandmother would be at her funeral two years later. It took me years to forgive my family for taking my grandmother away and leaving me behind. I always blamed myself because, well, I was the teenage addict, and they were the adults. Independence and self-sufficiency became my normal. When I turned 21, I met my children's father. To protect his identity, I will call him "Bob".was married at the time. I had been an addict for 6 years. I took my mother's advice and found men that would take care of not only me, but my mother, men that would feed both of our addictions. I always stayed in long term relationships for all the wrong reasons. I looked to others to provide stability for me instead of relying on myself. Hell, if I'm being honest, relying on myself was never an option for me. I had a bad self-sabotage complex. I would give up and quit before I even tried. I had no confidence in myself at all.

Looking back on my relationship with Bob, it was always off. The circumstances in which we were together in the first place were faulty. The foundation was weak from the beginning, but we continued to build together. He was 16 years older than me. Daddy issues much, Amber? I always held this man on a pedestal. He worked 6 days a week - sometimes 7 – to always provide financial stability for us. My mom had taught me that financial stability is the key to a successful relationship. Bob provided for me financially, but he would not provide for me emotionally. He was the type that held everything inside: every feeling, thought, and emotion. He would let everything bubble up inside of him until he would finally explode during an argument. He told me he loved me all the time. He would tell me a lot of things, but his actions never matched up with his words. He had confused lust with love, just as I confused money with love.

e both had our faults. I am a Pisces sun and a Cancer moon; I *need* to feel the emotions from my partner. I craved emotional connection as a child and as an adult - but my emotional needs were never met, therefore I never felt safe in any relationship.

EVOLVING ON PURPOSE

I always felt like I was asking for too much. My requests were unreasonable. My desires were unworthy. Nevertheless, I continued to stay. I made another mistake: I assumed that because Bob was a good father, that meant he was a good partner. I was delusional for years. I think we both were. The first six years of our relationship were a wild roller coaster. I was still using drugs and trying to hide my addiction as much as possible. He was still talking with and messing around with his wife while trying to hide it. We were both a mess. Our lack of emotional connection led to two different physical altercations. At age thirty, I got pregnant with our first child, and I knew I had to get clean. So, I moved to be close to my mom. She had moved to Maysville, Kentucky, which was the next county over and had been clean and sober for a few years. I remember feeling a renewed sense of self after moving. I had been given a clean slate, a fresh start, a new beginning somewhere new. I began to see the world through a wiser, brighter, and clearer lens. At that point, Bob and I had been broken up for maybe a month, but we started talking about trying to make it work since I was now pregnant. *I* made a promise to him that *I* would straighten up and get this relationship back on track (since the demise of the relationship was always *my* fault).

I spent 8 years proving myself to him, but nothing I did was ever enough. We both had severe trust issues with each other at that point, but we felt that we had to stay together since a baby was on the way.

On May 18, 2015, my mom's birthday, I was 8 weeks and 1 day. I was devastated, but I knew in my heart that there was a reason. Three months later, I found out that I was pregnant again, and her due date was May 18th, 2016. That was a huge sign from the Universe to me that this was all meant to be. On May 12, 2016, I gave birth to a tiny baby girl who weighed a whopping 4.4 pounds.

I suffered from severe postpartum depression and anxiety. I used to joke all the time that I was a single mom with financial stability, because he was always at work. Those old childhood wounds of feeling so alone had resurfaced. At the time, I was going to college and working towards getting my degree to become a Registered Nurse (RN). While I went to school, my mom would watch my girls for a few hours, and then when Bob would get home from work, he would take over kid duty until he went to bed. I always felt he held onto feelings of resentment towards me on that. It could have just been my own paranoid thoughts, sure, but Bob never asked me how I was doing in school, what my grades were, nothing. He just never seemed interested in my life unless it directly concerned him. A couple weeks before Christmas, my mom's boyfriend passed away unexpectedly. He had made such a positive impact on not only my life but on my girls' lives as well. I will always be grateful for the love he showed me and my children. After he passed, my mom and I were crying in the kitchen as Bob went on about his dad as if nothing had happened. I felt so hurt that he didn't even try to give me a hug or console me, but that's just the way Bob was ice cold.

We both had issues. I never worked through any of my own shit even after getting clean. I had abandonment issues, no confidence in myself, and was severely depressed. All of this was the perfect storm to cause a relapse. *If I use drugs to stay up longer, then maybe I can study more.* Boy, was I wrong! Instead, the drugs would cause me to be so distracted that I couldn't focus on my schoolwork. I would find myself scrolling through settings on my phone, looking up at the clock, and noticing that three hours have passed, when it felt like only 10 minutes.

On the first hit, I told myself, this must stop immediately. I knew that relapsing would not have a happy ending. I kept myself locked in the bathroom for hours while my kids watched their tablets. I was physically there, but I was checked out emotionally. I remember praying, *God, please help me out of this. I do not want to live this life while trying to raise my kids. How can I teach them to be responsible and to make good choices if i can't even do that?* And then surprise! I got pregnant with our 3rd child in March of 2021, while in the middle of a relapse that I hadn't pulled myself out of just yet. I can say that 2021 was the hardest year of my life. Bob and I both panicked about the relapse and pregnancy. He stayed hell-bent on me having an abortion. I would start getting major daily anxiety about an hour before he would get home. Every day he came home from work asking if I'd made the appointment, and if I hadn't, he would stand there and argue with me. Accusing me of planning this pregnancy, telling me the baby would come out deformed, anything to stress me out. I honestly went along with it because I thought he knew better than me. I had zero confidence in myself. This was a big decision.

I made two different abortion appointments, but both of those appointments were canceled due to situations out of my control. I knew then that this was fated. That's when I decided to have the baby no matter what. "You're not going to be able to take care of three kids!" he screamed at me. "Well, I'm having this baby whether you want to be a part of it or not! I'll do it with or without your help! Please let me go to rehab and get clean. I need to take care of my physical, mental, and emotional health." He shook his head, "No way! I can't take off from work to watch the girls. You're going to have to figure something else out." Again, I was on my own. No family. No friends. No support system at all. I had hit rock bottom with nowhere else to turn but to myself and towards God, the universe.

Please show me a way out of this. I prayed silently as tears streamed down my face. Within a few days of praying, I came across an app called Numerology. I downloaded it, and I started to learn what a life path number 9 meant for me. It was amazing the way it described my mind sets and tendencies, both positive and negative. Within that app, I read that if I could start practicing meditation, my life would change for the better. There was something else in me that told me to start documenting all of this.

So, I started journaling as well. It all just kind of flowed naturally thinking back on it.

The first time that I tried meditation, I was high on drugs. I tried to last just 5 minutes, and I would fail every time. Finally, after 7 months, I put the dope down and was finally able to meditate properly. Once I got the withdrawals out of my system, I really felt the benefits of meditation. I started noticing that I was able to navigate daily stressors with much more ease than before.

Every day, I would have a little more strength and patience with myself and my children. At this point, I was nearing the end of my pregnancy, and my relationship was headed even further down the drain since I got clean. I started seeing things that Bob was doing that I took as extreme disrespect and disloyalty. Our communication with one another was literally like the Twilight Zone. Funny thing is, it's the same way we've always communicated with each other, but as an addict, our poor communication seemed normal. By becoming much more self-aware through meditation coupled with a clear mind from getting clean, I started to become much more aware of our dysfunction. Any conversation between Bob and I was shrouded with confusion. If I was upset about something, Bob would play on my emotions. He would become all sweet and loving, then as soon as I started pouring myself into him, he would pull away again and retreat to the same old behaviors. This is my definition of breadcrumbing someone.

I couldn't deal with the emotional and mental abuse anymore after realizing it was so unhealthy for both of us. I pulled away from both Bob and my mother so that I could focus on myself. What do *I* want? What do *I* need?

"Bob, I am tired of being on this emotional rollercoaster with you. Our relationship is only getting worse, and I think it's time for us to separate." For the first time in my life, I managed to take a stand for my wants and needs. "I'm doing this for myself and our kids."

He had no reaction. No response. He said nothing for six weeks, then finally he gave me a handwritten letter with his response. He explained how he felt his age was a contributing factor on not wanting to have the baby. He never actually expressed anything new to me, it was just him repeating the same thing he had been saying for months, but at that point, I was done. In January 2022, I had my precious baby boy. The following month after everything calmed down from having a newborn enter the family, I told Bob that I was done, and we were over. Bob continued to stay in the family home during the next 4 weeks. The energy in our home was terrifying. Remember how I said Bob never showed any emotion? Those emotions and feelings bubbled up, and it became scary and uncomfortable. I could feel the rage every time he looked at me. I was sleeping in the kids' room with the baby and our middle child. Bob would make it a point to walk through my room to go to the kitchen. As he would walk by, he would glare at me with such deep hatred and anger. I felt like he was trying to intimidate me and to instill fear in me so that I wouldn't leave. That's when I started seeing Bob through a much different light than I had previously. If I would have a civil conversation with him, next thing I would know, Bob assumed that we were back together again. I would have to reiterate to him, "No, we are still separated," and then we would go off on a tangent, "Well, I don't understand why you're doing all of this! Why are you splitting the family up? You're doing this to be with someone else, aren't you?" I responded "Our separation is not about anyone else but me and you. I can't make you believe me, and I'm not going to keep wasting my time and energy explaining the same thing over and over to you."

He ended up moving in with my mother, which wasn't a surprise. They had stayed in close contact unbeknownst me for a long time throughout our relationship. So, then I had to deal with both Bob and my mother, trying to convince me to change my mind. I call it browbeating. No matter how many times I would tell the two of them "NO!", they would keep trying to get me to change my mind. There were so many things that came out over the course of the next 6 months after we separated. Bob had sent messages to his ex-wife telling her about how he wanted to hurt me so badly so that I could see how it feels. She would say, "Don't worry," she replied, "Amber will start using again and lose it all, and then you can take the kids." They don't know it, but all those awful things they said are what keeps me on track staying clean and sober.

For the first time in a long time, I was single and on my own. I told Bob that this was a journey I needed to take for me. I needed to prove to myself that I can be that independent woman like my grandmother tried telling me about. It was a time for me to work on myself and get to know my true self for the first time in my life.

Remember, I was an addict in a relationship from ages 14 through 30. I knew that I was valuable and worthy of anything I wanted in this life, so I began healing my inner child on my own through rituals, meditation, and journaling. I started pouring all the love I used to give to others so freely, and I began to pour love into myself. The truth is, we can't pour love into others if our own cup is empty.

Slowly but surely my negative self-talk started to fade away. I started practicing positive I AM affirmations, and within a few weeks, I realized the amazing benefits that affirmations can have on our thoughts and emotions. It's one of the quickest ways to build confidence within ourselves.

These last 15 years weren't a waste, but a valuable lesson that I needed to learn. Since leaving Bob 15 months ago, I have done very well for myself. I quit smoking, no drugs, or alcohol at all. I started focusing on my health, and through hard work and dedication, I was able to lose 106 pounds.

My mind is the clearest it's been in my life. I know I deserve to be respected and nurtured. And there will be no one to stop me from getting everything that life has to offer to me. I've learned to speak my truth and stand in my power – so can you!

It's time to shine!

About the Author

Amber Bridewell is an expert in learning life lessons the hard way. By making mistakes and falling forward, she has gained an immense amount of wisdom and knowledge that she has shared in this chapter, "Finding the Light."

With the odds stacked against her and no support system, she had to learn to be her own mother, daughter, sister, and friend. In doing so, she freed herself from the cycles of addictions and toxic relationships. She hit rock bottom, but that was the moment that she chose to take a chance at life: a death and rebirth for the ages. Through shadow work and meditation, Amber was able to heal her inner child by learning how to integrate her shadow to obtain inner peace and balance. Now, Amber helps women heal through building confidence and by making positive choices. By making small adjustments in their habits and their mental, physical, and spiritual health to come into alignment. Amber was able to switch from a negative mindset to a positive one with the help of I AM affirmations and speaking positively over her own life and the lives of others.

Amber is the Founder of Darkside of the Moon Healing where she gives guidance to the collective by divinatory means through tarot

cards and channeling. She is proof that addicts can change and live a productive, happy life without craving a substance to put into our bodies. We can effectively heal those past traumas and break through the proverbial glass ceilings that society has placed upon us so that we can all be the best version of ourselves.

Connect with Amber below:

- Facebook: www.facebook.com/Canttouchthisss86
- YouTube:

  www.youtube.com/@darksideofthemoonhealing
- TikTok: www.tiktok.com/@darksideofthemoonhealing

AMMA VENTELÄ

I am Light, I am Joy, I am Abundance

Finding and remembering your soul purpose is a lifelong process and the greatest gift you can receive. There are always new levels to discover, but fortunately, there are also stopping points where you can have a moment of understanding and processing. Discovering new aspects of your soul purpose ends the period of the quest at least for a moment and transfers you into the new space of implementation. The pieces of the jigsaw puzzle – once separated and in chaos – now form a new untouched landscape to explore.

EVOLVING ON PURPOSE

I'm now in a place where significant parts of my soul purpose have unfolded. It will be a totally new kind of journey from now on as the woman in me is not feeling lost and lonely anymore, but she has found the way to align herself with Source, the soul, and the loving helpers of Light.

I am Amma. It may sound funny to you, but I know that I am a fearless and peaceful intergalactic warrior. I came to visit the Earth tens of millions of years ago in order to help humans with energy lines and healing techniques, but I fell in love with this planet and its beauty – water, earth, air, and fire. I was not supposed to stay, and I first lived here as I was – the star being, but I wanted to feel the physical body, so I decided to incarnate as a human.

Now, as my current incarnation has started to get her memory back, I have to say that when choosing to have the human experience, I was not able to grasp the implications of the Earth experience: total amnesia, free will, feeling of separation, loss of inner power, and loss of connection to Source and to the loving beings of Light around me.

Not all incarnations have been this challenging. Sometimes I had the gift of being surrounded by those who already remembered, and the journey was easier. But often, like in this current incarnation, I was born into a family and a society with long and deep amnesia and disconnection from the spiritual world.

I share my story with you now so that you will remember yours quickly and easily and even with joy.

Deep Amnesia and Separation

My full name in this incarnation is Anne-Mari Ventelä. I have always been called Amma at home because my little brother didn't know how to pronounce my name. I was trained as a biologist, and now I am an adjunct professor of Aquatic Ecology at the University of Turku. For 20 years, I was one of the leading aquatic scientists in Finland. I have worked globally to save lakes and rivers. I am an author of more than forty scientific publications, and I have been a regular speaker in science conferences all over the world: in China, the United States, Australia, Mexico, Japan, and Europe. My last project was a collaboration with the Chinese Ministry of Water Resources, so I have visited China more than 30 times.

I was born in Finland to a family with a heavy religious history. The Finnish religious environment has been very monotonic. In the 1970s, almost all Finnish families were somehow linked to the Lutheran Church. My parents were from Northern Finland and had family roots in strict revival movements that emphasized sin and suffering. My first Sunday school, however, was Pentecostal, and my parents took me away when I started to preach to my baby little brother about Jesus when I was only 3 years old.

I understand now that I've always been connected to my angelic guides. I have heard them talking and guiding me all my life. I have muted myself for long periods, but the connection has

32

always been there. I just didn't have any connection to people with higher spiritual knowledge.

In 2009, I made a research trip to Seili Island where the Archipelago Sea Research Institute is located. The island has a dark history. There used to be a leprosy hospital where people were brought to be isolated from the outside world and, ultimately, to die. Once brought to the island, they could no longer leave. Many people were taken to the island to be disposed of – especially women. Not all of them had leprosy, and some lived on the island for decades.

I lived in a nice two-bedroom apartment in one of the old buildings. On the second night of the trip, I suddenly woke up to a child crying. My youngest child was two years old at the time, so for a moment, I thought I was at home, and she was crying. I opened my eyes and saw that there was a woman dressed in gray clothes standing at the door looking panicky with a crying little child in her arms.

I stared at them; the woman stared back. As the child cried, I could feel the horror that she felt. Suddenly, I woke up and turned the light on. Little by little, the woman and the child disappeared. I laid in bed with the lights on for the rest of the night, and I didn't tell anyone about this mysterious event.

I returned to the island again the following week. This time, the program included a guided tour that talked about the history of the island. The guide said that because many people had to live on the island for a long time, relationships between them started to form, and sometimes children were born. Illegitimate children were taken away from their parents and taken to a special building. One room, in particular, was used to lock up the broken-hearted mothers after their children had been taken away. The room was exactly the one that I had stayed in the previous week.

Even though my experience was real and true, I still struggled to understand and refused to tell anyone else about it. Following that supernatural experience, the spirit world left me alone for a few years.

In December 2012, my friends lured me to an evening where a local medium was present. I resisted because I knew that something was bound to happen. First, we would relax in a sauna, then we were going to enjoy dinner together, and at the end of the night, we would contact the spirit world.

Before going into the sauna, I realized that I had to get something from the car and went out. A short elderly woman was standing in the yard by the doorway covered in a cloud of smoke and the scent of strong cigarettes. I recognized the woman and the smell. It was my grandmother Tyyne, my father's mother. She died in the early 1990s, and she was short and always smelled of cigarettes.

I ran back inside and told the people that my dead grandma was standing outside. Grandmother Tyyne came again to me through a medium in the evening and talked to me for a long time. She also showed up two more times later at my house. I told my mom but not anyone else.

After this, I started to become more aware of the invisible world, especially my inner guidance, which consistently criticized my life and my choices loudly. I focused on my work and filled my life with all possible hullabaloo to distract myself from the "now" moment and my spiritual guides. I remember saying that I can't be alone without an audiobook or music in my ears because I can't stand the inner mumble of my head. This must be quite common, so perhaps you can relate to this too.

Time to Remember

2015 was the year of Divine intervention. I was living a hectic and busy life. I was working 10 to15-hour days as the head of the aquatic division in a research institute. In addition to my work, I was also raising 3 young children. Needless to say, I was burning my candle from both ends. I was surrounded by the energies of struggle and lack – lack of time, joy, support, and pleasure. I had a deep feeling that whatever I did or achieved was not enough. *I* was never enough.

In October, I hurt my knee and needed an operation. I had a long sick leave from my daily work at the Institute. My knee was in so much pain after the operation, so I took painkillers and slept the first month of my sick leave. It may be hard to believe, but I really did! I was physically and emotionally exhausted and could barely stay awake for longer than 30 minutes at a time. There was absolutely no way that I could continue like that. For the first time in decades, I was forced to be present in the now-moment. I hated the way that I avoided my feelings by working too much or filling my spare time with too many gym hours, always away from home. I needed to make a change.

During that time, my husband was really keen on family roots, and he was playing with My Heritage, an app that will help you to search for your ancestors. One Friday, he suggested that I search for my family roots too. During that first day, we found out that all first Swedish and Danish kings were my great grandparents. These royal ancestors went back to the time before Christianity – and were found not only in Scandinavia but also in other parts of Europe and even Asia. I found a group of ancestors (my great grandmothers and grandfathers) who later turned out to be my spiritual guides.

After learning of my heritage, the spiritual world started to approach me in many ways. I was led to places, where I was able to sense spirits around me, although I didn't know how to communicate with them – and, to be honest, I didn't even want to! Then another family member also started to see spirits in our house. I had a friend called Riitta who had a specific clairvoyant skill to sense low vibration energy by dowsing, and she was able to explain our experiences. The spirits in our house were negative earth-bound spirits who had not been able to go to Light yet. Riitta knew how to send the spirits to Light and clear the energies in our house. She cleared our home energy many times in 2016. I was still resistant and didn't really want to know too much about spirits.

Then one family member got cancer and another one had severe anxiety symptoms. Riitta advised me to seek help from the spiritual association she belonged to as they had some powerful healing methods. I contacted the head of the association, who then did energy healing to both family members.

The cancer patient received significant relief of his cancer symptoms several times. Once, his tumors had even disappeared when scanned in hospital. Also, the anxiety patient was healed so that there was no need for any medication, and she was able to continue normal life.

I was extremely grateful and finally gave up my resistance.

I should learn more about this myself. I signed up for an online course, and I immediately got back my clairvoyant skills, my ability to sense, count, and analyze the types of entities and the energies with the dowsing stick and to clear them. I started practicing so that another person could see the spirits with her third eye. I was sensing them with my stick, and the observations matched. It was easy for me as a scientist to adapt this modality as it was so logical and based on these double-checked observations. I remember being relieved that I would not have to be more woo woo.

I quickly further developed my skill of sending earth-bound spirits to Light, and in my work trips, I was often called to do some service work with that. I went to Hawaii, sat in my hotel room, and saw thousands of earth-bound spirits (even from distant history) that were coming and seeking the way to Light. I sat there for hours helping them and more and more just continued to enter my room. On another trip, I was staying on the 43rd floor in a hotel in Nanjing. I made a group healing for all earth-bound spirits in the city view below me and watched in awe as more than 30,000 spirits from WWII went to Light. In 2018, I was taken to places around Finland where the victims of the Finnish Civil War (1917-1918) became visible for me, and again, I sent thousands of them to Light.

Remembering My Spirit Team

In 2017, I made a work trip to Mexico, Yucatan, and I had a chance to visit the ancient Mayan city, Zizen Itza, and several other Mayan museums. That was a life-changing experience, as I remembered and knew that I had been there several times in my past lives. The Mexican energy opened my portal of remembering, and the next day, when I was doing my meditation in the hotel room, my great grandmother from 32 generations ago, a Viking queen named Thyra, appeared to me in meditation. She said, "Anne-Mari, it's time to remember who you are! You are the daughter of powerful healers and seers, and you have strong powers within. It's time to start using them." Thyra was one of my spirit guides.

I also learned to know my other guides. In 2018, a beautiful woman with long, brown hair just jumped into my meditation and said, "I'm Miriam. We'll start healing now."

I asked if I should take a reiki course, and she just laughed. "No! No need for a reiki course!"

Immediately, my hands became very warm, channeling her healing energy. Later, it has been confirmed by many events and people, that she actually carries the energy of Mother Mary.

One of the first Ascended Masters I recognized and remembered was Quan Yin. I started to cry when I first heard her name. She came very close to me, especially in China. In 2019, I made four trips there and connected with Quan Yin each time. I saw her name and figures daily in temples, museums, and even in the restaurant menus. I remembered that I knew her when she was incarnated on Earth, because we lived and worked together in China.

Although I was now connected to spirits and my own spirit team, I was not happy or in high vibration myself. I didn't have many spiritual people around me and my spiritual knowledge was very limited. However, in 2019, I was strongly guided to go and meet a Mayan astrologist, Päivi Kaskimäki.

I told her about my experience in Zizen Itza. She was able to see that I had past lives as a Mayan, and I had been planning and working with the Mayan calendar in my earlier incarnation. She also told me that science was not my future work, but she saw me channeling high vibrational galactic angel energies and singing to ley lines. The information blew my mind, because I had always imagined that water protection work would be my soul purpose.

However, I immediately felt that she got it right. I had another purpose to quest.

During the session, I saw something that took my breath away: Diana Cooper's Dragon oracle deck on her table. We didn't talk about it; I just saw it. I had never heard of Diana Cooper, so immediately after I came out of Päivi's house, I googled Diana and found her teachings about the archangels and dragons.

I have always felt the connection to angels and had a love for dragons. During my trips to China, I often asked about the dragons that seemed to be everywhere.

"Oh, dragons are just old legends," people would often share, but I knew intuitively that was not true. Somehow, I remembered – or perhaps, re-remembered – the truth about both angels and dragons. My mind and soul exploded with the joy of discovering the truth that I already knew.

Transformation

The connection to angels, Masters, and my other guides finally led me to the point where I was able to see myself, my life, and my circumstances without illusions or show. I was joyless, close to burn out, and far from excellency at my work. I was just barely surviving and performing my life. I was surrounded by suffocating scarcity energy.

My life was also strictly divided into "normal" and spiritual parts. I had my secret spiritual life with powerful experiences and a strong connection to my Spirit team, but the idea of telling someone else was horrifying. I was fully aware of the potential conflict there would be. The research institute where I worked was really non-spiritual and science based. I was totally blocked by the fear of visibility.

I started to feel more and more frustrated at my work. I found the Narnia of Young Living essential oils, and it was like a mental oxygen mask with new people, new ways of thinking, and a new way to talk about energy, vibration, and the power of nature. I didn't realize how these magic and miraculous oils started to raise my vibration and how their crystalline structure started to re-create my soul mandala. I began my own company Thyra&me Oy, thinking that it would be my vehicle to fulfill my dreams and even the highest soul contract – although I had no idea how it would happen.

After the pandemic started in 2020, everything that I had been able to cope with and persevere with in my working life was removed. The work trips with many social contacts ended both in Finland and internationally. I was doing administrative office work at home and was getting more and more frustrated. Also, the world around me began to change at an accelerating pace.

In 2020, I joined a longer spiritual course with focus on manifestation. I first started with very material requests (without too much success), but gradually I was guided to change the focus to the energies I desired. I felt my life needed more light, and I had no idea where my inner joy was hiding. I had lost my joy somewhere during my serious work years. As I had been fully surrounded by the energy of lack, I had a deep desire for the energy of abundance. So, my manifestation took a form:

I AM Light.
I AM Joy.
I AM Abundance.

At the same time, I really started to remember and connect with my soul mission, Lightwork. I began a constant manifestation of becoming a Lightworker. I had no idea how that could happen as I was very occupied and economically tied to my long-term work in the research institute.

In spring 2020, I took an International Lightworker course. It included all the basic steps needed to start a Lightwork business, and it also included the Angel Light Hypnosis modality, which felt easy and natural. The practice sessions opened a new world to me as I was really able to connect with angelic energies and guide these meditations successfully.

I continued manifesting, and in the fall of 2020, I got my first international healing customers. I struggled to make myself the first version of my web page. I had no budget to buy the service. Nevertheless, I started to become visible, but only to people outside of Finland. To be honest, I was terrified at the thought of someone in Finland learning of my new business.

What was I so afraid of? I was afraid of the collapse of my life scene at that time. I was a docent, head of a research group, in an organization where spirituality and all kinds of woo woo were laughed at in the coffee room. In fact, I had laughed along for 20 years, even when I myself thought otherwise. I was afraid of the judgmental reaction of my friends and my community. I was afraid of acting differently from everyone else around me.

Unbeknownst to my colleagues, I was already doing spiritual client sessions, and there, I experienced a new kind of joy and success. I started talking to the head of the Institute about wanting to leave the leading and administrative role – at least for a while. We agreed that I would be allowed to focus only on China work for a year beginning in February 2021.

In January 2021, I had a zoom session with my New Zealand client, and I completely lost my voice. We were surrounded by angels, and I knew there was a deep learning lesson involved. My guides said that I wouldn't be able to do both healing sessions and my normal day job. It was time to make some decisions. I later discovered that my astrological chart was perfectly in a position where this choice was inevitable.

I decided that I had to reduce my working time in the Institute and China project to 50% and devote the rest of my time to my own healing work for my own company. I had to share this plan at work with my work mates, so during one of our weekly team meetings, I blurted out, "I need to cut back on my hours and invest time in my own business." I couldn't avoid telling them at the same time about my spiritual awakening, my esoteric abilities, and there I broke free from the spiritual closet where I had been hiding.

At first, I continued my work only with the foreign clients. However, I felt strongly that I needed to become visible in Finland, as well. I started, surrounded by strong fears, with my Facebook friends, to whom I told what and who I had become. My guides gave me the right words and I was able to share my transformation story in a gentle and understandable way. I explained the story as I have told it here and received a lot of supportive and loving comments. I also received some hesitant and even judgemental comments, but it was surprisingly easy to stand in my truth in a loving way and let them have their opinions.

I opened a Finnish Facebook group, and I invited my Facebook friends to join it. At the beginning, my group had less than fifty members, but I was really surprised that so many joined. I started to do Facebook lives, where I just talked about my experiences. I also started to do lives with free angel oracle card and energy readings, where I picked up angel cards and clairvoyantly studied the energies of the participants. The number of participants grew quickly, and new people found my group.

In July 2021, I did the first Finnish courses, and a nice group of people came to them. I had found Joanna Hunter, and with her business guidance, I started to find my own way of doing this spiritual business. I also found Elysia Harzell's soul alignments that resonated completely with my own guidance. With their help,

I was able to work on money-related beliefs and energies in myself.

In the fall of 2021, I first channeled the Step into the Light course, then the Valossa (In Light) program. I received full spiritual downloads with all the details, and they became the core content of my work. I was able to raise my course prices significantly, and 32 people signed into my program. That was my first financial success! I became very empowered by this and decided to fully resign from the Institute. After 21 years of service, I was ready to set myself free.

Initiations and Miracles

Despite the empowerment and the first taste of success, the year 2022 did not start well. The war in Ukraine raised strong fears, which I had to face and battle. I struggled to earn the monthly income that I needed in the midst of challenging energies, and I again found myself working long days and nights. I was quickly going back to my old ways of struggle and battle. However, I received strong support and guidance from my spirit guides. I was guided to hire an assistant, who helped to expand my sales activities.

I was given several new courses as full downloads, and they formed The Academy of Joy and Light, which I launched in Spring 2022. I started to see the basic annual structure of my Lightwork, it was formed of two annual Valossa periods and shorter courses like *Askel valoon* (Step to Light) and *Rakkaus itseen* (Love yourself).

The first six-month period of the Valossa program was a real success, the participants experienced beautiful transformations, and the testimonials after the program were amazing. It was not difficult to make another successful launch of the next round of the program.

Despite all the progress and wins, I still had some initiations and learning lessons to face. After Lion's gate in August, I started to face some unexpected difficulties in finding customers for my short courses. In spite of all the difficulties, somehow, I felt the most powerful presence and guidance of my spirit team all the time.

I knew that the courses and content were exactly as they were meant to be, but almost nobody joined them. The situation didn't improve, and by October, I had to take out a loan to pay my assistant's salary and for family expenses, as I wasn't able to pay my own salary.

I promised my husband that I would look for another job if I couldn't get sales to grow in the next month either. I did not. I saw an open job position on LinkedIn which exactly suited my biologist training, and I decided to apply. I thought that I could keep another assistant running the company while I go to work elsewhere and get paid for it.

The job interview was a catastrophe! I was guided to the wrong place twice and found myself speaking so arrogantly and self-empowered that the condescending boss who was looking for a humble subordinate hated me. I knew I wouldn't get a place.

Then the miracles came. Numbers 12 and 21 had been following me for several years. I keep on seeing them, and in my "Angels - Amma" dictionary, they meant: "You are doing fine. Keep going! We are supporting you!"

In November 2022, in the middle of my financial struggle, I realized that there would be only two months left with these special number days with only 1 and 2 in the date. I started to celebrate them in my Facebook groups and soon noticed that they eally were special! I received significant downloads, course contents, and teachings every time there was a number day.

I also received an invitation to the newspaper interview with Ilta-Sanomat, the biggest tabloid in Finland. I almost refused because of the fear of such a huge visibility, but the guidance in my head was saying that it would be a reward, not a punishment. The interview was done, and the story came out at the beginning of December. The article received a lot of attention, and I had tens of messages and contacts from new clients.

But that was not all! I was also invited to do a YouTube live event on 12/12/22 with the famous Finnish astrologist, Seppo Tanhua. He wanted to do an astrological reading for me, especially from the context of my total career transformation. More than 1,000 people were watching.

We talked about me, my dramatic life events, and my astrological chart for over an hour. He explained that all the phases of my transformation were written in the stars and explained by my astrological chart. After we finished, my email was filled with messages and the booking calendar was fully booked for weeks. My Facebook group expanded from 400 to 1300 in the next two months.

I later understood that as I was sharing my awakening experience, there was some kind of collective code of remembering hidden. When I had sessions with those clients, they all had the same story: "I was listening to you for a while, and I just had a really strong intuitive feeling that I need to talk to you, that I know you already." And that really is true. I'm able to do the Akashic record readings, and we really have had past incarnations together, often Lemurian or Atlantis lives.

I received confirmation – also finally in the form of financial peace, as 41 people joined the third round of Valossa program in December 2021 – that this spiritual work is my soul mission and soul purpose. *Evolving on Purpose* has been an amazing journey, and I know it will continue to be so. I am learning and still having human struggles, but I am also fully supported and loved by the Universe – and so are *you*.

Now, in July 2023, I'm working as a full-time Lightworker. I have studied many kinds of amazing spiritual modalities, including angelic and crystal healing, but I'm now mostly using my own techniques, guided by my guides.

My business of Thyra&me Oy is growing quickly, and my assistant is working full-time for me now. In addition to Finnish

Facebook group, I also have an English-Finnish Facebook group called "Healing Us, Healing Earth" where I'm channeling a weekly free bilingual service meditation, which is about filling one's own energy reserves with Source Light and sending it to the Ley lines and humans in need. We are connecting the ley lines by singing. That's an old Lemurian way. My Finnish Facegroup group "Iloon ja valoon" has now over 2000 members, and that number is quickly increasing. I'm committed to further develop and implement The Academy of Joy and Light. The content of my courses is all about I AM Light, I AM Joy, I AM Abundance.

I know there will be much more as I further evolve in my purpose, but right now I'm happy to be and stay here, every day co-creating with the Divine. The most important finding on this journey is that I'm exactly where I'm supposed to be, and nothing could make me happier than all this that I have now.

About the Author

Amma Ventelä is a channel of the Divine galactic energies, an intuitive psychic, and spiritual healer living in Finland. She is the CEO of her fast-growing spiritual business Thyra&Me Oy, named after Viking Queen Thyra who is one of her spirit guides and her real life great grandmother from 32 generations ago.

She has a PhD in ecology, and for 25 years she was fully devoted to an international aquatic science career. In the 2010's, she experienced a transformational spiritual awakening which has turned her from a work-oriented, stressed out, joyless woman, to a happy, inspired, and enthusiastic queen of woo woo energy.

Amma has received full downloads of spiritual courses and programs since 2021. The academy of Joy and Light has already more than 200 students and both her personal mentoring and the group sessions with clairvoyant energy healing are currently very popular.

She is now remembering the Lemurian way of connecting with ley lines and healing them by singing and chanting. She has a weekly service meditation for this on Facebook, and people are joining the public live event from different parts of the world. She is offering both group and 1:1 sessions for healing and coaching.

Connect with Amma below:

www.ammaventela.com

CELIA LOUISE

Enchanted by the Divine

Simple Joys that Enchant

B ring to mind the simple joys you have experienced. My mind rushes back to my childhood: the freedom I felt when I was on my bicycle, the exhilaration of jumping into a cold lake under the hot summer sun, the excitement of seeing how high we could get on the old fashioned rope swings in the playground, the anticipation of hanging over the neighbour's fence, talking and giggling with my friends, enjoying the stretch on our backs after sitting in school all day.

EVOLVING ON PURPOSE

My heart soars when nature speaks to me in the beauty of a place I am visiting. When I am near the ocean, I am infused by the scent of the saltwater - the air feels more alive to me here than anywhere else. Walking along a beach is a beautiful way to take a meditative walk, to listen to your heart, and to experience one of life's rhythms in the waves crashing on the shore. Forests, with their soft, rambling paths under a canopy of majestic trees, envelop me in a safe, warm embrace that feels like home. A light breeze on my skin gives me goosebumps. A wild wind followed by lightning excites every cell in my body. Anticipating the roar of thunder that follows the lightning, and then feeling it vibrate under my feet is thrilling!

I love to be soaked in the rain, allowing mother nature to shower me unexpectedly. While living in a remote community in Timor, the local children would grab their soap every time the rain fell. With no access to running water, they knew the joy of showers in nature. The giggles, the smiles, and the feeling of being so clean after the long, hot dry season was infectious! To walk in a coastal mist is a magical experience of gentle droplets of water on the skin, a fog so thick you cannot see more than a few feet in front of you!

The night sky filled with stars brings me to tears. The full moon pulls me out of bed to witness its beauty and whispers to me the truth that we are all divine beings of nature. Have you experienced the northern lights dancing across the sky above you?

It looks like Mother Nature invited angels to help her put on a show to remind us of the mystery and the beauty that we live in.

As a child, I was fascinated and surprised by my experiences with the outdoor world. Summer always included sleeping in the screened-in porch in our backyard. Once it was dark, I would dance with fireflies for as long as I could stay awake. I will never forget how seeing them filled me with wonder. It is why I fill my house with fairy lights, so I can continue to delight myself with this memory.

Have you seen the ocean glow at night? When I worked in Aceh, my colleagues and I went swimming in the ocean one dark, hot night and were surrounded by sea sparkle! It is bioluminescence that creates this magical experience. It was like swimming with the fireflies of my youth. With every stroke from my arm as I glided through the water, the ocean lit up around me. I am still enchanted by the memory of the twinkling and glowing of this night. Later, sitting on the beach, we could see this glow when waves broke on the shore.

Consider: Do we need more therapy for our mental health, or do we need more enchantment and reconnection to our own divinity? I am advocating for the latter. When we don't feel a deep sense of the meaning of life, we distract ourselves with shopping, alcohol, drugs, or sex in the hope of creating happiness, but instead we end up numbing the inner call that we don't understand. Our inner-standing changes our outer-standing. The way that we experience ourselves, our circumstances, our world. Allow yourself space for inner joy to grow. Like Michelangelo said about his carving of David, "David was always in the stone, I simply took away everything that wasn't him." When we remove all the beliefs that do not belong to us, we reveal our true divine self, allowing ourselves to feel the most alive, the most enchanted, in this mystery of life.

The Heart of Enchantment

For years, I felt that something was missing from my life. During this period, I would never have imagined that what I was experiencing was a lack of spiritual connection. After years of being mad at the very idea of Divinity for what I saw as injustices that never should occur, I resisted this all the way. But the Divine has a way of insisting we pay attention, and I began to notice experiences that shifted my inner-standing of the universe and the perception that I held of my role within it.

At church and home, I was conditioned to be separate from love. Love was something to be given or to be taken away depending on how I behaved. Good behaviour would allow me to receive love from God or my parents. Fear created this separation, and I experienced the hurt and anger in the world in ways that felt unbearable some days because I had disconnected from my source of Divinity. Some of us were raised to fear the Divine (as I was), some to not believe in the Divine, many of us to misunderstand the

Divine, while others have tried to describe it through stories, poetry, and art. I believed my heart's purpose was to give love to others and to receive romantic and familial love. I could not begin to ponder the depths of my heart's deepest desire - to connect to the Divinity within me. When I released this misunderstanding, the Divine began to enchant me. I could feel the truth of the Divine mystery of life; that we are love, we come from love, and we return to love.

Divinity is a sensation of deep love and wisdom that you become aware of. It is not an intellectual knowledge, but rather is a feeling of reverence for life that permeates you. Your heart is the essential bridge between you and the Divine. We have learned to look to others for love, but the truth is that love is who you are. When you place your hands on your heart, you are giving your soul the message that you are paying attention to it. The touch of your hands on your heart releases oxytocin, the "feel good" hormone of love, then your nervous system begins to relax, and your mind begins to quiet.

Divine love is more an energy than an emotion: it is the most healing, transformative, and creative energy in the universe. The human heart is a source of intelligence that signals the brain and body and produces a powerful electromagnetic field imprinted by your emotions. In fetal development, the heart forms and starts beating before the brain begins to develop. Opening and healing your heart is your way back to this transformative energy.

EVOLVING ON PURPOSE

Your heart sends more messages to your brain than your brain sends to your heart. It produces the strongest electrical and magnetic fields in your body. In fact, the heart's magnetic field is up to 5,000 times stronger than the brain. A heart has 40,000 neurons that can sense, feel, learn, and remember independently of the brain. These neurons form your heart brain which communicates with and has an influence on your cranial brain. Scientists only made this discovery in 1991, publishing the results of their studies in 1994. Prior to this, it was believed that only the brain sent information to the heart. With this expanded understanding of your heart, reconsider what love means to you.

As I began to release the walls I had built up in my heart, I came to understand the greater love and wisdom that is in us and all around us. Our love for ourselves and for others is infinite, and we each can access this Divine love. When I first heard the term "surrender," I didn't understand it. It isn't the word that evokes the divine to me. The word that does is love. I was enchanted by the infinite, exquisite feeling of inner joy that Divine love is. I know the walls I had built up around my heart kept me from understanding this. The beliefs I held about the world held me away from this truth. I believed that the Divine was outside of me. I believed that nature was outside of me. And then enchantment began to work its delightful spell over me when I was in water, under trees, watching the sky and the Northern Lights. I came to understand and feel safe in knowing that the Divine is in each of us and that we are part of nature. Whether I am walking along the city street enjoying the gardens and the creativity of the gardener, or along a path where the forest meets the ocean, or underneath the northern lights beside a prairie lake, each of these experiences reminds me that we are a tiny particle in something so much grander than we know.

Rhythms are the hum of the universe: the seasons, the tide, the sunrise, and the moon. We can maintain our personal rhythm by becoming enchanted with our own breath. The spirit of life is a sea of love and wisdom that we are surrounded by. This spirit of life is in us and is also what we breathe. Do not take your breath for granted. When I accepted this animating principle that gives life to and influences everything as my truth, my life immediately felt more enchanted. I was no longer outside of the spirit of life; I was the spirit of life. I was free of the label from the school of "consumer." I was also free of the label from the church of "sinner."

When I forget this, I miss out on the beauty of life, and I bury myself under the minutiae of daily tasks I assume I need to do: watching the news, getting angry at all the injustices, and wasting my precious time in conversation about the behaviour of others instead of improving my own behaviour. I could invest my time in creating a magical life rather than complaining about the life I have.

Making the shift from "life happens to me" to "I am the co-creator of my life" was what allowed me to open to the Divinity that we each have within us. Our hearts are the home to our souls, the infinite part of us that never dies. This is our connection to the greater life we are meant to be participating in. We are as much a part of Divinity, as Divinity is a part of us. We are co-creators in life. What we say and do to others, we therefore say and do to ourselves, both the good and bad. Bad is simply the absence of good, and when we embrace our true Divinity, our good grows and our bad shrinks.

Many people are enchanted by nature or animals but refuse to be enchanted by humans or the human experience. The truth is there is no separation. We are each a part of nature – not apart from nature. When you allow the Divine nature of your soul to enchant you, then you no longer take the world for granted. The reality behind the appearance envelops you in a warm embrace, and suddenly, you are open to receiving the love and wisdom that life has been offering you all along.

Allow yourself to be astonished by the nature of your own existence and allow the flood of wisdom to flow through you. This is the creative power of life. Here you begin to co-create with the Divine. Awaken to your true self as Divine creative energy. Feel the truth of your Divinity and the Divinity of others too.

Prejudice and judgement block your instincts and your intuition. Love is effortless while hate requires a lot of effort. I am grateful that my parents taught me the importance of caring about and connecting with other people from all walks of life. Curiosity about others leads you on enchanting voyages, real or through books, exploring life through the eyes of another. This is the opportunity to reveal the love we each hold inside our hearts. Allowing yourself to be enchanted by the Divine is an exquisite experience. A spark of the Divine may feel like joy washing over you, even for a brief moment. Be grateful for this, talk about it, and recall this spark often. Awaken to the mysterious Source of you.

Connecting To Enchantment

Divinity in life is a sensory experience. Observe the Divine in nature - the sights, sounds, smells, and touch of it. Explore your experience of the Divinity of life coming through pleasing music, delicious food, exquisite art. Feel the Divine in the hugs of friends and family, and especially in looking in the eyes of whoever you are with. Witness the Divine in everyone.

I am being inextricably drawn, pulled by a force stronger than me that I feel through all my senses as Divine love. The further I allow myself to receive this love, the more inner joy I experience. Some days it feels like a bubble machine or champagne bottle is inside of me, bubbling over, tickling my insides, and filling me with joy. Other days I react with the emotions of frustration, hurt or anger and these fear-based emotions remove me from Divine love, forgetting so easily that I have the choice to direct my thoughts back to love. In hindsight, I see the blocks I created.

In Sanskrit, there is a term, *Indriya*, describing the senses as the companions of the Divine. Enjoy your senses as gifts of the Divine for you to delight in life. They are to be celebrated. We are meant to live with deep inner joy in life, and our senses are how we experience this. Cultivate and savour every touch, taste, scent, sound, and sight that you love. I like to think of this as enchanting the Divine. Find little things each day to move you from ordinary into extraordinary. Enchantment is the Divinity of our life; it is our birthright and our legacy. To experience Divinity is to be enchanted. To experience enchantment is to be Divine. Will you join me here?

Engaging your senses ignites your imagination and your imagination is your greatest gift. Think of how a movie or book takes you to a place and fills your imagination with joy, with fear, or with laughter. It's your imagination that fuels your desires and propels you forward. Try it: close your eyes, place your hands on your heart, and bring to your imagination the thing you want the most right now. Here's the truth that the masters have been sharing for centuries: in order to co-create with the Divine, you need to become curious enough about yourself to allow your heart to speak and then hold your heart's desire firmly in your imagination.

When you courageously move toward the Divine, the Divine moves towards you. You are enchanting the Divine, while the Divine is enchanting you and when you pay attention to the signs and the synchronicities, you will walk directly into your desired life. This doesn't happen sitting on the couch and daydreaming. It happens by holding your desires and courageously co-creating them with the Divine. Invest your imagination into your desires not your worries or your annoyances.

Inviting Enchantment

Invite the Divine to you daily by walking in beautiful places, meditating, or enjoying candlelight. Create your own rituals of inner joy. Close your eyes and imagine the feeling of being washed over by the warm, loving embrace of the Divine. Invite the Divine in and ask for guidance for your day every morning. What would Divine love have me do today? Create and celebrate your life. Write yourself a love letter from the Divine describing the exact life you desire. It is all within you. Your imagination is wisdom and love and is the creative energy of your desire. Desire to be a student of the spirit of life.

I invite you to join me in being enchanted with life. I was enticed here by curiosity about the mystery of our life and a very fleeting sense of Divinity. I took the scenic route here. Like a scrappy barn kitten that refuses to be caught but is also curious, I was skittish and hung out on the outside of the Divine aspect of our life until it made sense to me.

I had to unlearn what I had been taught and release judgement of the mysteries of life I did not understand. Millions of people throughout the centuries have been taught that Divinity is outside of us, but that is not true. Your part is to be curious, courageous, and connected to this Divine energy. You are a spiritual being having a human experience here on earth. This is a beautiful framework for living a life that you love.

As I embraced enchantment, I was led deep into the meaning of life. I embarked on an exploration of life from a feeling of love, rather than the feelings of fear and anger that I had embraced during my years working in the humanitarian field in conflict and post conflict zones.

Although I was witness to the very worst of unconscious human behaviour at work, I also saw amazing examples of human resilience, kindness and love in the people who had experienced the worst atrocities. This kept hope alive in my heart, and the glimpse of a side of the human spirit I had forgotten.

I slowly gave myself permission to change my perception and rediscover that we are swimming in a Divine Sea of love and wisdom. This warm embrace of Divine love and wisdom was strong when I was a very young girl, dancing outside with the fireflies or playing make believe games with my dolls.

I experienced life through the senses, and I was curious about and delighted by everything. The deep inner joy we each desire to rekindle is the bubbly feeling that we see in young children as they explore the world that they have arrived in.

I saw this very same delight of being alive and curious in my daughter in her early years and did everything I could to extend her time being enchanted by life, creating magical experiences in the garden, walks in nature, and during story telling time. Now I am grateful to play in this energy with my young granddaughters, and for a third time in my life, I am reminded that the inner joy of a child is so alive, so true, and so Divine. Inner joy is our natural emotional state that gets covered up by the beliefs and emotions we absorb, learn, and hold onto in life. That inner nudge you feel, listen to it; it's your Divine inner joy begging for you to uncover it!

How to Co-Create with the Divine:

1. Be CURIOUS. Explore your perceptions and where you might want to explore a renewed understanding of your life experiences.

2. Be COURAGEOUS. Listen to your heart, appreciating that you are a part of something so much bigger than you know.

3. Be CONNECTED. As Rumi so wisely said, "Stop acting so small; you are the universe in ecstatic motion."

With a brain in our heart, and stardust in our body, we don't need magic, we are magical. Every atom of oxygen in our lungs, carbon in our muscles, calcium in our bones, and iron in our blood was created inside a star before our earth was born. My invitation to you as the co-creator of your life is to make each day a masterpiece.

About the Author

Celia Louise is excited to return to Soulful Valley's Evolving on Purpose series in "Co-Creating with the Divine." Celia wrote the chapter "Acknowledging Your Instincts" in the first edition of the Evolving on Purpose series, the international best-selling "Mindful Ancestors Paving the Way for Future Generations," published in 2021. This chapter led Celia to write her first solo author book, The Champagne Chakra: Seven Steps to Elevate Your Energetic Frequency, published in May 2022, as well as the Champagne Chakra Guided Journal Series.

Celia's mission is to help her readers reconnect with their instincts, intuition, and inner joy through her writing, energy healing, and coaching. Celia loves to share the practices that radically reset her energy and joy when she felt a deep ache inside her heart that told her something was missing in her life. She was very surprised to learn it was her connection to the Divine that was missing!

Since her days of teaching others to farm organically, in Canada, California, and Indonesia, Celia has been fascinated with the idea that we live in a connected energy field. Her second career focused on international peace, human rights, and humanitarian aid in the conflict and post-conflict zones of El Salvador, Indonesia, Pakistan, and Rwanda, teaching her the truth of human resilience. She has owned two art studios, one in Manitoba, and one on Vancouver Island, because the world is always better with a little art to play with. She shares her best practices so you can live and love your best life and embrace co-creating with the Divine too!

Celia's curiosity about life has led her studies to a Diploma in Agriculture, a Master's Degree in Human Security and Peacebuilding, and Certifications in HeartMath, Brain Story, The Emotion Code, Tantra, Yoga, Reiki, Instinctive Meditation, and Conscious Reading.

XO
Celia

Connect with Celia below:

www.celialouise.com

CHERISE GRESKI

A Journey with the Divine Starts in the Dark

As I held her hand tightly, she took her last breath. As I took my next breath, tears streamed down my face.

"Mom's dead!" I screamed in my head. My heart broke even though her death was something that we had been expecting for a few weeks.

When I was only seven years old, I made a promise to my mom that I would care for her until her last breath. Now, at 60 years old, I had kept my promise. My mom had been in at-home hospice for the past nine months. I chose to take care of her in my home, which proved to be the most challenging, loving, and growth-filled experience of my life.

When I made that promise, all those years ago, we were facing the possibility of her father, my grandpa, dying in the hospital or in a nursing home from liver failure.

"Promise not to put me in a home, Cherise. Promise not to leave me." I recalled those words so well right then, as she took her last breath. Thankfully, Grandpa pulled through and lived for another dozen years. Yet, those words and that promise were always in the back of my mind – for almost 55 years.

Quietly, I said to her, "Mom, I honored your wish. I did all that I agreed to all those years ago. I love you so much. I will miss you so much. It will be like a magic carpet ride. The angels will be there. Grandpa and Aunt Mandy are waiting for you. You're going home now, mom. You're going home."

My mother left the hospital on New Year's Eve 2022. Every single week, she'd ask me, "What is my prognosis?"

Each week, I'd reply with a shrug, "I'm sorry, mom. I don't know." I wanted to comfort her, reassure her, but I couldn't. I had an idea that she was dying of cancer. However, I could not be certain since she refused any medical tests. Medical procedures of any type frightened her. In the past, she had procedures that left her in pain for a long time. While those procedures were not around cancer, they had left her in pain and depressed for a long time afterwards. I had prayed and had received guidance that my intuition was accurate. Cancer is such a scary word, and I did not want to bring it up. I knew that even saying the word would not change her attitude. She had seen too many suffer through cancer treatments and the debilitating effects on the person and their family. The doctor had come to a similar conclusion. Yet, he could not confirm without tests.

What if I tell her, and she just gives up and dies even sooner? What if, in the sharing, I influence the outcome? A part of me was very aware and clear that I could not actually do that, her soul was in charge – not me. Yet, it is a very human idea that we have so much control over the lives of those around us. In fact, I balked at revealing what the Divine was telling me.

Each time she asked me what her prognosis was, I grieved. Experts call it 'anticipatory' grief – the feeling that you know you *will* have when the person you love will die in the near future. Anticipatory? Ha! Grief is just GRIEF, and it all hurts like hell. However, there is grace in this process of grieving.

Grief is normal, natural, and something to be embraced as it unfolds in our lives. Grief is the Divine's reminder that this physical life is transitory, that we each need to daily commit to experience the moments, not the memories.

While in the hospital, my mom had made a clear and definitive statement: "I want comfort, and I want to go home to my baby girl." She had refused any tests, any treatment beyond comfort care. She died without ever knowing her true cause of death - which meant that I would never know either. It was so difficult to be unable to give her a more complete answer. Yet, through it all, the Divine was at work in our lives.

Each day, I tried to be present with her and with her soul, allowing that 'anticipatory grief' to quietly guide me in the now. Thankfully, the first few months were 'easy' in that she was aware, awake, and could do many things even though she was in a lot of pain. She worried that she would never go to the casino again. My partner, Chuck, somehow figured out how to get her in the car with the least amount of pain. We took her to the casino several times while she was in hospice. She even won a several thousand dollar jackpot the final time she played!

She missed her daily shopping trips as well. Again, the Divine stepped in and inspired Chuck to create different contraptions to get her into the car, get her through the store, and allow her to shop until the pain overwhelmed her. Truly, she exemplified the term "shop til you drop"!

However, one of her favorite trips was to cemeteries. She had always admired their peace and their beauty, and she would ask me every month to visit a cemetery. Now, I found this a bit morbid to go so often. Yet, Chuck humored her all the time.

If I ever doubted that the Divine is with us, creates with us, and watches over us, then our experiences at the cemetery, eating ice cream, and my telling her stories that going to the other side will be like a magic carpet ride would have convinced me beyond doubt.

EVOLVING ON PURPOSE

About six months before that fateful trip to the ER on Christmas Eve 2021, mom had started to get very agitated about getting her affairs in order – especially about where she'd be laid to rest. She loved – really loved – cemeteries. This conversation had been an on again, off again discussion for the past 38 years. I never really wanted to have the discussion. Really, what 22-year-old wants to start talking about burying their mother? I certainly didn't.

Why was it 38 years of talk?

When my grandfather died in 1984, my parents had been divorced for over 15 years. My grandparents lived with us. My grandmother bought two crypts for her and my grandpa. Mom had asked grandma to buy a crypt for her so that she wouldn't be alone. Due to my grandmother's mental state (bi-polar), she agreed and then refused. My mom was devastated and felt abandoned all over again. When grandma died in 1995, all crypts had been sold, and so there was no way that my mom could be laid to rest with them.

Sadly, this situation had been a continual wound ever since my grandpa's death. Her own feelings of abandonment as a child by my grandmother, being sexually abused, and an abusive husband did nothing to give her a sense of safety or security during her lifetime.

At a very young age, I stepped into the 'mother' role in our relationship. In fact, it was a running joke between family and friends, that *I* was the mother all along.

While my mom had expressed that she wanted to be buried with her parents, truth be told, she secretly wanted to be buried with me. Between my grandfather's and grandmother's deaths, I got married. While she never said it directly to me, her words and actions showed that by getting married, I had ultimately abandoned her as well. Her natural assumption was that I would want to be buried with my husband.

My husband, a Vietnam veteran, died in 2008. It was a sudden, dramatic death – one minute I was talking to him on the phone, but just five minutes later, his work called to tell me to come to the ER as soon as possible. (The Divine had a strong hand in this set of circumstances… a story for another day.)

Since my husband's death was so unexpected, we hadn't made any plans about dying or death. We had talked about it often enough because of the fifteen-year age difference between us. But, no, we didn't have plots or specifics about anything. Yet, I knew and even said – "I am going to *feel* everything. I don't care what other people think or say if I 'lose' it and cry in the grocery store." My mother was NOT thrilled with my choice that I would feel it all, in the moment. She believed that feelings should be addressed in a more private way.

I had decided to keep his ashes until I found the "perfect" cemetery. Oddly, I had a choice of three cemeteries within 2 miles of the house. And, yet I couldn't bring myself to pick one. A dozen years later, I still had his urn at home. I was waiting for the right time, the right place. I found comfort in having his ashes at home.

During the 12th year after his death, mom, Chuck, and I stopped at the Abraham Lincoln National Cemetery in Illinois. Mom adored Abraham Lincoln, and she loved the cemetery. Walking around, she wistfully commented how she'd love to be buried there. Since it was a national veterans cemetery, only veterans and their spouses could be buried there. Sighing, I said, "Mom, I know I can be buried here, but I don't believe you can. And I know that you don't want to be buried alone." She slowly walked away, recognizing the facts of the situation.

Now, while I knew it was beyond time to lay my husband's ashes to rest, I am both very practical and spiritual about death. I have always subscribed to the belief that the body is just a container for my soul. I really didn't have a preference for what would happen to my remains.

My belief system is that I trust Spirit, so it doesn't matter what happens to my body when I'm dead. I know that I am Spirit, and I don't need a stone or a plot to be remembered. I live my life in such a way that I either leave my mark on the hearts of those I've interacted with, or I don't. Remembering me will be a perpetual thing and not something someone has to go and view in a cemetery.

At that moment, though, I was so very sad. I was grieving all over again for my husband, and for what I couldn't do for my mother. I wanted to comfort her, assure her that she would not be alone. But how could I do that in this very final decision?

At just that moment, in a quiet whisper on the wind, I felt my husband call me by his nickname for me, "Sveetie, it's ok. I want to be here, and I am not – and I will not be – alone. It really is okay to put my ashes here. You don't have to be here with me. We are always together anyway. I love you." I knew it was him because I heard the odd way my name was called. He always used a 'v' in the word. His way of telling me he loved me *very* much.

So comforting and loving, wise and kind. The Creator knew what was in my heart to be close to my husband even in death. My husband gave me one of his greatest gifts: peace.

That was 2019, and time marched on – especially for those things we don't really want to think about. How quickly we forget!

Back to July 2022…

Mom's anxiety about where she was going to be buried was getting stronger. Now, at this time, there was no indication that her death was imminent. She was older, true. She had aches and pains, and she was starting to slow down. Yet nothing could have prepared us for the year ahead.

Her burial location was clearly weighing on her mind, and there was nothing that I could say or do to comfort her. And then one moment, inspired by Spirit, I blurted out, "Mom, I'll be buried near you."

Of course, she lit up like a star with those words and was happy at the thought that she would not ever be alone again. However, in that moment, I was surprised to feel an overwhelming joy that washed over *me*! This had been Spirit's desire for me all along.

Now with a decision finally made, we began our search for a burial plot for us both. Mom already knew of all the cemeteries near me. In fact, because she loved cemeteries so much, we used to drive through several of them every month or so. There is one near me, Queen of Heaven, a Catholic one, that she truly found beautiful and had once mentioned that this was where she wanted to be buried.

Since I had finally decided this was the way forward, I now had an opinion. Wow! I was surprised by my own reaction. Being buried in a Catholic Cemetery was not even remotely what I had in mind since I had stopped being a practicing Catholic over 40 years ago. However, I knew that if I could pull it off, mom would be overjoyed about being laid to rest at Queen of Heaven.

That night, I prayed. "Creator, I ask for the highest good, a place that both of us are happy with, and arrangements that are easy for us. Guide us to somewhere with angels and flowers that always bloom, a place where my mother will find comfort and peace. Reminder her that I will be with her... always. Please, Creator, guide me to this best location swiftly and calmly. Thank you. I love you."

The next afternoon, I went online to see if any burial plots were available and scheduled times to visit the different cemeteries in the area. As it turned out, the first one I looked at, Queen of Heaven, had opened a special Archangel Gabriel Garden about 18 months earlier. It happened to be one of only two created in Illinois at the time.

Instead of a wall of crypts, there were both inground plots and statuary crypts. Most of the statuary were Bibles, benches, lambs, crosses, and other Catholic imagery – nothing that I would have ever selected. Yet, there was one designed as an angel. Remembering that she never wanted to be in the ground, I thought, "Wow! My mom would love a statue, and an angel statue? Now, that is something we could both definitely agree on!"

As I scanned the site, I noticed "SOLD OUT" on the page. Crestfallen, my heart cried out, "Creator, why did you show me this when I cannot do this for her? Why, on my first attempt, did you bring me here, only to be unable to do anything?"

The Creator whispered… "Look again, my child."

Reading more carefully, I scrolled to the very bottom of the page – which read: "We've since added a few more statuary to St. Gabriel's Garden in the past month. If you are interested, please call…"

I immediately called and asked if there were two locations left in the garden.

"There is space for one more statue," the consultant shared. "You are welcome to come and look in the next few days."

"Do you have an angel statue left?" My heart was beating loudly as I sat in silence eagerly awaiting his reply.

"I don't think so."

My heart sank, but nevertheless, I printed out the page explaining the garden, pictures of the statuary, and the other information to give to my mom. We spent the rest of the evening talking about it.

The next morning, my mom was up before me – dressed and ready to go, and as antsy as a child. I cautioned her that we might not be able to get one and that all we were going to do was look. She chided me, "Cherise, you are always so positive that Spirit guides you. You're the one always saying, 'Trust, believe, know that God provides,' and it is in an *angel* garden. The angels always come through for you."

Appropriately chastised, I quietly agreed while saying prayers to every guide, angel, saint and, of course, Spirit.

Since this is a story about co-creating with the Divine, I'm certain that you can figure out the rest of the story. Yet, allow me to share the details.

Mom, Chuck, and I arrived at the cemetery, and we were greeted by the consultant. He gave us directions to the garden. As we arrived, I thought, "My God, how have I not seen this before?"

There was a fifteen-foot-tall statue of Archangel Gabriel! We drive past this part of the cemetery nearly every week, and I never noticed this. While we pulled up, mom squealed in delight because she had spotted something I had not. At the bottom of the garden was a large Victorian style wooden gazebo. My mom had wanted a gazebo in her yard forever!

This was *her* sign that everything would work out.

When the consultant arrived with the available plot locations and pictures of the statues, mom rattled off her mental laundry list! She wanted an angel, a space along the walk, a statue under the outstretched hand of St. Gabriel facing the gazebo so she could 'look' at 'her' gazebo every day. She wanted flowers and flowers and flowers.

I looked over mom's head at Chuck. He smiled and whispered, "Keep the faith, love. Keep the faith." All the love I ever felt for my mom, bubbled over me. I don't remember praying so deeply in my life as I did in that moment. Then a sense of knowing and complete calm came over me. I, too, knew that everything would be alright.

As the consultant looked at his maps, books, and options, he 'discovered' that the last spot available was directly along the walkway, at the bottom of St. Gabriel's left hand, facing the gazebo, surrounded by bulbs that bloomed from spring through fall, marked to be filled by an angel statue!

"Mom, did you hear that? This is the last statue and the last space!" She was so thrilled that her wish list was fulfilled, she didn't hear a word I said. "I just wish I could keep my promise to be buried near you."

The consultant heard my comment and said, "You *can* be buried with her. The statue holds space for up to four urns."

WOW! The Divine truly co-creates with us when we are of pure heart and full of love. We finally knew – without doubt – that she would not be alone, because I would be with her when it was my time to leave this plane of existence. She was overjoyed and could barely wait to sign all the paperwork.

In a bit of a daze, we got back into the car to drive to the office to make the arrangements. Once we had finished signing, my mom couldn't stop talking about her new "home". She called her friends, she had Chuck take her there every week to see the garden, sit in the gazebo, gaze at her space. She even had him take pictures of her 'home'.

Ironically, she was just like my grandpa, who used to say that he would be in a 'condo' when he died. She invited her friends to come see it and visit with her. I never saw her so consistently happy and joyful as she was when thinking or talking about 'her' garden.

As time progressed and she weakened, it became every other week drives to the cemetery, looking out from the car. She'd take the pictures out so she could look at them and feel the safety and security of knowing what would happen when she died. Every other week visits turned into monthly visits until three weeks before her death.

"I don't want a funeral."

"Mom, what are you talking about? That's not fair! I need to have something to say goodbye to you!" I retorted.

"I mean it – NO FUNERAL! If you need to do something, then just have an ice cream social in the gazebo."

"Oh, mom," I shook my head. "An ice cream social in a cemetery? How in the world am I going to pull that one off?"

"I don't know, but I need you to promise me. No funerals."

During those last three weeks, as her strength waned, her soul prepared, and I stood vigil, I shared those pictures with her. She would smile, nod her head, and whisper, "My angel, my garden, my baby girl." I knew how Divinely led I had been. Then, she'd tag on, in a whisper, "my ice cream social."

Honoring her wishes to not have a funeral, I had a visitation for a few friends. Again, Spirit was in charge. While the cemetery wouldn't allow an ice cream truck on the premises, Spirit did guide me to contact her favorite ice cream shoppe, which created 12 ice cream sundaes. A loving friend picked them up for us, delivering them to the cemetery. Everyone knew her love for ice cream.

Standing in the gazebo with melting sundaes in hand, we celebrated her life as a gentle rain fell around us. We celebrated her garden, her zest for life, and, of course, her favorite ice cream.

It took me a month to organize a celebration, and it took 38 years to give her the peace and happiness that she had longed for. I certainly was aware of her feelings – or so I thought. Her friends told me during her celebration that they had never heard or saw her so full of joy as they did since we bought the angel statue in the cemetery. And, again, Spirit came through for we had another ice cream social at her celebration.

Yet, Spirit was not done with me… or with us.

Although my mom had passed, she was still communicating with me loud and clear – lights, popping noises, bells, birds, butterflies. It started the day before she fully left her body, and her communication was constant and insistent. I'd acknowledge her, and I'd thank Spirit for allowing this communication. I grieved, yet I was constantly aware of how supported I was, how supported and loved she was and that all was well. My only regret is that she did not really realize how loved she was while she was physical.

Over the next few months, I had a few readings from mediums. Now, mediums often tell potential clients that you should not try to communicate with the other side because they are not ready. Intuitively, I know that isn't quite the case. It is more likely that *we* aren't ready. Our energy is so low because of our grief that we can't let our loved ones into our energy. Since I was already communicating with her anyway, I knew that we could and would connect. Yet, it is nice to have a third party interpret things for us, as long as we are open, have no expectations, and trust Spirit to guide our way.

Like any child or mother, I had some concerns about how she was, what she was doing. But, mostly, had she connected with grandpa? Did she finally feel and know how loved she is? Did she feel safe?

Over the next several months, I had several readings from mediums. The first reading was a gallery reading. She came through loud and clear. There was no mistaking her energy, her joie de vivre. I was thrilled for her and happy that she had transitioned so well. There were a few comments that were unmistakably hers, and I was satisfied.

The second reading was a one-on-one experience. The medium said, "I keep seeing angels having ice cream. I understand the angels, but I have no idea why I see all this ice cream." I couldn't stop laughing as I explained to her about mom's last wish and the two ice cream socials.

We both laughed about her love of ice cream and how she was determined to let me know that she knew I had honored her wishes. Again, it was clearly her. However, her other message was, "You were right. You were so right! Everything you told me happened and is happening. It is so wonderful here. Grandpa is here. It is beautiful."

For some reason, this last message had me quite distraught, and I had no idea why. Who wouldn't want confirmation that everything you ever believed is true? Really, isn't that what we all *hope* is true? And, yet I could not seem to get past this confirmation.

I cried out to the Creator. "Help me! I don't understand why I am so upset. It makes no sense to me. Shouldn't I be ecstatic?"

And, slowly, quietly, the Creator shared that when faith without proof becomes true knowing, the mortal mind is awed by the reality of it – even becoming a bit overwhelmed.

I was definitely feeling overwhelmed. My belief had been an ever-present constant in my life. Mom would even chide me for just how much I believed, saying that I wore it 'out' there – often relating every little thing that happened as some Divine event.

Sometimes my ever-present belief that everything was a Divine really irritated her.

However, like everyone, I have had my moments (sometimes months) of doubt, confusion, worry, and fear. My mom had to remind me of my own trust on that day in the cemetery. And, yet, I have always believed that there is a Divine purpose for every action, situation, feeling – I just don't know it yet.

I've always trusted that someday, some way, I will know. Usually, I do discover the reason, like why it took 38 years for mom to find her final resting place. Yes, I now know why.

My last medium reading, though, was even more profound for me. Having gotten over my angst about belief and true knowing, I figured there wasn't anything that could come through that would upset me. I mean, how could there be?

In fact, I had such connection and confirmation from Spirit and from mom, that I had totally forgotten that I had even scheduled that third reading!

Usually, when I am working with another person with Spirit, I spend a few hours preparing for the session. I center, meditate, smudge, and light a candle. This time, because I only realized it when my calendar reminder came up 15 minutes before the call, I only had time to say a quick prayer, light a candle, and ask for the highest good for all.

The medium and I connected. Yep, mom was there in her full glory. She was so darn funny this time. Again, I was thrilled with her light-heartedness and joy. But then, the medium said to me, "I keep seeing a flying carpet. You know, one of those carpets from Aladdin with angels all around it."

I've been working with Spirit for nearly 55 years and, rarely, does something that is awing truly stop me in my tracks. I usually take a moment in appreciation, acknowledgement, and gratitude. Yet, this comment did stop time for me. The medium had to ask me several times if I knew what it meant.

Of course, I did…

For, the last words I spoke to her were:

> *"I love you so much. I will miss you so much. It will be like a magic carpet ride. The angels will be there. Grandpa and Aunt Mandy are waiting for you. You're going home now, mom. You're going home."*

The Divine does truly work in wonderful, amazing ways – if we can but trust that it does. We may not understand things while in the experience, but the experience expands our understanding of how very much we are loved.

Thank you for allowing me to share my experiences in co-creating with the Divine while my mom transitioned to her next adventure. It is with true joy and gratitude of the Divine as well as deep love and appreciation for my mom that I was given these tremendous gifts of her soul. Through her life experiences, her sacrifices, her pain and sorrows that I am who I am today.

My mom's journey to the other side has prompted me to help others create their final dying and death plans so that the last months and weeks of a loved one's life can be filled with connection, love, and peace. Spirit led both of us down a path of healing and growth, and I too, have dedicated my life to help others ease their sorrow, find their peace, and complete their relationships through grief coaching while discovering the joy of being present in the now.

My deepest hope for you, dear reader, is to discover being in the present moment, being fully aware of how the Divine is always with you and loving you where you are right now.

About the Author

Cherise Greski is an ordained minister and a certified spiritual, law of attraction, and grief coach who has shared her stories of forgiveness, love, and connection with those physical and non-physical for over 15 years.

Having been aware and connected with Spirit from the time she was a little girl, Cherise always knew that there is a reason for everything we experience – even if we don't know the answers at the time. Her awareness started in her childhood bedroom where she would gaze up at the walls that were covered in angels and talk with them in her darkest hours. And they, in turn, would share with her heart and comfort her.

When her husband, Alan Lesniewicz, died in 2008, she began in earnest to come to terms with grief and death. Reflecting on the many losses in her own life, she began a journey to better understand loss as well as how to embrace the joy that is ever present, if only we are willing to be open to see it.

With the death of her mom in 2022, she has chosen to dedicate the rest of her life to help others live their life fully connected to Spirit by accepting the inevitability of dying and the sacredness of death. As an End-of-Life Facilitator, Cherise guides those who are open to examine and document what they wish their last months and days will be like as well and to help organize the practical aspects of the dying and death process, encouraging others to 'play' in the gap between fully embracing life while acknowledging the sacredness of death.

Cherise's vision is to encourage others to give one of the most profound gifts they can to their loved ones: a fully recorded life and a completed book of directions for their dying and death experience - an End-of-Life Plan.

Recognizing that grief, just like death, are natural, normal parts of physical existence, Cherise also offers grief coaching and is a certified Grief Recovery Specialist (™) - the only program in the world that is evidence-based and backed by research from Kent State University.

Connect with Cherise below:

cherise@cherisegreski.com

DAVID KNIGHT

Awaken to Your Own Truth

I'm going to begin my story with a tale about fire and ice. My wife and I moved house in the last few days of 1999. It was an old, thatched cottage with a large garden full of trees and wildlife. Part of the property had an outbuilding (believed to be mentioned in the doomsday book), and ivy covered half the roof and walls which made the house feel quite magical indeed.

Apparently, around the eighteenth century (known as the "Age of Enlightenment") this was an ale house, and those travelling by with their horses and carts could quench their thirst and rest a while. We were not surprised that hard work and lots of tender loving care would be required to modernise and make it fit for modern living.

After spending all our savings on a new kitchen and central heating, I arranged a large loan to do major roof repairs. Every spare hour, we worked together – with blood, sweat, and tears – to try to turn this humble, historic house into a heavenly home.

At the start of 2001, we were almost finished with renovations. Then, on the first Saturday morning in January, I had a decision to make: begin decorating the main bedroom or fix the felt on the shed. Well, with the cold and frosty weather, it wasn't a tough choice, so I started decorating the bedroom in earnest while my better half went food shopping with her sister. While she was out, disaster struck!

In order to get some layers of paint off part of the window frame and lintel above it, I used a small hot air gun. But even though there was no naked flame, I hadn't noticed the heat building up in the corner of the window 'reveals.'

Suddenly, I saw a puff of smoke appear from a tiny crack in the wooden lintel above my head. Trying to peer into the crack, I could just make out a red glow and nearly crapped myself. Was the straw in the roof on fire? I rushed to grab a small squeezy bottle full of water (which I often used to wet the ends of my paint brushes) and squirted into the crack. I found out later that this is the worst thing to do, because it forces the fire back and helps it to spread.

After ringing 999 for the fire brigade emergency assistance, I waited for a minute or two which seemed like a lifetime, so I rang them again only to be told they were definitely on their way.

When they arrived, everyone seemed calm as I guessed there were no flames piercing the sky? I shouted out of the window to rush up to the bedroom whereby two fire crew proceeded to smash their way into the bedroom ceiling with axes. Pieces of wattle and daub plaster flew across the bed covers and plumes of dust were followed by the smell of rancid smoke.

"There's no way that I will fix this before my wife gets back!" I thought. Haha – not!

A firefighter rushed over to me and shouted, "You need to get out of the house now! Take what you can with you!" I was unaware that 9 out of 10 thatched cottage fires can't be stopped – dear me.

I ran into the back garden. I couldn't get my head around what was happening. As the billows of smoke escaping through the roof merged with the clouds in the sky, they became a reflection of the mental fog which had descended upon my mind. It didn't take long before I could hear the crashing of timbers leaving us with a derelict broken shell of a home. I felt traumatised with immense sadness.

My wife managed to get past the roadblock set up by the police. She found me in the garden searching for the cats. I will never forget her floods of tears as I held her tight. I cried, "I'm so sorry."

Neighbours rallied around and brought tea and biscuits for us and the fire crews, which was greatly appreciated. I recall the rear living room window blowing out from the heat and a shard of glass landed on a tea tray! Two fire crews stayed to continue dampening down overnight, and one was continually checking it for 3 days. They were brilliant.

Well, that was some New Year! But no one was hurt, thank goodness, and our pets were found safe, too ... having escaped into the field at the bottom of the garden. The only clothes we had left were what we were wearing. But more heartache followed as we discovered we were underinsured for the full reinstatement value, and after much debate decided to live in a caravan inside the garden for over two years until the house was rebuilt.

An interesting point regarding the house fire came from a special friend of mine called Jim, who was blessed with many spiritual gifts. We were both members of the Peterborough Sai Baba group – a meditation and healing circle – and we used to meet up at least once a month. After the fire, he received information (clairvoyantly) that there had been a previous fire at our home, perhaps in the 19th century. It hadn't destroyed the building, but the family member who was deemed to have caused it was vilified and overcome with guilt. Perhaps my karma was involved here, because Jim was being shown that a dark cloud had been lifted from that person's soul as if to say, "There you go, see how easy things can happen." It was as if his family could now forgive him. Perhaps everything happens for a reason, no matter what so-called joy or sorrow crosses your path.

This reminds me that we are all born with a lamenting cry, an acceptance of the 'body' in a material world. And on a soul level, you chose this life, and your karma and the choices you make will affect your day-to-day existence. In addition, your thoughts, words, and deeds are woven into the tapestry of both fate and destiny, which form connections that extend far beyond your next of kin, too.

This is why love and joy and fear and pain resonate deep inside you: to pour forth as emotions that transcend the physical into ethereal planes and dimensions. In fact, your feelings rise and fall as if you travel upon a rollercoaster, but you must treat these peaks and troughs with equanimity. Know that nothing is insurmountable, and whatever occurs, you are never alone. And even when you think God has abandoned you, he/she is not even a heartbeat away.

How can this be? Well, because you are a divine spark of creation. But even though the same energy and power flows through you, many opportunities are missed to create and shine the truth of you. In the same way, confusion, and illusion – like a splinter in the eye – cause an imaginary blindness to pierce the peace that is your inherent right.

It makes no difference if one's genes are male or female in design. Please comprehend that health and wealth, nationality, occupation, location, the colour of your skin and hair, and one's body shape and size do not affect karmic debt. All will face trials and tribulations on their journey. Appreciate that life helps you to learn and grow and mature as a human being and a soul.

Exterior circumstances may not be controlled, but our interior state/feelings can be. Please understand how you deem your experiences in life are entirely up to you. So, why should we perceive a situation as bad without even knowing that what occurs could become beneficial on a deeper, sacred level?

We gain knowledge and wisdom through our experiences, and to demonstrate this, I continued to experience additional trials and tests. My father was diagnosed with two types of cancer, and one of my best friends became very ill too. To compound matters, Caroline found herself out of work for the first time. Financially, we struggled to make ends meet, and paying monthly for the 5-year loan (on a roof that didn't exist) was galling.

Then, in August that year, there was a horrendous storm and lightning struck several houses on our street. Thankfully, we were both out, but later that day we discovered the caravan had been hit too, and one of our cats had died while hiding underneath it. Brand new items we had purchased for moving back into our home (like a new portable TV and microwave) were frazzled. 'Lucky' wasn't our middle name.

One day, while sitting alone inside the caravan, hours of torrential rain battered down on the tin roof which brought a constant and irritating hum. Looking out of the window at our derelict home, I thought I'd play some music. The CD player still worked, and I played Foreigner's 'I Want to Know What Love Is' (https://youtu.be/r3Pr1_v7hsw) over and over again on a loop.

Suddenly, I felt at a really low ebb. Darkness enveloped me like a shroud as if I wanted to die. I drove to a secluded countryside lane and pulled over to the verge. There was a large tree about twenty metres away on the right-hand side of the lane, and for the briefest of moments, I thought I would drive into it.

My mind was in turmoil, and my heart was broken. And yet I knew I loved Caroline, I loved my family and friends, and I loved God. Unexpectedly, 'his/her' presence descended upon me like a layer of soft silk. I felt like I was being cradled in the Lord's loving arms. Time appeared to stand still as I wept. It may have been some fifteen minutes or more before I drove away.

After many years of spiritual development through dreams, meditation, healing circles, and guidance from my spirit guides, I should not have been thinking, 'Why me (or us)?' or even 'Why am I here?' but contemplating 'what' am I here? (A soul within a body with a purpose.)

Nothing comes into our experience uninvited, and there are reasons far beyond our comprehension for the events in our lives.

Sometimes, work can bring some sort of solace because it provides a daily routine and allows us to serve fellow human beings too. But even my employment took its toll, like it was sucking the life force out of me. Working in a sales environment became cut-throat. After all we had been through, I was still hitting my sales targets, but there was too much management bureaucracy, small-mindedness, and favouritism.

I took time away from this rat race and, fortunately, got 'sick pay' for what a doctor deemed depression. A fog constantly filled my mind but I'm not sure I was depressed. Maybe I was angry with myself that I could have such negativity around me. And of how much hurt I could have caused if I had gone through with those suicidal thoughts. In reality, my faith and love kept me going – not drugs.

I went to visit my friend who was ill the day before he passed. He was in his own room and connected to goodness knows what machinery. Still jovial, we joked about "the good old days": the concerts, football matches, and the films we used to watch together.

The notion of sending healing suddenly filled my heart, and I imagined I could help him. You see, over the years I have been humbly blessed to express God's love through spiritual healing through the 'laying on' of hands – energy from spirit, through spirit, and to spirit.

For me, this is not some sort of business transaction. Others may well receive healing training, become 'certified,' have indemnity insurance and they like to practice it professionally, but I knew this was a precious gift that flowed through me. In any case, Jesus (the most powerful healer the world has ever known) didn't need — or show — any certificates, did he? Of course, I would always follow general codes of conduct by having another person present, especially where children or working with a female were concerned.

Rightly or wrongly, when I come into contact with illness or any form of disease (dis-ease), I try to induce it out of the person or animal. I'd imagine it coming up my arm and then ground it with an inanimate object. So, standing beside the hospital bed, I silently prayed and asked for protection for us both. I wanted God's mercy and grace and healing to wash over him, so I gently held his arm. But after a few seconds, I experienced this horrendous black mass — which could be the negativity or pain or the forebode of death — flowing upwards through me.

My mind started spinning, and I thought I was about to pass out, almost vomiting by the side of the hospital bed. I desperately tried to hide this from him (and the others present), laughing to one side, and smiling as we joked some more. It was an awful feeling and, fortunately, one I haven't had since.

Shortly afterwards, we said our goodbyes. The next day, he'd left his mortal coil – a very sad time indeed for all his family and friends.

Life's ups and downs continued. It was wonderful to move back into our home during 2003, but great sadness fell once more as my father passed away. Throughout his treatment, I never heard him complain at all, and he battled bravely right to the end. His strength inspired all those who knew him. And even though what we were going through felt like a huge karmic dump poured over us, Dad's courage and love became his lasting legacy. Surely, we must all try to live each day as if it was our last, because no one knows when the 'God' of death will call.

Regarding my work situation, a stroke of luck occurred, or was it destiny/fate? One day, I was thinking of handing in my notice but discovered that voluntary redundancies were soon a possibility. I decided enough was enough and applied for it. After all, a few months' salary would present me with the chance to do something else.

This was a sign of change and of hope. Likewise, I urge you to embrace change in your life, as it can become a catalyst for you to start anew, become fulfilled, and find your purpose. Your sojourn, your life's journey, is too short to be unhappy. Therefore, begin to follow your passion, and do what makes your heart sing!

In the end, I loathed the job, so the option of redundancy was a no-brainer. When I was about to drive away from the office for the last time, the sun was shining in a clear blue sky. I opened the car window and took a deep sigh of breath. A huge weight appeared to be cast from my shoulders.

I turned on the car radio and heard a chorus from the song "Free" by Ultra Nate (https://www.youtube.com/watch?v=JgRBkjgXHro) bellowed out from my car speakers:

'Cause you're free to do what you want to do.
You've got to live your life, do what you want to do'

A spiritual sign if ever there was one! The money would help me to become self-employed as a painter and decorator, which I still do today. So, you see, even when you feel the depths of despair, whether that's in your work, family, or home life, the phoenix will always rise from the ashes.

You may call this divine timing, God's will, or karmic balance, but you must simply trust the process. The mind will insist your future be judged only on past experiences, but you must break free from this flawed approach.

In fact, you may have already experienced your own 'signs' in the past. Or, in the days, weeks, months, or years to come, perhaps these will be revealed through your intuition or a dream.

What about one of many other things, such as a white feather falling at your feet or smelling the perfume or aftershave of a loved one who has crossed over? These are but gentle, wonderful reminders that we are loved and cared for.

Remember *everything* is energy/God. Love is the most powerful force in creation. And, if you are ever in doubt over your divine connection with a loved one, think of an object, an image, a place, or even a feeling that connects you both. Something simple would suffice. Ask the universe for a sign, and it will come. Allow creation to work through you with an open mind and heart, and it will speak back – just be ready to receive it! (By the way, gratitude plays a big part here, too).

EVOLVING ON PURPOSE

Since 1996, one of the beautiful aspects of my spiritual work are the words that flow through my inner voice, the 'Indweller' of my heart, in which I am co-creating with spirit, the source, our divinity – God. Some describe this as channeling, inner dictation, or automating writing. After watching the news late one night with distressing images of people in physical and mental pain and anguish whilst fleeing the bombs and devastation in Ukraine, a great desire to hear what God would say about these events overwhelmed me. I rushed for a notepad and pen:

A MESSAGE FROM GOD
REGARDING THE WAR IN UKRAINE

(5/3/22)
'SOMETHING NEW'

You hear me before I even call because truth and love resonate deep inside your core. It always has and always will. It's just that most people do not recognise me, but one day, all shall experience their own divinity by piercing the veil of hate and fear and anger and injustice of man versus man.

I am not blind to what occurs across — and through — the borders of your nations, whether they lie in the East or West or North or South. Such imaginary lines separate sons from mothers, daughters from fathers, and cause disdain and anguish between the brotherhood of mankind.

99

White, black, yellow, and red are colours of skin which bring prejudices and division, when all along, they bleed just the same and incur pain, be it physical, mental, or emotional, which transcends every person. Age, sex, nationality, and beliefs are not the prerequisites or the right to cut through one's eternal harvest of joy and peace and bliss, which is the birthright of every life and being.

During such times, it may seem a natural reaction to form opinions of right over wrong, and who is to blame? Should you suppress such feelings? No, because one always needs to say what they think and act on what they say. But again, this becomes difficult when fear for one's own safety or for their family is called into question. I do not intend to discuss karma or karmic balance in these matters but ask for each soul to remember I have given free will to express themselves from and through and to their heart.

However, the ego and the mind (which have their own attributes) often cause such devastation, whipping up a whirlwind of lies, tornadoes of grief, and oceans of tears. Homes may fall, towns and cities reduced to rubble and ash, but evil on any scale cannot deny me and my light and my love. And the same purpose and strength is within every one of you, too.

The world is beautiful. Though, of course, it may not seem this way when tyranny in its many forms and guises rears its ugly head. When electricity and gas and each form of fuel dissipates and is forcibly crushed, dismantled, or removed, know that I am the real power to sustain your soul. Love is the greatest bond and energy in existence, so send such thoughts through the ether to touch the hearts of both kith and kin and strangers alike, no matter where they may be.

Please do not doubt me – or yourself – because this will only attempt to hinder our connection. The hungry, the thirsty, the naked, the homeless, and the refugees will find this much harder to grasp or evaluate, but I implore you to simply believe. Yes, keep believing in me, for I am your true shield against seen or unseen foes in body or mind.

I urge you to hold on to the good both 'within and out' for a new dawn is upon the horizon. The sun and 'son' will rise and shine my glory around the globe. Shadows shall disappear, as there will be nowhere for them to hide. Broken hearts, I'll mend. Smiles and laughter so quickly forgotten amidst the depths of despair will return once more. And much blood will flow away, to be cleansed by the rivers of truth, the abundance of my grace and healing from my heart.

You already have hope, though you imagine it's buried under the weight of your expectations for change — a change of heart from those who believe they are in charge. Those in authority, in governments of false power, harbour human traits that, in reality, stem from an ivory tower.

Throughout history (and you know this), many men (with the masculine side of ego) portrayed dominance through violence or rhetoric with the flexing of physical strength and/or immature minds which sought to enslave, control, or eradicate people, towns, and cities from the face of the Earth. All have failed. Please take heart in this.

Ultimately, all *must live with their actions, no matter if one is a pauper, king, queen, religious figurehead, or a president. Do you get what I mean?*

So, take just a little solace from the past, which of course you cannot change. And while 99% of life imagines that the future can't be known, because of many spiritual gifts and free will that I have bestowed upon you from the beginning of 'time,' please understand we are all co-creators, and influence what has yet come to pass. In this process, I advise you that peace will overcome war and hate and anger and division.

Life always *finds a way; it is who you are and why you exist: to experience and to make things 'right' and to make things* new. *Therefore, think above the clouds if they torch the sky. If a building collapses (from a so-called earthly power) into rubble and dust, climb upon the debris to bear witness to new pastures. If home and the 'normal' way of life appears to be taken, snatched, grabbed, and pulled away from you with a vice-like grip, do not lose heart; never lose heart, because paradise and every comfort you could think of remains inside you, only a heartbeat or a thought away.*

Know that birds will still sing like lullabies to a child. Seeds of love fertilised in the furrows of your heart growing in the soil (soul) will rise to (and overcome) each challenge and reach upwards towards the light, your light, my light – our light. By empowering your own truth, you evolve – on purpose – and humanity will achieve so much more.

Therefore, please take each day as a precious gift, for no one knows if, or when, it could be their last. Each moment is an opportunity to shine or prove your real worth – not to me, but to each other. Every human being is like a star against the backdrop of a night sky, and you can illuminate and shine as a jewel upon my crown, or stay hidden, veiled, unable or unwilling to show the truth of you and me.

One must decide to act or to simply react to all walks of life. Will you lead and become examples of justice and fortitude, or will you retreat inside the hardened shell of despair and not care? Know you are also divine and possess the ability to create and unify like a link in my chain of love, so demonstrate this in every thought and word and deed.

I'll leave you now to contemplate upon these words, but I remain forever your father and mother and friend, your strength and power, through your faith in me. Amen.

I trust that what you have just read will resonate inside you. I also invite you to open your heart and listen to this beautiful song from Chris Eaton called, "Something New." (https://www.youtube.com/watch?v=899Q_kktrNo)

You possess the same ability to listen and have your own conversations with the Divine too. However, only in silence can you hear your own truth. And, your inspiration, intuition, spiritual, and psychic gifts are all latent within. They give you the ability to create. Only your false belief in your limitations can prevent your imagination from making the unknown 'known' and the unseen 'seen'.

In doing so you reveal your inner reality and become 'realised' in the knowledge you are already divine. This provides the basis for co-creating the life you wish to lead. You can and will evolve as a human being and as a soul, so prepare yourself to nurture your inner child. Reach out beyond the boundary of your senses to transform the nature of your life and the lives of those around you too.

When you are focused and passionate and excited about your goals and desires and 'receive' in gratitude, anything is possible. God can work *through* you. Do you always believe that you are the do-er, when the universe gave you the power, the fortune, the will, and the means? And God wants you to be who you were born to be. You have a place and purpose in this world, or you would not be here! Find, follow, and bask in it. Make your dreams come true.

Queen Elizabeth II once said, "We are all visitors to this time, this place. We are just passing through. Our purpose here is to observe, to learn, to grow, to love, and then we return home."

This is a wonderful statement indeed, and yet it also implies a 'to and from.' How do you know that you are not already living in heaven? What if you recognised that you are already totality and free? You would soon evolve from all self-blame and self-sabotage and self-doubt to self-responsibility! You would act consciously not compulsively.

EVOLVING ON PURPOSE

As I said earlier, one must embrace change and opportunity. There is no time like the present, for 'now' is all you have. It is a gift, pre-sent from the dawn of creation. The fact that you are reading this book indicates you have awoken from the sleep of doubt, and rather than looking back upon the imprint of your slumber with fear or dread of a new day, you will rise with gratitude and excitement for the joy and peace and bliss the day will bring.

Being compulsive in nature shall fall behind you like a dark shadow, for the way ahead is lit. The light of truth will lead you forward to living more consciously, whereby you reclaim the power within you and start to live a purpose-filled life. I wish you the very best as you continue your own journey.

About the Author

David Knight has helped to conduct spiritual development and healing circles for over 25 years. He has also been a guest speaker sharing his enlightened experiences to promote 'oneness' at various Mind, Body, and Spirit engagements in the UK.

Through inner-dictation, dream interpretation, meditation, mindfulness, precognition, and healing, the books he co-writes with 'Spirit' provide you with the foundation to discover your own path of truth. With a renewed sense of purpose, the spiritual guidance and education you receive can help you reach the goal of self-realisation and bliss within the permanence of love and light. David is tee-total and a vegetarian who loves the sunshine, nature, animals, and his wife!

Connect with David below:

On social media sites Facebook, Twitter, Pinterest, LinkedIn, etc. as @AscensionForYou and via his blog/website: AscensionForYou.com

ERICA MARTIN

"It's Going to Take a While, Miss Erica"

I think it's fair to say that we can all look back on our lives, in retrospect, and reflect upon certain events, people, and circumstances that have helped shape who we are or who we would ultimately become. As if it were an elaborate jigsaw puzzle, piece by piece, the picture begins to unfold. We can look back examining when we arrived at specific destination points throughout our journey and we begin to draw conclusions about the significance of these past events and encounters, or about whether they fit or did not fit authentically into our lives.

Perhaps, we may look back and see forced puzzle pieces where they did not naturally belong or how we had a preconceived notion of what the final product would reveal... sometimes only to be proven wrong. It is easy to place the puzzle pieces together from the perspective of the past knowledge obtained, but the challenge for so many of us is to allow this same sense of understanding or wisdom to come to our present circumstances...or our future.

Throughout my work as a psychotherapist, I am consistently drawn back to the power of the ego and the critical work of Carl Jung. The Ego, that brilliantly complex and magnificent mechanism, whose very existence is to create a sense of safety and control in an otherwise changing and chaotic world.

As human beings, we all crave safety and a sense of autonomy over ourselves and our environment. It makes sense that we would operate from a place of self-preservation and perhaps engage in the "magical thinking" that we can and should be able to control everything in our lives by sheer willpower and self-determination. Many people suffer with profound anxiety, which I would argue is really a crisis of the ego. When the ego and reality cannot harmoniously coexist, there will be a crisis and anxiety will be a symptom.

This inability to reconcile our ego (our sense of self and that which we believe to be true) with the realities we are faced with daily, creates internalized distress. This distress or "dis-ease" will be seen in a host of mental and emotional conditions which equally disrupts the overall function of the body, which I believe to be much smarter than the brain.

We see anxiety and depression as primary symptoms of this inner conflict, but there are a host of other mental and physical illnesses that are also representative including autoimmune disorders and other chronic conditions. The body is simply not built to undergo prolonged periods of stress, and we are far more likely to pay attention to the physical signals given to us by the body than the emotional ones administered by the brain.

So, what happens when we reach a place in our lives when all our constant worry, all of our fears, all of our perfectionism, all of our tireless efforts to control are simply not enough. What happens when we are left emotionally exhausted, mentally massacred, and physically failing? What happens when you try to pour from an empty cup?

Ultimately, we are presented with a choice. We can choose to continue to live by the ego, or we can choose to surrender it. I have come to call this process "the sweet surrender." We begin to let go of the old stories, wounds, traumas, scripts, and narratives that, by design, have kept us anchored to our past and to our own limitations.

Here, we can begin to examine with consciousness who we want to be, and our soul's purpose in this lifetime. Until we can welcome the soul's purpose into our lives, we will remain stuck in the intricate labyrinth of the ego. We cannot ascend to our highest potential spiritually and be living in the ego simultaneously. They cannot co-exist. So, we are presented with an opportunity to evolve.

When we begin to examine how much the ego and the need to control robs us of our joy, we can begin to make conscious choices of letting go and releasing ourselves from fear and from the need to be "right" or "perfect." With the release of this perfectionism comes the ability to be human. As we embrace our humanity, we allow space for error. And as we are open to error, we allow vulnerability. As we allow vulnerability, we become open and receptive to others and expand our ability to empathize. And then, we begin to learn that there is no greater strength than being authentically yourself, standing in your superpower - the ability to be *vulnerable.*

What does it mean to be vulnerable? It is giving ourselves permission to shamelessly express and share all our inner thoughts and feelings. It is granting permission to set down the protective armor that we have created in an attempt to shield ourselves from shame, emotional pain, and hurt. It is our willingness to share our truth and suffering with others. It is embarrassing humility. It is being utterly naked and exposed, understanding that there is a risk of being attacked or harmed and choosing to do so anyway.

With vulnerability comes the recognition that we may need to ask for help. Though this is something the ego would fight adamantly against, we begin to step out of fear and control. As we expand from that place of ego and fight through the initial discomfort of being vulnerable, we will soon recognize the increasingly deep and meaningful connections that we have with others. We will begin to see the deepening of connection with the world around us, and perhaps, most importantly, the appreciation and deep understanding of self. The realization that when we view each other with humanity and empathy and allow ourselves to be vulnerable, we open to an entirely new way of being and an entirely new type of energy. Once we understand and begin to incorporate these key concepts into our lives, we can now begin to "evolve on purpose."

We are all energetic beings, brilliant and complex. If we choose to come from the place of ego, we operate from a very low-vibrational energy, rooted in fear and limitation. But when we come from the power of our authenticity and soul's purpose, we raise our vibration; in doing so, we raise our awareness, connectedness, and our possibilities. As we ascend on this journey and release ourselves from limiting self-beliefs, we open to a new way of existing and to universal guidance and spiritual wisdom. Our construct of reality begins to shift, and we open to things we never thought possible.

We transition from the 3D to the 5D construct, and we begin "co-creating with the divine." The universe is always working on our behalf, and there are signs and synchronicities, divine alchemy, if you are willing to pay attention and participate.

We are blessed with a divinely created inner guidance system – our intuition – yet we are prone to reject that which we cannot see and quantify or that which goes against the "reality" that the ego has scripted. When we are ready and willing to expand beyond that which can be seen and felt and tap into our soul's purpose, we arrive at an entirely new vibrational level and a new state of consciousness and being. The story of how each of us will arrive or has arrived at this place is as varied and magnificent as each one of us. It is not uncommon for us to ignore or push away that which we do not understand, and oftentimes the universe will be forced to step in and help us through external forces. Here is my story…

It was a dark, crisp fall evening several years ago, and I was working in my office. I was struggling during this time personally and had somehow managed to put one foot in front of the other and throw myself into my work, likely as a life distraction. I stared at my desk and the remnants of a pitiful blueberry muffin, which was all I could somehow force myself to eat that day. It was about 8 pm, and I had one last therapy client in the waiting room, so I brushed the crumbs from my desk and went out to greet my client. To my surprise, the client's mother had accompanied her (we had met only one time prior a few years before), so we exchanged niceties, and I went back to meet with her daughter for our hour-long session.

After the session, I walked her daughter out and asked her mother, "Is there anything that you would like to speak with me about?"

She glanced coyishly and with a curious smile responded, "Yes! Actually, I would like to talk to you about you."

Inquisitively, I nodded to her, as her daughter continued to roll her eyes and I questioned, "You want to speak to me about *me*?"

"Yes," she insisted, "I would really appreciate a few moments of your time."

I indulged her (after all, she is my client's mother and a very well-respected doctor). I felt a sense of urgency in the air. "This must be something really important." As I began to escort this rosy-faced mother down the hallway to my office, her daughter yelled out to me, "This is going to take a while, Miss Erica."

My anxiety rose like a lump in my throat. The mother stepped into my office, I slowly closed the door, and she sat down on a chair uncomfortably close beside me and whispered, "I have been called to come and speak with you by your spirit guides."

I was like, "Oh boy, it's 9 pm, and this woman sounds like she needs to be hospitalized." I smiled slightly, nodded politely, and pretended to listen (while mentally planning my escape), but the look on my face must have given away my disbelief.

She looked at me wide-eyed and mouth gaping, "You don't believe me. Oh my God! It's so late. I worked all day, and now I need to provide you with evidence. She needs proof?!" She looked up at the ceiling with exacerbation then back at me before continuing, "Ok. I was sent to you by your two grandmothers."

She provided the names of each grandmother and intimate details about my relationships with them. My disbelief turned to anger. "How cruel and crazy this woman is! She must have

Googled me or something to obtain this kind of personal and private information."

She proceeded with great animation to tell me things that no one could possibly know, intimate details of my private life, that left me absolutely horrified. I began to cry. This was one of those crisis moments where my ego and my reality were at odds. She took my hand and whispered, "You are loved. You are not crazy. They have been guiding you and reaching out to you. You see it with the lights; they are connecting with you. It's you coming together with them. I know you sense their presence. This is a *gift*, not something to fear."

I nodded with creepy, mascara-stained tears rolling down my face. She continued, "Your grandmothers sent me to tell you that they see you struggling and that the guy was no good for you. They helped push him out the door." I felt as though I was about to have a full-blown panic attack when her 12-year-old daughter came barging through the door.

"Mom!" she exclaimed as she looked at my horrified face. "Not my therapist!"

I tried to gain some type of composure for the sake of my 12-year-old client. I asked, "Does your mother do this often, honey?"

"YES! She talks to spirits or whatever she calls them all the time, but upsetting my therapist is completely inappropriate!" Stirring in anger, as my client began wildly stomping on the floor, I may have levitated from my body, because the next thing I recalled was escorting both of them out of the office and assuring my client that I was okay and not to worry.

Her mother handed me a card and said, "You really need to go see this woman as soon as possible. The grandmother that you were named after will show up there."

I somehow managed through the emotional haze to get my belongings and drive home, all the while thinking about all these things she said. How could she have known these things? What was her motive? How could she have gotten all this information? Was she crazy? Was she spying on me???

Again, my ego and my reality were not able to co-exist, and I found myself in quite the existential crisis. "Ah ha! She is wrong!" I exclaimed like Sherlock Holmes. I found myself breathing air into my lungs for the first time since she and I spoke. I wasn't named after either of my grandmothers. She is a fraud. I knew it!

My analytical mind had solved the mystery, and my body began to calm down. I arrived home, took a nice, hot bath to wash the filth of the day away, and called my parents that evening as I usually do. In passing, just to be sure, I asked my mother if I was named after my grandmother in any way.

She responded, "Well, there was that issue with your birth certificate. The nuns wouldn't allow us to name you Erica, because it wasn't a Catholic name, so on your birth certificate, it actually says your grandmother's name as your first name and Erica as your middle name. We never paid any attention to it."

I dropped the phone. "Mom! How did I never know this? I am 40 years old?"

"I don't know, dear. Let me get your father for you." She handed the phone to my father, and he verified that my mother was telling the truth - I *was* named after my grandmother!

A very sleepless and restless night followed, and I had a stare down for several hours at the card that my client's mother had given me. It just said "Lois" and a number.

I went to work in a haze the next day, but all I could think about was everything this mother had said to me and the accuracy of it all. I dare not tell anyone about this experience for fear that they would think I was certifiably insane. After an internal battle of several days, I decided I would call Lois.

A rather unremarkable woman with a New England accent picked up the phone. I found it difficult to put words together and felt the endless silence as I heard her repeat several times, "Hello? Is anybody there?"

"Hello, I was given your card by a client of mine and asked to set up an appointment."

"What is your first name?"

"Erica," I replied.

"Thank you. That's all the information that I need. I'll see you in two weeks."

Two weeks? This would be the longest two weeks of my life.

Two weeks later, she called to cancel our appointment because she was sick with the flu.

By now, three weeks had passed, and my mind could think of nothing else. I was filled with anticipation and anxiety. I realized I didn't even know who this woman was or what I was stepping into. I felt totally out of control and yet excitedly curious. On the way to the appointment, I found myself driving into a very quaint little neighborhood on an ordinary street to an ordinary little house that matches the house number I was given.

"Could this be it?" I grumbled to myself.

There was a little garden and a pathway with signs that instructed me to a little cottage behind the home which was nestled in the woods.

I knocked.

A very ordinary woman answered the door. She seemed no different than any other soccer mom I would see at the grocery store on a Saturday afternoon. I don't know what I was expecting - perhaps a gypsy or a witch and her coven. Lois smiled at me with kind eyes and said, "Well, so nice to meet you. You have two grandmothers, an uncle, great aunt, and two spirit guides... heck, you have a whole army with you! I hope we have enough time to get to them all. We only have two hours."

As I entered the cottage, I remember the sound of the door creaking behind me. It was the closing of a door to the life I once existed in, the one driven by fear and ego.

For the next several years, I continued on this healing journey with Lois. I studied, expanded my knowledge, took courses, and practiced. I was quickly soaking up the spiritual energy of this new and fascinating world. Lois became my mentor and guided me as I began to tap into my spiritual gifts and nurture my abilities as a healer. Ironically, I had established my therapy practice 11 years earlier and surrounded myself with mind/body practitioners. My soul was guiding me, and I unknowingly followed without thought or complication. I slowly began to discover that I had been co-creating with the divine my entire life, but my ego had been the one taking credit.

At the earliest stages of my awakening, my ego would jump for joy, like an annoying and precocious child saying, "Look at *me*! Look what I can do!" The ego relished in the thought it could be so powerful, so special. I could not contain the excitement. The capabilities that I now possessed placed me on the "pink cloud," and it was as if someone turned on the lights in a very dim room The flowers smelled better, the sun shined brighter, and I was so in tune and connected with everyone and everything around me. But then, the ego showed up and asked, "So, what are we going to do with this?" Oh, the anxiety! The hamster on my perpetual thought wheel would circle, keeping me up all night.

My once spiritual playground filled with childlike energy, now became something of great responsibility and importance. I realized that I was working for and with the Divine. Oh, how I prayed that the ego would die! I imagined smashing it with a hammer... repeatedly. Once again, the ego and reality were on a collision course, but this time, the ego must be eradicated.

This period of time hallmarked for me the "Dark Night of the Soul" - a time of surrendering the fact that I am really not in control of anything and a time to begin the process of ego death, a painstakingly slow erosion that is necessary for all of us to be in alignment with the Divine. Do we remain in the human construct of all we have known and everything we have learned? Or do we follow blindly that which we are being called to do even when we cannot see or hear? Do we trust the gift we have been given, the gift of "the know?"

The "know," as I call it, is the way we receive messages or spiritual downloads from the Divine. The messages, at this time, were coming in with greater frequency and greater acuity. I was left to ponder how I would ever reconcile this with my work as a psychotherapist. If I surrendered fully to the Divine, then I would surely lose all credibility as a psychotherapist and would certainly lose the business I had built over the last 13 years. And so in the dark night, I sat... for quite some time.

It was around Christmas time that year when a dear friend of mine, Dan, asked if I would be interested in meeting with his spiritual guru, Michael.

I gasped. "Are you asking me to cheat on Lois?"

"No, no, of course not," he responded. "But I got you a session as a gift, and I hope you will use it. I think you could use the extra support."

At this time, I had been quite ill and struggling with an undiagnosed medical condition that had landed me in and out of the hospital for the better part of four years. On a snowy, winter day in January, I found myself deteriorating in bed for several weeks due to my medical condition, and I was quite miserable. I decided to take Dan's advice and contact Michael. I texted him, and he was quick to respond. Michael texted back and said that we would speak later that evening.

I waited anxiously.

The phone rang.

I began the call that would ultimately change the trajectory of my entire life.

Michael, a mystic and intuitive, since age 5, worked at a local church and was eccentric but spoke plainly without emotion. Within the first five minutes of our call, he told me that I had Crohn's disease and that my doctors had been repeatedly failing me (a diagnosis which was confirmed sometime later). He instructed me on the tests that I needed to confirm diagnosis as well as other tips for alleviating my symptoms such as eliminating gluten.

"You are a natural born energy healer," he said. "You have been healing your patients energetically for years without being consciously aware of it." He cited compelling examples that he could not possibly know and went on to explain that my gifts were always there and operational since I was a child.

In my career, my ego was trying to control things that it could not otherwise rationally explain, so I began to heavily focus on the analytics of my work as a way of coping. He went on to elaborate that it was really my energetic connection to my clients that was helping them to improve.

"You are a Reiki healer, and one day, before we meet in person, there will be convincing evidence that what I am telling you now is true." He offered to come from New York to Maryland (a five-hour drive) to personally train and mentor me in Reiki. "I won't take no for an answer!" he emphasized. "This training will heighten your ability to heal and help you to grow your therapy practice... You can also heal your Crohn's Disease." Three months later, I was preparing for Michael's arrival from New York, and I had set up a small intimate group for him to teach Reiki. The evening prior, I had been doing some Spring cleaning in my home and came upon a book on Reiki that I had purchased from Barnes and Nobles ten years earlier for $3 from the bargain bin on the sidewalk. I had never read a page. I think we would call this convincing evidence, just as he predicted.

The Universe is always providing us with signs and synchronicities and is always willing to partner with us to co-create. When we allow the soul to come forward more in our life and set aside the ego, we will see how our soul is always guiding us toward our authentic purpose. However, the soul will never, ever interfere with our free will. It may guide us to the book, but it will not force us to buy it, and it is for us to decide if we will pick it up and read it.

My long overdue journey into Reiki began the next morning, and my soul felt at home and at peace. It was such a beautiful experience and a deep bond for everyone in the class. Over time, I became very close friends with the five other students and remember Michael telling me that I should be sure to keep in contact with one member in particular - Diane.

Four years later, I am now a Reiki Master, incorporating a number of healing modalities into my work with clients. I am in total remission from my eight-year struggle with Crohn's. And Diane, the very woman with whom Michael told me to stay in contact, has become a part of my business. Diane had contacted me four years after that providential Reiki class with Michael. She had started her own business and had become certified as a yoga instructor and was looking for a place to expand her yoga practice. I just happened to have an empty studio… just waiting for her.

Oh, how those tricky, little jigsaw pieces of life all come together effortlessly, when we stay out of our ego and out of the way of spirit. There is no need to force the pieces of our lives to fit, because when you are "co-creating with the divine," they will always fall perfectly into place and without effort. I am so grateful for the wisdom and faith that I have gained along this beautiful journey, recognizing there is still so much more to learn. When the Divine leads, I will follow. And yes, in the prophetic words of my 12-year-old client, "This is going take a while, Miss Erica."

About the Author

Erica Martin is a licensed clinical psychotherapist and the founder of Martin Counseling and Associates, LLC, a dual diagnosis treatment program that supports those suffering with mental health issues, addiction, and trauma. Erica has spent the last 20 years in the mental health field, increasingly recognizing the importance of incorporating mind/body/spirit elements into the recovery process. Erica is a Reiki Master and instructor and is also certified in Auricular therapy. She incorporates these complementary elements into her work to enhance the client's therapeutic experience. As an intuitive, Erica has a very niche part of her practice which is devoted to supporting empathic clients on their spiritual journey to include exploring child parts and shadow self.

Inspired by Covid, in 2021, Erica began co-hosting a podcast entitled "Two Italian Women and the Stories They Tell." A podcast devoted to educating and empowering others, especially when so many felt isolated and alone during the pandemic. The podcast focuses on overall wellness, while bringing laughter and joy to people's lives.

Erica has always been passionate about helping adolescents and young adults find their authentic voice. She began her career as a secondary education teacher and special educator. Erica earned her B.S. in Education and English Literature from Pennsylvania State University in 1995, before receiving her master's degree in clinical social work from the University of Maryland in 2005. Her early years in teaching included educating children in inner city schools, group homes, detention centers, and alternative schools. She also served as an educational liaison between the schools and local school systems.

Erica also worked for the National Security Agency (NSA) supporting agency personnel, military families, and their dependents. She continues to serve military families and devotes much of her time and experience to those suffering with complex PTSD and other trauma-related disorders.

In 2018, Erica was elected to the Board of Health in her local jurisdiction in Maryland, where she continues to serve as a Board member and was also nominated as the head of the Mental Health Sub-Committee. Erica's sincere and dynamic nature allows her to be a strong advocate for improving mental health services locally and abroad. She is a driving force for the de-stigmatization of mental health, as well as a proponent for alternative and holistic treatment options. Erica speaks out and advocates for those who have been failed by the health system, especially those suffering with chronic medical conditions from which she has also suffered.

Erica believes in living in gratitude, "paying it forward," and giving back to her community. She is involved in several philanthropic projects and is an advocate for entrepreneurial women. Erica also provides educational training to those in the mental health, medical, and legal fields, in hopes of expanding their content knowledge and educating them about the importance of the mind/body connection.

Connect with Erica below:
www.facebook.com/notagranolagirl?mibextid=ZbWKwL

FIONA BLACK

From Sacred Suffering to Sovereignty

There's a tower moment in everyone's life – perhaps even multiple. You know the moments I'm talking about, the moments where nothing makes sense anymore, and you question everything and everyone – especially yourself. Maybe you lost your job or got sick, or someone you love has died, or perhaps suddenly, you wake up one day, and you've become so disillusioned with the world that you wonder: *"What's the point?"*

The tower moment is meant to be your wake-up call, a sacred alarm that alerts you to your deviation from the truth of who you are, a loud and undeniable event that pulls the rug from beneath your feet and leaves you free falling into the abyss of the unknown.

Perhaps the wake-up call is a little gentler. It starts with a sense of uneasiness in your belly, a growing dissatisfaction with your life, a deep yearning to know: "Who am I? Why am I here?" And this yearning and desire to know the truth gets louder and stronger by the day until eventually, your search becomes all-consuming.

Once the alarm clock sounds, you can keep hitting snooze for as long as you want, but the alarm will keep ringing until you're able to stay awake long enough to not fall back asleep. And this is how it starts: the conscious journey of awakening. This is the beginning of co-creating with the Divine.

My awakening experience happened in waves. Each wave seemed to build upon the next until one moment in 2015, a wave came along that was so powerful that it wiped out all that I thought myself to be and turned my life around forever...

The Beginning of the End

I was born a deep feeler and thinker. Ever since I was a child I remember being extremely confused and sad about the amount of pain and suffering in the world. I couldn't understand why people made the choices that they made and why adults were so unhappy and dishonest to others and to themselves. It made no sense to me and hurt my heart. So, in an effort to fit in, I tried really hard to be the best I could be. I shut down a lot of my sensitivity and turned off my ability to 'see' in order to survive.

I coloured inside the lines, followed the conveyor belt of schooling, and chose a practical University course to study. Once I finished Uni, I traveled to Australia for three months, and suddenly, I could breathe again.

I could see all the ways I had squished myself into a box, and I was ready to break free. But when I went back home, the need to make money led me back to my previous life, and I shut down the possibility of living any other way.

By the time I was in my mid-twenties, although I enjoyed my job as a Physiotherapist in London UK, I could also see ahead and practically predict my future. I began to understand that I was following a society defined program of 'go to a good school, get a good job, marry a well-paid man, and have children'. Every single cell of my body began to scream, "NO!"

I yearned to experience other countries and explore different places. My feet were itchy, and my heart was desiring more. So when my friend invited me to a last minute holiday to Thailand, I jumped at the chance. While there, I met my soulmate from British Columbia. After just 6 months, I decided to follow my heart and moved to be with him in Canada. That's when the awakening truly started to speed up.

Although my new life was full of excitement and adventure, the grief I experienced was immense. I grieved the loss of my family and friends. I grieved the loss of my identity, the loss of my profession, and the loss of my "place" in society.

One day, I went tree planting with my partner for the first time, and my grief amplified in a way I could not have anticipated. With each tree that I planted, I could feel the grief of the land, the death, and the destruction. Driving up to a once pristine forest after it's been logged is like arriving at a battlefield with the bodies of trees slain and left for dead on the ground. There were slash and burn piles everywhere, replacing magnificent trees and vegetation that was once home to countless animals. This destruction of nature broke my heart.

Along with the grief came waves of anger and rage. I was angry because, in many ways, I felt completely powerless in this new life I had created. I was angry at the world, angry at society, and I was angry at my soulmate for not having to change any part of his life to be with me whilst I had to change everything. I was full of rage at the perceived injustice of it all.

Then I became a mother, and my struggle increased. I thought I would feel empowered, but that was not my experience with my first child. All my karmic patterns and beliefs came to the surface. With no physical family support to help me raise my daughter and a partner who worked away for months at a time, I felt alone and exhausted in a foreign land.

Everything's all on me. There's no one to help me, and I have to do everything alone. These disempowering thoughts were my constant companions. Every day, I told myself a 'poor me' story. I was a true martyr.

Guilt and shame accompanied me along the way.

Why am I so angry? Why do I feel so much rage? What's wrong with me? I have so much: a loving husband, a beautiful daughter, a wonderful home, and I live in an amazing country. I'm so privileged. Who am I to suffer when I have everything? I should be happy.

If I'd gone to see a health professional, I'm sure I'd have been diagnosed with postnatal depression and given medication. I felt like I was losing my mind, because in many ways, I was.

One day in 2015, the weight of my thoughts and feelings about my reality became too much. I felt so completely desperate that I was literally on my knees. I didn't know how to continue. I didn't know how to be a mother, a wife, a daughter, or a friend. I didn't know how to navigate this human life when nothing felt true anymore.

Everything that I had once believed felt so fake and pointless. The foundations of my life began to disintegrate beneath my feet. I felt utterly alone and didn't know who I was anymore. I just wanted to go home, but I didn't know where home was. And, perhaps, the scariest feeling of all, I could feel that part of me wanted to die, the part of me that was experiencing so much pain and suffering.

I reached out to a friend and spiritual mentor of mine, and she offered to hold space for me over a Zoom call. I shared my utter desperation and paralyzing fear that I was going crazy. She kept asking me: "Where are you? Where is this Fiona that's in so much pain and suffering? Where are her edges? Where could this Fiona be found?"

I'd sat with these questions many, many times before, but there was something different about this day. Eventually, after about an hour of searching and searching, my mind just gave up. I surrendered. I didn't know where I was. I couldn't find *me*.

When all attempts to find myself had been given up, there was a split second in time that seemed to last forever. Something subtle – but powerful – shifted inside of me. Instead of my consciousness residing inside Fiona as a separate self, all of a sudden my consciousness exploded into becoming everything.

I knew at that moment with every fiber of my being that I was not a separate person living a life; *I was life itself!* I was the breath moving through me, the bed I was sitting on, and the person staring back at me on the screen. The illusion of a separate self fell away, and I was left with the absolute knowing that I was pure consciousness.

I laughed because it seemed so silly. This peaceful state that I had been longing for, this enlightenment that I had been searching for was here all along. I was not the person that felt peace; I *was* peace and always had been. My laugh was quickly followed by a thought that felt like the biggest unburdening I'd ever experienced: *If I am consciousness itself, then I'm free to play the role of Fiona. I'm free to be me!* What a relief!

My entire body relaxed. For lifetimes upon lifetimes, I had been trying to be someone or something that I wasn't. Now, those feelings had lifted.

I'm free to be me. I'm free to be ME! I kept repeating this in my head over and over again. To be liberated from the need to be anything other than who I was in that moment awakened a bubbling joy inside of me that I hadn't felt since I was a child, and I found myself dancing for no other reason than the sheer love of it!

This new consciousness had me gliding through life for a couple of months. A veil had been lifted from my eyes. Everything seemed brighter and more vibrant, especially when I was out in nature. I could see patterns of energy around people and between people. Instead of getting drawn into my own ego patterns and those around me, I could observe them and choose not to participate. It was like experiencing life in the complete reverse! Instead of seeing through the eyes of my small self, I was seeing life through the eyes of everything. What once was the foreground became the background, and my overriding experience was a feeling of peace and flow.

This flow state did eventually dissipate, and there was disappointment as my old ways of being began to resurface. The first time in a long time, I felt the familiar feeling of anxiety in my belly when I woke up in the morning. I panicked because I so desperately wanted to keep hold of the flow state. But then I realized that my ego wanted to try and control my experience, and when I shifted back to the observer, I felt free to feel anything and everything without judgment. I could choose my point of attention. Any time my ego tried to get a hold of something and get upset or make myself the victim, the expanded version of me came to the forefront again. This knowing that I was always free to choose changed everything. Suffering ended for Fiona.

As the years passed, I continued to live my life. Whenever Fiona took center stage, her drama didn't last long, and peace became my resting state of being. From the outside, it would have looked like nothing much had changed.

It wasn't that everything became 'perfect'. I still got angry, had arguments with my spouse, and worried about money, but none of those emotions lasted long or held much weight anymore. I witnessed these very human moments as my conditioning 'playing out,' and the less attached I was, the quicker these 'waves' passed.

Ironically, the more I knew that I was not a 'separate self,' the more grounded I became in my body, and I began to show up in my physical life in a more practical and powerful way. The exhaustion lifted, and I felt more ease. With no desire to push, prove, or pretend to 'be someone,' I became free to be myself exactly as I was, and my nervous system continued to heal from lifetimes of fear-based living.

I kept following the whispers of my heart and soul, and one day, I found myself exploring Soul Realignment: an intuitive healing modality created by Andrrea Hess that uses the Akashic records to explore Soul level information. I started accessing the Akashic records regularly for myself and my clients, which helped to skyrocket my intuition and psychic abilities.

Integrating Soul-level guidance into my life and business over the last 3 years has been one of the most profound experiences of my life. I feel freer than ever before to shine my light, do what I love, and support other women to understand a deeper truth about who they are and why they're here. And because I've had this powerful glimpse of knowing that we are all so much more than we think we are, I wake up every day feeling privileged that I get to be Fiona and share this 'work' in the world. I finally feel like the empowered co-creator that I was born to be.

The End is just the Beginning...

As we navigate the 'enlightening' process, our mind tries to trick us into believing that awakening is the end point. But in my experience, the very opposite is true! Where there is death, there is always rebirth, not just for us as individuals, but for humanity as a whole. We are now experiencing this on a global scale.

The collective is waking up from thousands of years of unconscious living. We are waking up from our slumber, and Great Mother is awakening, too. Our bodies are not separate from the body of the Earth. We're not separate from our brothers and sisters on the other side of the planet. We are all connected, and every single choice that we make affects the whole.

Every human on this planet has the potential to be a Divine Creator. We're all God-Consciousness in a body made of the same non-stuff that creates mountains and valleys, forests and lakes. And we each have a unique Divine Soul Blueprint that holds the key to living a life of infinite joy, peace, abundance, and possibility.

Every person is literally walking around with the winning lottery ticket in their hand – a ticket that holds all the information about who they are and how they were designed to create abundance in their lives. Yet, the majority are completely unaware of this magical essence inside of them, and this unconsciousness causes a whole lot of suffering.

When we're walking around, identified as a singular person who's at the mercy of the actions and circumstances of the World around us, we feel disempowered and small. We continue to lead our 'fated' life. This is a life led by our programming, our conditioning, our family's thoughts and beliefs, our karma and societal expectations. Our choices are inevitable, predictable and don't deviate much from those around us.

When we begin to wake up, the light of awareness shines upon all the parts of ourselves and society that are out of alignment with Truth. This initial wake up is often the most difficult to navigate. It's uncomfortable and painful. There's a lot of repressed emotions to feel and beliefs to dismantle. Any old way of being in the world literally has to die in order for us to live authentically to our true nature. We can feel very alone and like we're going crazy. We may want to go back to the blissful ignorance of sleep, but once consciousness has shone the light of awareness, we can never forget it. We are forever changed.

On this journey of awakening, we suffer for as long as we need to suffer in order to come to a place of surrender. True surrender happens by grace. In my experience, this is not something that we have any control over, which is the reason that we have such a hard time letting go. Our ego thinks that enlightenment or peace is something a person achieves and is a place to 'get to,' and we try so very hard to 'make it,' but this is one of the biggest misunderstandings there is.

When we realize there is no person to become enlightened, then we're free to simply be as we are: a beautiful, magnificent expression of the Divine in human form. The weight of being this perfect human that must achieve anything in life is lifted. And ironically, that is when our human expression is liberated to truly co-create a life of joy, peace, and abundance with the Divine.

A Message Just for You

Your suffering is sacred, and it's the key to your sovereignty. Every single choice you've made and every experience you've had has brought you to this exact moment in time where you're holding this book in your hands. It's no mistake.

EVOLVING ON PURPOSE

This has not happened by chance. You have created this moment by listening to and following the whispers of your heart and soul.

Your entire life can change on a dime once you make the empowered decision to never go against the integrity of your Soul again. You can choose to stop suffering *now!* You are that powerful! And instead, you get to live your destined life, co-creating a life of infinite possibilities with your eyes wide open. Anything - and everything - is possible for you.

I love you!

Fiona xo

About the Author

Fiona Black is an intuitive, channel, and midwife for the Soul. Her passion is to support conscious, creative women to deeply integrate their Soul gifts and wisdom into their life and business so that they live a truly purpose-filled, powerful, and prosperous life.

Specializing in the Akashic records, Fiona tunes into 5th dimensional information to support her clients as they increase their clarity and capacity to make conscious soul-aligned choices. This leads to greater freedom for her clients as they understand how to liberate themselves from karmic cycles and ultimately remember their Sovereignty.

Originally from the UK, Fiona now lives on the West Coast of Canada on Vancouver Island with her husband, two beautiful children, and two magical cats. She loves being in nature, hiking, mindfully moving her body, eating clean, and being with family.

Fiona's mission is to ground unconditional love on the planet and to be an integral part of a network of global light workers who are here to assist in the ascension process of humanity.

Connect with Fiona below:

www.freedomwithfiona.com

GISELLE LORENA HURTADO

Divine Emergence: Rebirthed and Risen
from the Darkness of Our Past

Love and fear rises from the collective stream of consciousness. As creators of our experiences, we can control how the confluence of these energies shapes our reality. Love radiates acceptance, trust, and unity. Fear radiating threat, illusion, and separation of the self. Two powerful emotions that can't control the challenges we face in life, and influence how we approach the next ones.

The moment flashed between "I need you to find my phone now," to several whips from the metal parts of the belt lashing against my skin.

I cried, "Stop! Please!" and the more I seemed to yell, the more she seemed to get into hurting me. With nothing on but my arms covering my red, ripped body, I saw the fresh scars all over my legs and arms.

"STOP!" I screamed from the top of my lungs and jumped out my window one leg first, falling on the ground. I ran with no shoes and felt glass shards stab into my feet. I couldn't run any longer, until I fell on the ground, crying in the middle of the street in pain.

I didn't understand why I was being punished badly for losing a phone, but my mother had her reasons.

All I could think about was my sister, and I ran to her for comfort. I saw her as my only friend and mother figure. I knew I didn't deserve such pain and felt distorted in what just happened. Mother later apologized, but the scars remained. In a home where punishment was a way of showing necessary correction and love.

As a child, my sadness developed into love. My anger forged a path for my resilience, and my pain became the foundation for my power.

Over the years of enduring mental and physical abuse, my pain became the driver of my life. I created my cycle of depression, avoidance, and lack of self-love. I was both the tsunami and the aftermath. As with any disaster, I tended to linger in the destruction, rather than move on or find closure.

I'd always disappear somewhere in my apartment or the same yellow slide that became my comfort. After never-ending fights and frustration and disagreement, I learned to spend a lot of time watching the view from my window and looking up at the star-filled sky to calm my sanity. The moon would always glisten around a million stars, and the wind would always soothe my mind. Stargazing became a getaway for escape and opened a connection to the universe and me.

The universe brought me in on a wave of curiosities on November 23rd, 1997. In a small Chinatown named Flushing, New York City, after years of planning to move to the U.S, my parents decided to part ways, and he would return to Ecuador to care for my grandma. The move would be the last time I saw my father again. The next 18 years of my life would continue without him.

I was the only one of 3 siblings that had the chance to move to the US. My sister and brother had been in Colombia and suffered their trauma and fear without a mother to bring them sooner than planned. She held hope to bring them after working and saving a few checks.

However, life had other plans, and they had to adjust to having a new sister. Our family had been broken up for years - literally and figuratively.

My family wasn't to blame for our imperfections. We all had suffered individual trauma before reuniting together again – refracted pieces of ourselves reflecting on each other.

My brother Jonathan, suffered from alcoholism and daily rageful outbursts. Every morning, he would play heavy metal music and drink a beer for breakfast. I would lay in my bed in the room next to his and try to drown out the noise by blasting my favorite songs on my headphones. Some days, I couldn't stand to be there a moment longer, so I would lock my bedroom door and sneak out of my back window just to find some peace and quiet... I loved my brother, but sometimes I didn't like to be around him.

During the summer, I would often sneak out at night to go on a walk in the woods with insect traps. I needed to escape the chaos of my house in order to create peace both around me and within me. A getaway from home was necessary to keep the peace. I had only one goal: capture the creepiest critters! I became an expert at finding all the little ladybugs, rolly pollies, and ant farms. Unlike most little girls, I was not afraid of bugs or spiders; instead, I would climb trees so I could sit even closer to them. I would stare at them for hours with awe and wonder. The bugs would never bite, and for that, I loved them. As the sun would set, so would the clock for my time outside. "Giselle!" No matter how far from home that I roamed, I could always hear the shrill sound of my mother's voice as she called for me to come home. It was time to shut down and go to my room for yet another sleepless night.

EVOLVING ON PURPOSE

I loved waking up to the sounds of nature: the birds singing in the trees, the leaves rustling in the wind, and the hum of the bees buzzing by. At night, I would gaze up at the star-stained sky shining through the tall, intertwined trees. Sparks of kindled fire would pop like fireworks, and the smell of the smoky wood filled the air. I promised myself that one day I would run off into the wilderness, create a home, and allow the animals to stop by for tea. Maybe by then, the world would have invented a device to invite them all in, and I could forget my identity and be free like the wolves yet deep into the Earth like the depths of the oceans.

I discovered that pleasant imagery and visualization were incredibly healing. It's essential to have a happy place or memory to return to when feeling your lowest. While in the darkest times in my life, I would allow my mind to wander in the universe and let the images of my soul's desire flow in. Flowing freely, I would imagine myself traveling to different planets, spiraling into different dimensions, and always being loved and greeted by many strangers I didn't recognize. Sometimes, I would even see children I don't yet have, yet the love that I had for those strangers was there. I could feel my energy shifting into different places. All these colors would flow through my mind and body. The more I wandered in the depths of my mind, the more I recognized beauty in all things in front of me. Outside of this matrix, the reality I escaped to was far more real. Waking up to my reality felt surreal.

Wherever I would run off to, I'd fall into hypnosis with the sky and trees. The sounds of music or nature would swirl my emotions into one symphony. Suddenly there was no pain, no anger, and no tears left in me. Before I got here, there were dark secrets that haunted me for what seemed to be an eternity. Before I saw the brightest dawn, I saw the darkest hour. Before I knew love, I knew pain, and anger. Deep, deep, anger.

The ones we trust the most are often the ones who let us down. When I was 11 years old, my grandpa was the only one I confided in. We would take long walks after I got home from school, and I would hold his hand when walking him to work. One day after another, Grandpa decided to hurt and betray the trust we had as a family. As hard as it is to say, the abuse started with sexual comments and bribing me for acts I could not commit. Manipulation at its best, he would threaten me with my mom if I didn't do what he asked. I felt my heart sink to my stomach after school and began running away from home. One of the hardest things to do was tell my mom. We were not as close as I wished us to be.

I've never felt more lonely or more scared in my life. Many times, I tried to run away for good, and every time, I ended up in the same cold, yellow slide in the middle of the night, with nothing but a fluffy elephant blanket, some headphones, and my green iPod. My head would lie backward on the slide. I would face the stars and stare into the cold night. Too many tears would fall down my face and I could feel an itching anger of pain and rage bottled up inside me.

I was never the same girl anymore, and that perception of being shattered would change my life for the worse. My future relationships were never the same. My self-love was non-existent, and my trust for anyone on this Earth was gone. My heart was destroyed; I was destroyed. The excuse for him, of course, was that "the Devil got inside him," but I couldn't understand why he would blame the Devil when *he* was the one that was doing something evil.

I had to live with him before he decided to leave back to Colombia. In the meantime, I avoided going home. My life took place more on the outside of the world, and one escape that helped me through this, was boxing. I spent most days after school boxing at the Boys and Girls Club where I found friends, discovered dance revolution, the chess club, art, and boxing.

Out of all things, boxing helped me through my anger and lack of confidence. My hands would cramp and bleed after punching the back stuck in my thoughts. My shadow boxing intensified by the anger that waved inside me like a storm. Every Time I got into that ring, another side of me would come out. I'd face my survival mode in the face, in the flesh, without fear or worry. I boxed for 6 years, and my coach told me my 18th birthday would be the last time I could box there. I moved forward, a part of myself felt healed.

The memories of my past carried on and became faint until adulthood. Eventually, I found myself in abusive relationships and narcissistic abuse. The battle had just begun for me, and the war was against myself, trapped in my walls I created for my enemies. Before I knew it, I was the enemy. I was subconsciously lashing out at those I loved, rejecting love, and creating hatred for myself. I couldn't seem to find the joy in my life and did not understand my hateful reactions and negative self-talk.

The day I left; I stopped feeding my demons the negative energy that they desired. I decided to stay silent, remain calm, and think before I reacted to external negativity. I was no longer disturbed but the observer at hand, watching my darkness with a magnifying glass and paying attention to my reactions. I needed to accept ALL parts of me- including the darkness.

Many years later, as an adult, I began to practice meditation, listening to sound healing and solfeggio frequencies, taking sound baths, and practicing breathwork every night. I started reading and learning about the universal principles of existence. I came across a channeler named KYRON. His teachings of the lightworker and love changed the purpose of my existence and my being. My curiosity to become a better person pushed me further into the ancient teachings, and our star family of light that are always there for us. I began meditating every day, breathing the air, and feeling the wind. I felt connected. There was finally an at-ease love feeling bubbling inside. My emotions felt harmonious, and I could actually breathe away my pain and had an intense sentiment of joy. I didn't fear death, nor bad situations. Too many of them kept happening, and I realized that shit storms come in. The way I approached them changed, and the way I thought and reacted changed. That's when the practices got deeper, and my energy work expanded. I would practice energy body work and could feel the crystals tingle my body. Each one had a different feeling. I became infatuated with the idea of energy body work.

I began to practice self-reflection and played my day in reverse every night. This practice helped my mind to work a new power because human beings usually think ahead – not behind. This can help reset our subconscious inner programming. Self-reflections bring self-awareness. Becoming aware of our state of mind and thoughts can help us grow out of old thinking patterns and limiting beliefs.

The more I learned about these teachings and my connection to the Universe, the more my Spirit filled me with joy, love, and compassion. From a time of pain and desperation, my heart was my sacred home of GOD. It was not superior to me, nor out of reach, but a matter of turning a light switch on.

Trauma created an entangled web effect on my mind, causing me to believe I wasn't worthy of love. I went from hiding in isolation to avoid getting hurt and creating these walls of distrust with anyone who came into my life. Limiting beliefs and emotional reactions happen subconsciously. I had to ask myself why I was so defensive and often reacted in a fight or flight mode. The answer was survival. I felt I had to survive my surroundings. I would eliminate any potential factor in my pain.

Human consciousness is a form of awareness of our environment, and if raised to be in survival mode, then that's exactly how we live our life. Subconsciously surviving. I'd be lying if I said the process was easy, and the first steps were even harder. Isolating my thoughts so that I can focus upon them. I would think about why I was thinking negative thoughts. Sounds paradoxical, but to think of why you're thinking that one upcoming thought, is a big step in finding much needed inner healing. Focusing upon our thoughts can help pinpoint the trauma, which clouds the lens we see our life through.

The wounded healers here hold extraordinary power. Tender-hearted beings offer their pain as a soothing whisper, easing the minds of those in desperation, consumed by their darkness. I recognized a part of their soul, a heavy familiar heart, a nightfall that is not new to an experienced soul.

I realized darkness is the absence of light and doesn't hold an energy of its own. When you put out a light, there is darkness. When you turn on a light, it disappears. In this way, the wounded healer learns to heal others by transforming their pain and profound sorrow, turning these emotions into compassion, comprehension, and love. Love amongst similar souls just like you and me at some point, hurt, lost, or tired of endless suffering. We all come together when evil hits, and the light we create is quite extraordinary.

Furthermore, I've put together three initiations to journey into your inner realms of Divinity. We are all part of infinite love from the Universe, the Creator, and Spirit. Use these three initiations to help train your heart to see the Divine within.

Divine Light

Looking at a lighthouse, we can see its meaning and purpose is to shed light in the darkest waters for boats and ships to find their way. The lighthouse always stands strong, shining its light while the waves constantly hit against them, shining the light in a dark sea so that others may never lose their path. We all hold divine light, although the nighttime always comes around. There are ways to move through the darkest of times and adapt our hearts to becoming even brighter within ourselves. The following three practices will ground your heart and help you to stand firm as a lighthouse so that you may shine the light amongst yourself and those still lost at sea.

1. **Unconditional Compassion.** Love others – and yourself – without judgment. Love and compassionate action are unconditional and a catalyst for healing trauma. By radiating our light, we can help others tune into a higher

frequency with love. Our emotions can block our understanding of ourselves and others. See-through a different lens and try to understand the perspective of those hurting. Remember, all of us are a part of the Source and come from unique backgrounds. To see others as less than us is not accepting the Source in them. We all are capable of non-judgmental, unconditional compassion. We allow our consciousness to expand through breaking the barrier of disagreement and accepting others as they are and not allowing our reactions to get the best of us. When we integrate compassion and light, some people may feel uncomfortable. Some people may not understand you, and in some instances, you must learn to let go. Letting go is a painful part of accepting that we cannot change anyone else. However, you *can* change the way you react to others, and know that behind the lost connection lies Divine Source.

2. **Hold Spiritual Sight.** When you look at a stranger, see them as a part of GOD and a part of you. To see divinity in others is the beginning of the understanding of love. Spiritual sight allows you to see beyond the physical world and perceive from the other side of the veil. It brings unity and connection to those around us and helps us see the good in others. The divine seeps through all of us, and this change of perspective allows you to understand and see GOD work in our lives.

3. **Laugh More.** This one is simple. Laugh more, enjoy more happy memories, and be more involved with your playful side. Creative and sensual energy derives from joy, the ecstasy of happiness. Feel free in your heart and enjoy the essence of your passions, your Earth, and your inner-being connection. Light is spread in many ways, and one of those ways is laughter, love, and joy.

Divine Power

When we think of Divine power, there's an idea of GOD or a Creative Source with this Divinity somewhere, a place that is superior to us or out of reach and one we hold our prayers and problems to solutionize. There is no place or time in a quantum state, so how could GOD be somewhere other than ourselves? There is no separation of place or time, the present, the now. To hold Divine power starts with accepting that Divinity is a part of *you* and that the system of the Creative Source is *you*. Your base thought of yourself should be acknowledging you are Divine with a piece of GOD within you and not apart.

1. **The Power of Your Words.** The first catalyst of healing is with your words. Repeat three repetitions throughout the day in the mirror, acknowledging you are Divine. Affirm this thought as a base belief about yourself. The chemistry in your body starts to change as you talk to it. Everything

we say is affected by our feelings. Create a space for positive self-talk and reflection. Talking to yourself and your body activates light quotients in your DNA and changes your actual chemistry. Emotions can make this challenging but remember: you don't own your emotions. They are a state of consciousness in lower vibrations, along with fear. Love is the highest vibrational state of consciousness, and fear is the lowest. Align positive thoughts with actions. If you experience negative self-talk or thoughts, remember this very moment is an experience of your conscious being. You are in control of feeding fuel to the fire or diffusing the fire by recognizing and releasing these thoughts.

2. **Raise Your Vibration**
   o Be in nature
   o Meditate daily
   o Practice breathwork, tantras, and mudras
   o Listen to high vibrational music and frequencies
   o Create art
   o Observe sacred geometry
   o Gain higher knowledge of ancient teachings
   o Ingest raw, natural foods and pure water
   o Fast occasionally
   o Expose your auric field to monotonic scaler crystal energy

- o Do Vedic yoga
- o Practice self-love and healthy self-respect
- o Practice shadow work
- o Heal your inner child

3. **Being present in the NOW.** Fear of the past and future can hold you back. You can temper the past with wisdom. Understand why something happened in old energy so you can move on and tap into a different frequency. Ground your Divine power by living in the present and stop pondering the past. Living in the present moment allows gratitude to fill up your cup.

Divine Connection

1. **Trust in the Universe and Co-Create with the Divine.** Trust in the Universe allows limitations and expectations to drop and helps manifest our dreams.
   - o Practice A - Repeat: *"I surrender and let go and follow the path the universe has for me. Dear Spirit, I trust in synchronicity and listen to my intuition so that I am in the right place at the right time. All I ever will need will be provided for."*
   - o Practice B - "Manifestation Dancing." Flow and dance freely to high vibrational music while visualizing your soul's desires – not your mind's. See the images of your soul's yearnings, claim them to be yours, and let them go.

2. **Communicate with the Great Spirit.** Talk to yourself. Spirit is always listening. Your innate body takes your thoughts and your words and works them into your physical and Spiritual bodies. Speak with your Higher Self and ask for signs and intuition. Your Spirit speaks. Your body and Spirit were designed to work together to activate your cells, your DNA, and your intuition. Practice meditation to silence your thoughts and help eliminate random thoughts blocking the voice.

3. **Communicate with your Family of Light.** We are all part of a big family of light. Prayer, gratitude, and communication with these beings will allow them to interact with you as they can. Through signs, numbers, dreams, or images, they communicate to our physical realm with your permission only, as it is ruled by free choice. Practice meditating on your inner temple and create a space with yourself. The inner temple is unique to everyone and subconsciously travels into your inner realms. Here, our guides can be with us. Once inside your visualized temple, breathe up to the Source, through your inner temple, down to Gaia, then back up to you.

From warrior to warrior, the wounded, and the healers, keep shining your light wherever you are on your journey. Remember, the one who is evolving and bringing light to the world is crucial to our shift and is beyond amazing. You no longer are separated by religion, color, and race but by evil and good, dark, and light. You corner the darkness, stand against evil, and illuminate those dark corners. You want good and no longer stand by evil when civilization decides that is the reality you're going to get. You are that powerful. You are living incarnations of the SPIRIT. You are creators of the DIVINE!

About the Author

Giselle Lorena Hurtado is a survivor of domestic abuse who has evolved from a time of darkness into an advocate for spreading messages of love, light, and self-mastery. Giselle guides others with processing their experiences and moving forward from trauma toward healing. Amid chaotic situations and having a passion for writing, she has moved forward with a desire to teach others about the Divine as a lightworker. She has dedicated 7 years to various practices, such as energy body healing, meditations, and spiritual self-awareness. Her knowledge expands to ancient hermetic teachings, universal principles of law, and esotericism.

Giselle's journey has not been easy, and she has had to overcome sexual abuse, childhood trauma, and breaking free of narcissistic relationships. Her mission is to help others connect with their inner masters, teachers, and ancestors to embrace their light, love, and compassion. She teaches women to deal with obstacles and to live happily, regardless of their past. She believes if we look further into our thoughts and state of consciousness, we can raise our emotional intelligence and bring awareness to necessary inner healing.

Giselle Hurtado is also a passionate writer, herbalist, and spiritual enthusiast who shares wisdom of our divinity and mastering our emotional, mental, and physical bodies. From darkness to a life of light and love, she continues to learn and create transformational guidance to help seed a new generation of joy, peace, and inner freedom.

Connect with Giselle below:

www.facebook.com/jennifer.lorena.7

JENNIFER ELIZABETH MOORE

Letting Go of the Good to Welcome the Great

I don't suppose you'd be interested in moving to Portland?" my colleague Chris inquired dryly.

An inner voice whispered, "This is your True North. This is what you've been waiting for. Say 'yes!'"

I'd watched my inner Wicked Witch of the West write "Surrender Dorothy" across the sky enough times to know my ego was no longer in charge.

Up until that moment, my life had felt like a maze. After a few steps forward, I'd hit an inevitable wall. Sometimes the turn led to a clue. Sometimes I had to back out of a dead end.

At the seasoned age of 36, I'd had my share of failures and near misses. I'd bounced from one eager attempt to another. I'd had great ideas but no sustainable successes. I'd tried to make it as an artist, spiritual teacher, psychic, and energy healer, but had little to show for my efforts. I'd tearfully returned a vintage diamond ring to my ex-fiance. I'd walked away from two coveted tattoo apprenticeships after circumstances became too precarious for my sanity and well-being.

I had plenty of evidence to prove my inner critic was correct: "I don't have what it takes. I'm destined to fail despite my intelligence, talent, and ambition. I'm doomed to push the boulder up the hill for the rest of my life."

Despite my spiritual practice, I liked to be in control. I thought I knew what I wanted. I believed I knew how to make it happen. In reality, most choices were actually attempts to avoid pain. When I said "yes" to co-create a custom tattoo studio with my soon-to-be business partner, the unpredictable maze I'd been stumbling through for my first three decades became a single route labyrinth offering a clear way forward. All my near misses, random detours, exertion and years of trial and error began to make sense.

I experienced flow from the moment I committed. I was carried by currents of Divine possibility. Within a month, we found a property to lease. We bought discounted cabinets and countertops at a liquidation sale. We went from raw industrial space to a fully operational studio in less than three months!

I'd taken a massive leap into the unknown. I was becoming the person I was destined to be. I'd claimed my purpose. The Universe said, "JUMP!" I responded, "how high?" I was invited to drop everything familiar. I moved away from all my friends and family. I invested every penny I had with no promises that my plan would work or guarantees that my efforts would pay off. I just had a profound sense that I had to try. I knew denying this opportunity would be worse than failure. I desired this more than anything I'd ever wanted before. Simultaneously, I was willing to surrender all of it.

This marriage of determination and detachment was the special sauce. My life unfolded miraculously. Six months after leasing our studio, I was thriving in Portland. I met my future husband. Business blasted off. Plenty of wonderful clients hired me. We were well on our way to becoming one of the most successful, popular, and award-winning tattoo studios in our region.

Though inner demons of self-doubt, unworthiness, and low self-esteem still lingered, I'd stopped waiting for the other shoe to drop. I believed I'd finally landed. I'd found the place I would put down roots and dedicate the rest of my life to.

This heralded eighteen years of creativity and delight. I said, "yes!" and in return my life was filled with gratitude,

160

prosperity, and good, honest work. However, as the saying goes: "This too shall pass."

In the autumn of 2013, I had my butt handed to me. I won't share the litany of woes, other than to say I experienced nine human deaths in less than eighteen months, the sudden and traumatic loss of our beloved pug Maya, family health crises, and a bout of pneumonia that left me depleted, vulnerable, and struggling.

I slept through most of October, November, December, and January. I tried to return to normal, but every time I'd exert any energy, I relapsed and ended up back on the couch streaming mindless TV for hours without end.

Finally, in March of 2014, I received a conclusive diagnosis for Lyme Disease. You might imagine that I felt devastated. In truth, I was elated. I finally had the key to address my actual problem. I'd spent what felt like an eternity pulling my exhausted body out of bed, hauling myself to the studio, and rallying to work with clients. After ten months of debilitating fatigue, brain fog, and intermittent bouts of fear, depression, and existential foreboding, I turned a corner that August.

The spring in my step was restored. I'd regained my sense of purpose. I was finally feeling hope: "I can do this! Not only can I do this, I was *made* for this." Then the co-owners of my business called for a private meeting. I did not anticipate what was coming next.

Lyme is often an invisible illness. Weariness and distress influence everything for the one who suffers. However, these challenges frequently go unnoticed by outside observers. I'd gone to great lengths to put my most cheerful and engaged self out to the world. In truth, I'd been running on fumes for nearly a year. My colleagues had no idea the struggle I experienced everyday. Without inquiry or expression of concern, they'd become irritated with my need for time off and my challenges with time management.

"Lyme disease has kicked my butt. I drag myself to the studio. I give every drop of energy I have to serve my clients. I go home and collapse." I explained. Brandon and Steve offered no sympathy or understanding. Instead, they told me to "suck it up and do better." I felt blindsided. During the meeting, I stood up for myself. I firmly stated: "As the senior partner and original co-founder, I'll run my part of the business as I choose." I kept it together through the rest of the meeting, but once it was over, I felt gutted.

That's when I realized the friction that I'd been overlooking had become too big to ignore; my illusions of respect and safety were balanced on a precarious fault line. My days were numbered in a business I'd already poured nearly two decades of my heart and soul into. Our conflicting goals and communication styles made common ground impossible.

I was shattered. I cried for days. Yet on the other side of those tears, I sensed keys to my freedom. Keys to possibilities beyond my wildest dreams. I was called to reveal my magic without constraint or attempts to appear "normal." I became "willing to be willing" to surrender my first identity as a success. That was when I realized I would have to *let go of the good to welcome the great.*

I had been quite content with life as it was. I could have continued on that trajectory for another decade or more. It would have been easy to stuff my lingering sense of betrayal. As long as I focused on my own work and my client's needs, I could overlook the studio politics and interpersonal conflicts. This had been my golden goose, so why would I want to kill it? Logically and financially, remaining in the business made sense. However, the Universe kept delivering hints and whacks upside the head. Anytime I'd deviate from the flow, I'd be thrown a curve ball.

So, I formed an exit plan. I found support to leverage my way from my thriving business to something even juicier. With the help of mentors and coaches, I developed systems for a viable online business. I upleveled my marketing and writing skills. I earned accreditation as an advanced EFT practitioner. Eventually, I became a Master Trainer for EFT International. I created a program for empaths and began to write my first book, *Empathic Mastery.*

In the last week of 2017, I shed the final vestiges of my role as the co-owner of an award-winning brick-and-mortar business. I took one last look at the studio that had supported me for 18 years and handed over my keys.

It took time to let go of the part of me that still felt hurt. I could absolutely see that everything unfolded in divine and perfect order, yet my bruised ego nursed my grievances and losses. Until I addressed the pain that prevented me from seeing beyond their harsh words, only part of me could say "no harm, no foul." I returned to the memory of that pivotal business meeting and used EFT/Tapping to release my pain. As I released my grudges, I became able to move forward without resistance. I could recognize that this confrontation needed to happen for my destiny to unfold. What came from this letting go was the revelation that those business partners served as divine agents for change. It took this discomfort and anguish to push me out of my cozy nest.

If that meeting hadn't happened, I could have stayed for years. In that reality, I wouldn't have followed Divine Guidance to refinance my mortgage and build the space of my dreams. I wouldn't have written and published my own book (or chapters for this and three additional collaborative books). I wouldn't have become a Master Trainer for EFT International, nor would I have mentored students to become impeccable practitioners who change people's lives with their skills.

I'd have been utterly unprepared for the COVID lockdown when everything came to a grinding halt. In this new life, I was already working virtually with all my clients. I could see the Universe had started preparing me for these circumstances eight years earlier. Had I resisted, had I not responded to the clues and followed the trail of lights along the way, I would have been stranded.

Co-creating with the Divine isn't always easy. It often requires stepping outside of our comfort zone. However, the price of playing safe and staying small is even higher. The thing is, it requires more than intellect and strategy to manifest our dreams. It's rare when thoughts and plans alone transform our lives. Co-Creating with the Divine requires five conditions:

1. Preparing the way by recognizing and releasing our pain, trauma, and limiting beliefs.
2. Grasping our lessons and adjusting our behaviors and attitudes so we can live differently.
3. Connecting with Inner/Divine Wisdom and trusting the guidance we receive.
4. Taking small but significant steps, consistently and persistently, to actualize possibilities.
5. Going all in and allowing ourselves to share our unique magic with the world.

In the next part of this chapter, I'm going to focus on two actions: releasing our pain, trauma, and limiting beliefs and cultivating our connection to Divine Source.

There's one tool I've discovered and worked with that surpasses the rest in efficiency, gentleness, and sustainability: Emotional Freedom Techniques (EFT), which are also known as "tapping". This modality is incredibly versatile and can be used for nearly anything. EFT is like mental and emotional acupuncture. We identify an issue, we rate its intensity, then we speak our truth while tapping on our head, torso, and hands to shift distress frozen in our physical, mental, emotional, and energetic bodies.

EFT is easy to learn. It can be self-administered to bring relief after just a few rounds of tapping. In its more advanced and nuanced forms, EFT can be used to release old trauma, ancestral legacies, past life challenges, physical pain, sensitivities, habitual patterns, mental and emotional wounds, and unhelpful conclusions we've formed. I've yet to find anything that tapping can't benefit in some way.

You could spend years exploring, studying, and practicing EFT and still have more to learn. Therefore, I'm going to share a simple but specific way to gently release memories and to connect with your Higher Power.

One of the benefits I love with tapping is that we do not have to dredge up a memory or relive the past to clear it. Instead, we set an intention to shift while maintaining a safe distance. If you've been on a healing path for a while, chances are you've been encouraged to take a deep breath and dive into the gnarliest stuff. It may feel counterintuitive not to jump into the deep end.

Perhaps you've heard the saying "no pain, no gain," or you've been taught that anything other than facing your demons head-on is resistance. With EFT, we do address our issues, but we use leverage and precision to deal with them from the shallow end of the pool. The key to success lies in targeting an issue as precisely and specifically as possible while simultaneously maintaining distance. The basic protocol is something you can do yourself. However, there are times when it helps to enlist the support of a skilled, accredited EFT practitioner.

Perhaps the most difficult part is learning to recognize when you're diving into your story and triggering old distress. The following approach might seem too basic or easy; as one who's facilitated countless sessions and witnessed miraculous transformations for many, I invite you to simply experiment with the technique as I share it with you. Once you get this down, you'll have plenty of opportunities to learn more. My approach will help you to develop good tapping habits from the get-go and give you a taste of what's possible.

The Basic EFT Recipe

EFT has three components called "the Basic Recipe":

1. Identify and Rate
2. Acknowledge and Accept
3. Tap and Notice

This basic formula works whether you're addressing memories, physical pain, negative self-talk, cravings, or any other kind of stuck energy.

Step 1: Identify and Rate

EFT starts by noting sensations, feelings, thoughts, or memories to identify what to tap on. In this chapter we're going to focus on tapping for a specific event. It's most effective to target a brief period of time - no more than a few minutes. Even with longer, more complicated situations, we break the story down into segments and tap on one "scene" at a time. The goal is to work incrementally and thoroughly.

The key to this technique lies in *not* unpacking details until most of the intensity has been discharged. We come up with a neutral title, as though we're casually mentioning a movie title. We choose words that won't provoke a reaction. For example, a name such as "Boat on the Water" is preferable to "Scary Shark." You can even call it "The Event" if you can't find a better neutral title. Though you're targeting a very precise and specific moment, you'll keep your distance using a detached title.

Here are some examples:

- Lost Keys
- Coffee Mug
- The Bathroom Floor
- Bridal Shower
- The Football Field
- Water Balloons

Without recalling your memory or trying to access any feelings about it, rate its level of intensity on a scale of 0 to 10.

Zero has no energy whatsoever. Ten is so extreme you can't imagine anything higher.

Don't overthink it. Just ask yourself what you *guess* the number would be. Go with the very first number that comes to mind. Write the number down to keep track of your progress. This way of gauging your SUDS (Subjective Units of Distress) is called "Tearless Trauma," which is just a fancy term for guessing.

Once you've established your words and their SUDS, you can start tapping. There are two distinct elements to the tapping part. First, the Set Up, and second, the Sequence, or Round, of Tapping.

Step 2: Acknowledge and Accept

EFT allows us to acknowledge our situation and introduce a different perspective. We achieve this first by using the Set-Up Statement and reinforce it as we move through the full tapping sequence.

The Set-Up Statement has two parts. Part one states what is: "Even though I experienced *The Event*." Part two offers a counterbalance: "That was then. This is now, and I'm okay."

The Set-Up has three purposes:

1. To access your issue and express your truth,
2. To neutralize resistance by creating space for both negative and positive perspectives, and

3. To define and express what you'd like to feel instead.

The traditional balance statement is: "I deeply and completely love and accept myself." At first, many people used this affirmation exclusively. However, those words didn't resonate for everyone. It even provoked dissonance for some. It's more important to use a statement that works for you than to force something to resonate. Take a moment to consider what feels best. It's essential to use words you agree with.

Here are some possibilities:

- I recognize that it's over now, and I'm okay.
- Maybe I can love myself anyway.
- I'm open to the possibility that this can shift.
- I did my best, and that was good enough.
- It's safe for me to let this go.
- I invite a surprisingly easy new experience.

Step 3: Tap and Notice

The first two steps helped you to tune in, define and acknowledge your issue. Now, we tap!

Using the tips of your index, middle, and ring fingers, tap gently on the outer edge of the opposite hand just below your pinkie. As you tap on the side of your hand, repeat your Set-Up Statement: "Even Though... (I experienced "movie title"), I... (use any positive or neutral statement you prefer)." For example: *Even though I experienced the "Lost Keys event," it's over now, and I'm ready to release it.*

Tap and repeat your Set Up three times.

Next, move through all the tapping points (see next section) as you only repeat a simple reminder phrase aloud. The point of this approach is to take the charge out of a memory and release the intensity without going into any details. Instead of trying to feel into it, try imagining there's a wide gap of time and space between you and the experience.

After you finish the first round, take a deep breath. Notice how you feel. Then, *without recalling the memory*, guess your new SUDS. Write down the first number that comes to mind. Even if new thoughts or adjacent issues arise, stick with your original issue until the SUDS is as low as it will go. It's okay to adjust to words that feel more accurate. However, though something new might bubble up while you tap, stay with the same words through the entire round of points. This allows you to thoroughly clear an event one scene at a time.

Even when it's tempting, avoid stories and emotional sinkholes. Keep it simple. Bringing up multiple details complicates the process. I encourage you to stick with this protocol as it's written. The purpose is to defuse intensity without engaging; it's not to air every piece of dirty laundry or dig into the drama. EFT allows us to address issues gently, from a safe distance. While it may seem counterintuitive, less is more.

At the end of each round, return to the top of your head and take a deep breath. Scan for shifts. Re-rate your intensity 0-10. If your rating is a two or higher, repeat the tapping sequence. Repeat your one title as you tap through all the points again.

10 Tapping Points

1. SH: Side of Hand (the outside edge of your hand, below your pinkie)
2. TH: Top of Head (the crown of your head)
3. IE: Inner Eyebrow (just above the bridge of your nose at the edge of your eye socket)
4. OE: Outer Eye (on your temple, just past the corner of your eye)
5. UE: Under Eye (directly under your pupil on the ridge of your eye socket)
6. UN: Under Nose (the philtrum, aka the groove between your nose and lip)
7. UL: Under Lip (the space between your lower lip and chin)
8. CB: Collarbones (the often tender spot just beneath your clavicle and above your nipples)
9. UA: Under Arm (on the side of your upper ribs past your breast, just below your armpit)
10. TH: Top of Head Again. Take a deep breath. Rate your intensity.

Using EFT to Connect with Divine Source

As effective as it is for releasing distress, EFT is also fantastic for tuning into Divine Source. Now that you've learned how to tap, I'm going to teach you one of my favorite ways to amplify your connection with Spirit. This technique combines tapping with breath. In its simplest form, you tap through all the points, inhaling and exhaling while inviting Spirit in.

You might start by tapping to release an issue and then finish with a few rounds of tapping and breathing. You can also use a set-up, followed by tapping through the points, or just start with a round of points. The following is a script I use either alone or in conjunction with a longer session.

Set-Up (Repeat while tapping on SH)

"Here I am, just being present and breathing into this moment. I'm ready to welcome my deeper connection with Divine Source and invite Inner Wisdom to guide my heart. I breathe in the light and energy of Sacred Presence (inhale), and I breathe out any illusions of separation and static (exhale). I am a beloved daughter of this Universe, and I embrace my magic" (repeat three times).

Sequence (Inhale and exhale at each point while either tapping or applying gentle pressure and repeating the following).

"I breathe in Light and invite my connection to Divine Source" (inhale). I breathe out static and distraction and claim my place right here, right now" (exhale).

After the first round, return to the top of your head and take a deep breath. Tune into your heart and feel how your connection to Source has shifted. Return to the side of your hand for another round.

New Set-Up

"Now that I've tapped, I embrace my sense of deeper connection with Divine Source. I invite the guidance of my Inner Wisdom and welcome clarity. I breathe in the light and power of Sacred Presence (inhale). I breathe this Light and Radiance out around me (exhale). I recognize that I am Divinely supported and claim my holy purpose" (repeat three times).

New Sequence (inhaling and exhaling through all the points)
"I breathe in my even deeper connection with Divine Source" (inhale). "I breathe out light and love and send it all around me" (exhale).

Return to the top of your head, take an extra deep breath. Notice how you are feeling. Reflect on how the round felt, and any insights you might have received. At this point, you might adapt the words of your set-up and sequence to reflect any shifts or revelations you've experienced. If you received a message, you might tap it in as an affirmation. If you are still seeking more guidance, you might try another round where you say something like: "I breathe in Wisdom; I breathe out Clarity" or "I breathe in Divine Inspiration; I breathe out Willingness and Love."

As you may imagine, the possibilities are limitless.

Once you've reached the point where you feel complete, you might simply end with a final deep breath, or offer a prayer with one final round of tapping. Here's one I created to enhance my connection:

TH: Divine Source, I open my soul to you.

IE: Allow me to know you ever more.

OE: Amplify my faith.

UE: Help me trust your sacred plan.

UN: Fill my heart with love.

UL: Use my hands to heal and serve.

CB: Reveal each right step before me.

UA: Guide my feet on your path of light.

TH: Make me a channel for your magic, hope, and wisdom that I may fulfill my holy destiny

–Amen

(Deep breath)

As you might imagine, this journey has taken me on a path of glorious surrender. Every day, Spirit guides me to the next right thing. "Do what is before you, and the rest will be revealed." This is Divine Guidance's firm but gentle reply whenever I get ahead of myself and start asking for more information. When I try to take back my will or persist in asking questions, Spirit reminds me they've already revealed the one baby step I can handle.

There is a serenity on the other side of allowing. There is an ease that only comes by handing the wheel back to Divine Source. There's also a paradox: the more I release control, the more I'm supported and provided for. Every time I try to figure life out, predict my future, or endeavor to exert my will in an attempt to pursue success by my ego's terms, I wade through glue. As long as I keep my focus on the one breath, the one step, and the one action, I remain in the flow and life unfolds with Grace.

Here are a few discoveries I've learned on this journey. Divine Surrender is an ongoing process. Our heart's desire is not fixed. Even the surest goals are destined to change. Co-creating with the Divine means being willing to feel the fear and do it anyway. It means we must acknowledge when we've hit a wall and have the willingness to adjust. It requires a capacity to dream bigger and follow our spark.

I'm deeply grateful for the life I live today. I'm blessed with love, plentiful resources, clients and mentees I adore, creative projects that delight me, colleagues who inspire me and an abundance of natural beauty that surrounds me. This life is what it is because I was willing to say "yes." I was willing to let go of the good to go for the great. I didn't give up before the miracle happened. I took incremental steps towards my divine goals. I cultivated the capacity to stop and celebrate each win along the way.

Instead of focusing on all the issues that appear to be wrong in the world, I return to my Divine connection and appreciate the simple delights and pleasures I experience daily. With the help of prayer, breathwork, EFT, meditation, willingness, and gratitude, I get to be the unbridled, magical fairy godmother I was born to be. I get to show up every day ready to serve, to notice and savor beauty and miracles, to contribute to the ease, grace and flow we need right now. I'm beyond blessed to empower other magical women to do the same.

About the Author

Jennifer Elizabeth Moore Fairy godmother to many, Jennifer is a healer and mentor for highly sensitive empathic women. She's the author of the Amazon bestseller, *Empathic Mastery: A 5 Step System to go from Emotional HOT MESS to Thriving Success*. She's also written chapters for 4 multi-author books and is the host of The Empathic Mastery Show which, as of this writing, ranks among the top 10% of all podcasts. In addition, Jennifer is the creator of the photographic Healing Tarot deck and two oracle decks.

Intuitive from the get-go, Jennifer experienced her first prophetic dream at the tender age of nine. She's been navigating her extrasensory awareness ever since. Jen (the name nearly everyone uses for her) has well over three decades of professional experience as a psychic, shamanic practitioner, and energy healer. She holds a Master's degree in Psychology and Religion and has earned the distinct honor of being among the 115 accredited Master Trainers for EFT International through which she offers professional EFT practitioner training along with individual and group mentoring for students seeking certification as well as support for established practitioners who need annual supervision.

Jen brings depth, compassion, and practical woo to her work. Jen's greatest passion is to support intuitives, lightworkers and creatives to express their truth, reveal their magic, and use their abilities for good. Jennifer lives among the great green pine woods and horse pastures of coastal Maine. She shares this bee and elderberry covered paradise with her husband, David, LeeLu, the pug, Livi and ZuZu their two black cats, a sweet young porcupine, a herd of deer, a nest of phoebes, one fox, and a few groundhogs.

Connect with Jen below:

Learn more about Jen and grab your illustrated EFT Guide at: EmpathicMastery.com/cocreating

JOS POUNE FAE

From Darkness to Light

🌿

I was so scared for so long to expose myself – my *true* self. If I spoke of all the darkness, the hurt, the pain, my soul contract with my earth family.

Being an indigo child means to go through many phases of pain, lying, cheating, manipulation, stress, anxiety, depression, feeling the waves raveling you up like a tsunami. Eventually, you need to go through the waves and learn how to surf. It takes time and energy, but mostly it takes love. Love is everything, and love for yourself comes before all.

I have transformed into the Quantum energy of light, when unraveling all the loopholes of darkness and facing them head on. No one can escape the darkness. It hurts, I understand, but it's necessary.

I went through my soul's darkness at the end of 2014 after the loss of my grandmother. While she may have been my father's mother, in my heart, she was *my* mother. She was everything to me. When she died, a part of my soul left with her, and I coped by making one bad decision after another!

I had a partner at that time, he came from Orion, the darkest planet in the Universe, offender, abusive. I lost everything but mostly my two oldest children! Today, we have both worked so hard to become better co-parents, we have a good relationship, I am very proud of both of us, we are doing an amazing job!

In 2018, I went from shelter home to shelter home with my three oldest children Eventually, the whole earth system was against me. They helped him out at that time. I didn't get it. I couldn't understand why. The truth is the system is full of reptilians! We need to go through our soul's darkness to become light.

At the end of 2018, I felt completely disconnected from my body and my soul. A part of me was gone forever. As time went by, I was less and less connected. I may have been physically there, but my mind was elsewhere. I was a vampire – appearing to be human on the outside, but dead on the inside. My humanity was completely gone. My feelings were shut off. I felt nothing. It was easier to feel numb, because if you don't feel, then you don't hurt. In 2018, after we got a police raid, I decided it was enough!

In April 2018, I met the father of my youngest children not long after we had a miscarriage. I have to be honest, I didn't feel hurt, but I felt something. Today, I understand her mission to come help me wake up from the darkness. Thank you, little one, for being part of my soul's growth to light. I feel you. I see you.

In August 2018, a month after my miscarriage I found out we were pregnant again. Slowly, I was having a rebirth. I also gave birth to a beautiful magical human: my little fairy in April 2019.

It wasn't even a month after I found out we were pregnant again. I wanted to wait a little to make sure, but by that time, I was already five months pregnant with twins. When the father of my youngest children came home one night, I told him, "I need to go to the hospital!"

He flippantly replied, "You will be fine. Just eat a little."

My heart raced. "I don't think you understand. I see my mother and other spirits which aren't in human form!"

He immediately brought me to the hospital, and when I arrived, I told them, "I think I have HELLP Syndrome." I was 33 weeks pregnant. The twins were in danger, and so was I.

The Doctors obviously did their tests, and when they came back, I had HELLP syndrome, which I knew because spirit told me.

They wanted to do an emergency C-section, but I refused. I called my doula, and she came as soon as she could to make sure my wishes were respected. I had made a birth plan. When the gynecologist arrived that morning, he was worried, I was open to negotiate, but I felt the whole universe with me. They whispered that everything was in the Divine plan.

Around 1 PM, the nurse came to see me. "We are ready to proceed."

I put a little bit of glitter on to meet my babies. "I'll be ready in 10 minutes!"

The nurse looked annoyed. "But we have been waiting all morning, and the emergency staff will be leaving at 5:00 PM."

"Don't worry! This will be fast. I will give birth by 5:00 PM." My little super girl arrived at 5:11 PM. I call her "super girl" because her little arm was in the air when she arrived. Luna cried right away, but her twin was breech, so I had an inversion.

I pushed and pushed, but I knew there was no way the baby was coming out. The doctor took his hand – or rather, his arm – and shoved it inside of me to pull my baby out!

Everything was silent, and I started to fear the worst. I waited and waited, and then finally I heard her cry. I cried as well. I was so relieved! She was born at 5:23 PM. I was 23 minutes late on my timing, but the medical staff were amazed that both twins were delivered so quickly.

After both girls had been delivered, something went very wrong. I started bleeding, and it wouldn't stop. I stared at the doctor in his eyes and said, "I am going to die."

"If you don't let me continue, you will die! You need to let me continue!"

I sat up and asked, "What was it that you wanted to give me?"

The nurse gave me one shot of fentanyl, and I fell into a very deep sleep. While sleeping, I was with my galactic family and my higher self. They had two questions for me: "Are you going to start all over? Or will you finish your mission?"

When I woke up, I was in another bed getting a blood and iron transfusion. "Where am I?" I asked the doctor.

"You just gave birth."

"What?!" I didn't remember anything. I could see the word "maternity" on the hospital bed, but everything else was a blur.

"You lost a lot of blood," the doctor stated. "You can't walk, and you will also need to stay in the hospital for a while with the twins. You will need blood transfusions, and the twins are in the NICU."

When the father of my children arrived that night with my ten-month-old baby I told him everything that the doctor had said. He smiled and told me, "You will be fine."

A full 24 hours had passed before I was able to go see my little rainbow babies. A nurse took me in a wheelchair to the NICU, and as soon as I saw them, my heart sank. They were covered in tubes, and one of the twins had a needle in her head! All I could hear was the constant beeping sound of the monitors and the beating of my heart within my chest. They both seemed so fragile.

Slowly, I started to remember. My first child, Luna, read her soul contract and I strongly feel that she has come to connect on a deeper level to help elevate the collective consciousness. The second twin is my mom. I feel her soul. She came here for me. We named her Yvonne after my mother.

Shortly after giving birth to my twins, another part of my world collapsed in August 2020! My second oldest child left. It was obviously a very hard relationship before our departure! This is part of the fifth step of awakening when your world as you know it shuts down. You are in the dark, but you need to be in the dark to understand more of the light. The desire to be alone, to be in nature, and to be a hermit burns inside you. You feel alone and lost because no one understands all that you are going through. You have nothing to cling to except to seek the answer to the question: "Who am I?"

In the sixth stage, I experienced immense gratitude, peace, and love in my heart. I am blessed to have chosen all these beautiful souls to help me become the person I am today. Our soul contracts were not easy. I found the urge to study spirituality, and my perception of the world changed. I realized that I was sent to earth for a higher purpose.

In the seventh stage, I started to appreciate the interconnectedness of everything: nature, animals, the stars... I felt, I *feel* that I am part of the universe. As my consciousness expanded, I began to see the world more deeply and more connected.

On October 23, 2021, we welcomed our tenth child to the world– a little quantum baby boy from the Sun. His birth was very Zen – full of candles, magical oils, and meditation. Both of us helped him out. We welcomed him together as both our arms were ready to receive him. He is such a calm baby; he hardly cries. Baby Coconut is very joyful. He has helped me become even more connected to nature and those around me.

At the end of 2021, I created my business. I became the CEO of LunaStar Magical Fairies, offering products, spiritual classes, energy healing, akashic soul purpose, and blueprint reports. The Universe helps me every day to create, develop my psychic abilities, and realize that my thoughts and emotions shape my reality.

I feel so grateful every day that I have chosen this last mission on earth, to help with the new frequency of the new earth. It's a very Magical time to be incarnated, and I am here to remind people who they are and where they have come from. I help women, men, and children who have karmic relationships to tear apart their soul contracts in every dimension and in every life – past, present, and future. I help them heal so they know how to heal themselves and can then help to heal others! I create my products with the energy of the Fairies, Mermaids, and the Galactic Family. Every product is made with so much love and protection!

We come to earth to heal and will reincarnate as many times as we need to, so we can learn and then understand. When we finally heal ourselves, then we can move on to a new frequency. When this happens, we tap into our higher self, our inner God or Goddess. We are the actor, the author, and the Director of our life, and at any time, we have the power to change our life. We can choose to live in full abundance in every sense of the word in all Dimensions of time and space.

Many people associate darkness with evil and thus try to fight it, but what if darkness and evil were unrelated? What if darkness, just like light, was a source of enlightenment and spiritual growth?

When you do shadow work, the goal is not to eliminate your darkness but rather to integrate your shadow, acknowledging that everything you hide is still part of who you are and that accepting this as such will help you feel whole.

For years, I unknowingly fought my own darkness. I was scared of it because it used to get me in trouble and my cells still carry those memories. I was rejecting it out of fear of being hated or feared by others. I was ashamed of it on such a deep level that I couldn't see how I'm not actually being who I truly am to my full extent but today, my Higher Self finally showed me something I couldn't see before.

All parts of me come from Source. All parts of me are important and necessary. None of them are corrupted. It's just a matter of perspective. But when you remove this duality and understand that everything was created by Source, you can accept both darkness and light as equal.

When you look inside yourself from the position of your Higher Self that's a fractal of Source rather than from your mind, you'll understand that the war you lead inside yourself is unnecessary, and you accept all aspects of you as Divine.

About the Author

Jos Poune Fae is a spiritual life coach and self-love advocate. Her main mission within her business is to help people fall in love with themselves and their lives. She is the owner of LunaStar Magical Fairies and offers many services and products.

Following a near-death experience in 2020, Jos remembered her previous incarnations and the true beginning of her journey. By going through the darkness of her own life and facing death, she became light! Now she helps others to step into the darkness and free themselves from their own mental prison. She also helps her clients and students to connect to their soul families and to fulfill their mission.

At any point, you have the power to rewrite your story. You have the power to become all that you want for your life. When you realize this your life changes forever!

Together, we can create the new frequency of the new earth!

Connect with Jos below:

- Website: lunastarmagicalfairies.myshopify.com
- YouTube channel: youtu.be/93eKPi2ba08
- Facebook group:
  www.facebook.com/profile.php?id=100082765721357&mibex
  tid=ZbWKwL

JULES IMPICCINI

Right Where You Are

For most of my life, I have either been searching for or aware of a greater presence. In the early days, I was taught and knew this figure as God, 'the Creator of all.' A Pentecostal surge saw me buried in the bosom of Abraham and bible studies, fellowship and praising the Lord. A turn of events planted me in a space of reflection where nature became my constant amidst the chaos of life, and its complexities echoed a greater energy in play.

I have always asked questions and appreciated the artists and creatives who are able to prompt the mind to consider an expansive universe of theories, truths, and beliefs. The values, beliefs, and cultural practices of people groups around the world have contributed to my personal understanding of a Spirit entity from Christians to Catholics to Latter-Day Saints to the Pentecostal and Indigenous peoples and their sacred storylines. Similar stories, tellings passed down through generations upon generations and captured in word, creative forms including music and art, as well as dramatic forms strengthened my belief in this greater force, collective energy, Divine source. I, like many, became curious and open to the stories of people and their experiences with the Divine.

To understand life and its complexity, I have often turned to nature. I have been inspired by the seasons that reveal so much about our own existence. Spring, Summer, Autumn, and Winter bring us full cycle by bringing forward new life, fresh starts, rejuvenation, intensity, a falling away of that which is no longer necessary, and a crystallisation of sorts, and thus, the cycle repeats. Recycling is something we have become good at naturally. Nature has always been our greatest teacher. Nature supports our existence; thus, the concept of 'Mother Nature,' the nurturer, resonates greatly as depicted through time.

Flying over land and looking down at the natural landscape, there is so much to see that becomes one mass at a higher altitude. Up there in the clouds, you can see a whole different world, gazing through the oval window, down, over, and across the horizon. Perspective is all important. There are people down there, individuals, communities, all bustling around, maneuvering, and experiencing season after season this thing called 'life'. People in their own little worlds, jostling with others, connecting. From this vantage point, one truly appreciates the interwoven 'fabric of humanity' and the idea that the threads pull together to make one whole garment. Up there, in the sky looking down, our greater purpose is highlighted.

At one point, each of us must consider the question: 'Why? Why am I here?' Over the years, I have come to learn that relationships are critical to discovering our purpose. Even in the womb, a child's relationship with their mother is critical for survival and development. Being shaped by our environment rings true here in this cocoon like space more than any place. This relationship births family, partnerships, then community. In all of this, though, a personal relationship with self and the Divine calls for most at some point in time.

To truly value life, we must understand that we are relational spirit beings, travelling within physical vessels for a brief timespan. More than that, we can be reassured knowing that we are never alone, and we never have to feel alone because there is a greater energy at play. Whether it be family, friends, community, or Spirit, in the toughest of times, the greater energy, or source, becomes a calming force and guiding entity. The Divine centres our existence in the hustle and bustle of life. Take a step back and realise your need for connection. Daily meditation is a part of this rich experience; that moment in the day where you allow yourself to breathe deeply, calm your mind, slow it all down, and just breathe in and out and engage in the stillness.

Sometimes, stillness is found in the early hours of the morning, when all is quiet, and the world is still sleeping. It is here at this time that you can connect with the Divine. Then comes the moment for devotion, requests, appeals, whisperings, ideas, and inspirations. Sometimes this starts with gratitude: *I am grateful for life. I am grateful for my partner, my family, my pets, workplace, colleagues, and friends. I am grateful for possibilities, and I am open to new opportunities. I am willing and grateful that I am able.* Never underestimate the value of being grateful. Gratitude will lift your spirit and help you feel taller.

Other times, stillness is found on a walk up a mountain, a hike through a cavern, rainforest, or just down by the seaside listening to the ebb and flow of the waves lapping at the shoreline. Take a moment to connect with nature: a force that teaches so much about existence. It starts with calming the mind and making time to connect with the energy of Source.

As a writer, I love the power of the word as it spills onto the page and then is scooped up again by the reader to comprehend or delight in. Through writing, contemplation, and reflection lead to awareness, understanding and revelation. Writing or journaling is a powerful way of connecting with self, the Divine, and others. Sometimes a poem or lyric will flow onto my page. Other times, I find myself scribbling or doodling absent-mindedly which ironically resonates powerfully. At times, I feel compelled to write an extensive letter to self; a message to the Divine asking for guidance, or a clear sign to help with moving forward.

Whatever the format, we find synergy through the focused effort to communicate and realise our thoughts and intentions. When considering the life plan, writing, or journaling is not merely a written expression of feeling and thought, intention, or affirmation, but a reflective component that can be utilised to observe how far one has journeyed, and even a record keeper to acknowledge the journey and reset the course if need be. Here we can toy with ideas, thoughts, and emotions and create blueprints for our existence.

Make time to journal. Keep a record of your thoughts, insights, and plans for now and the future. Return to journaling often, so you can follow your path, plan the journey, celebrate in the ventures, and reflect on the direction you have taken.

Pivotal points in life help us understand that the Divine is always present, sometimes just waiting for us to stop and realise that we are never alone on this journey. Most times there are signposts along the way to guide us in a given direction. Events and people that lead us to a Divine calling. Sometimes, we have a picture in our mind of the direction we need to follow, only to have it thwarted by circumstances or decisions made by ourselves and others that can be life changing.

What if we decided to not just be blind-sided by these moments? What if we committed to living a life where we co-created with the Divine and sought guidance, direction, and support? What if we didn't need to feel total desperation and despair in these times? What would life look like then? What pathways would open? What direction would our lifespans take? What would our influence be? It is in these moments that the Divine calls us back to honestly appraising our journey, to questioning our course, and to consider our future endeavours.

The greater calling comes when we stop still in our tracks and ask, "Why am I here? What can I possibly contribute to the life force on this planet?" Can you pinpoint those junctures in your own life where you have had the opportunity to reflect on what you have been spending your time on and with whom? Realising that we are all journeying and have the capacity to offer so much to one another, learn from each other, and support fellow beings has become an affecting awareness.

So, what is co-creating with the Divine? The answer to this lies in knowing your calling, following your calling, and living your calling daily. For some, the knowing is apparent from an early age. For others, knowing your calling comes later in life. No matter the time, the realisation that the Divine works with and through you in both your personal relationships and career is truly life changing and life giving. You will know that you are walking in your calling because you will feel like you are living in the zone.

EVOLVING ON PURPOSE

What does a day in the zone feel like, look like, and sound like? Can you think back to that one day, or even, a moment, when everything felt like it should? Can you? Or do you continuously relive those moments known as the pain points? Tears in the heart, that lump in the back of the throat, tears that well and you can taste the salt as it flows down your face? Messy face, messy everything.

These days define you. Learn from the hard moments of your past and live in the zone. A day in the zone is that day when your heart sings, your energy vibrates, and everything resonates. The day in the zone sees you acknowledging where you are, how far you've come and envisioning your life dream, one that is co-created with the Divine and seeking life-giving moments for you and others. Again, we need to dig deep and tune into our true purpose here on this planet.

Do you ever get the feeling that doors are opening up for you? That there seems to be more light on the situation? This is it. You know that your path is unfolding, that things are making sense, and you are empowered to move forward. Living in the zone has more of these moments and less of the moments of feeling *blown by the wind*. Yes, there are more days of focused direction and intentions that will help you create something purposeful in each moment. We must understand that possibility sits in the present – not the past – and can be actualised *today*.

Take action – today – and realise that which you have imagined, desired, and wished to be. Manifesting is not just thinking, planning, or dreaming about something. Manifesting is actioning and implementing that concept, idea, or goal. Write it out. Speak it out. Act it out.

Remember, *actions speak louder than words*. Check your course and align with Divine principles that are life giving. For example: love always; it is better to give than receive; honesty is the best policy.

Patience is the biggest lesson of our era. Know that even as you move forward there are lessons to be learnt. It seems to be that these lessons will continue to appear in our lives until we learn them. My biggest lesson to date has been learning to listen to that still, small voice, to be still enough to hear the gentle whisper. We must take the time to listen to avoid stumbling through the dark and venturing without direction.

Life can be filled with memorable moments, pivotal points, or jagged junctures. Co-creating with the Divine calls us to aspects of divinity like graciousness, humility, honesty, and gratitude. It calls one to understanding the importance of humanity, the individual and the role each plays in mirroring a divine order. This is a daily experience, one which needs a mindful approach. There are so many obstacles that can get in the way when you determine to live a life of purpose and when you take your lifespan into your own hands and say, "What shall I do today to support myself and, more importantly, to support others?"

EVOLVING ON PURPOSE

This awareness leads us to knowing *why we are here* and *the difference we can make*. This awareness causes us to discover the community we can travel with to make a lasting effect or endurable impression - no matter how large or small. Living for self becomes inconsequential when you become aware that there is a greater purpose for each and every one of us.

Enrichment occurs as we pursue our purpose asking questions like, 'What next and with whom?' As you commit to co-create with the Divine and those with similar callings, you will find yourself on your intended path. The Divine is often present in the lives of others, and it is more so a truthfulness, authenticity, compassion and sense of love that we appreciate in those that are guided by the Divine and walking a life of Divine purpose. Seek out fellow travellers. Cultivate community. As we walk together, the presence of the Divine becomes more evident.

Harmony is found in community. A community provides support and strength. Kindred spirits are like birds of a feather, they flock together. In the ups and downs, we can find great comfort in knowing that we are all in this together. It is also good to remember that most of us are like the rest of us. We all experience humanity and its joys, fears, hopes, and moments that sometimes, inevitably lead to speed bumps or stopping still.

What happens, though, when you reach a dead end? A place of stagnation, a place of exhaustion, a place of loss? Over the last 50+ years, I have experienced things that have stopped me still in my tracks or thrown me off course: divorce, battling cancer, loss of loved ones, chronic health concerns of family members, and the severing of opportunities.

I used to describe these happenings as complete overwhelm and derailments, but now I realise that each and every moment was really a part of the evolution process, prompting the pressing in and co-creating with the Divine. Each and every happening helped me to understand that the Divine is wanting us to move through the moments of change or difficulties.

When you feel overwhelmed or too tired to work through something, what do you do? Some of us sleep. Some of us eat. Some of us escape into fictional worlds via social media platforms and narratives. What's your coping mechanism?

Ask yourself: *How long can I afford to stay on pause? How much time do I have?* Unfortunately, the problem that you want to escape or avoid is still there once you come off pause. When it feels like you can do no more, and you have flailed around way too much, the stillness that you come too often reveals that indeed, everything will be okay, and you are not alone. The Divine is there, right where you are. Guidance is there, as well. For some, it is a still small voice, a sign, or a supportive friend or family member that sees you and extends a hand to help.

For others, like me, guidance can also be found in oracle cards that have been carefully created to intuitively speak to the card reader and act as messages, promptings to press in and seek that which is supportive or to let go of that which no longer serves us and instead follow that which is life-giving.

For most of my life, I have used oracle cards as a form of guidance and have found that the images and messages of these prompts have spoken to the heart of many concerns or questions that I have had. Often, I am amazed at the accuracy, the relevance, the poignancy of the oracle cards that speak to the situation being experienced.

The key here is to seek guidance, to hear the messages, and to allow the mind to respond to the message and the wisdom being channelled. A daily, weekly, or monthly practice of drawing a card of guidance can make a significant impact similar to meditation. It is important to find an oracle deck that you can relate to, and this is definitely a personal choice. I have had the privilege of working with several decks including teaching and instruction around using the decks as personal growth tools over the last 5 years and understanding the power of the oracle decks as a link to the Divine and universal truths.

Oracle decks, like sacred texts passed down throughout the ages, bring clarity to life and its complexities. My personal favourites include Wisdom of the Oracle, the Map, the 7 Energies and the Shaman's Dream by Colette Baron-Reid, and the Modern Oracle and the Modern Oracle of Essential Oils by Katy-K.

My love for aromatherapy sees me using the Modern Oracle of Essential Oils on a daily basis, as essential oils support our human existence in profound ways including physically, emotionally, and energetically. Guidance around past, present, and future time frames can be readily questioned with oracle cards and both images, messages, and recommendations for future action are often provided within these decks.

We must learn from experience, seek guidance to spiral upwards, and realise that when we evolve on purpose, we can move through the narrows. Only then do we understand what it means to thrive and co-create with the Divine. So, let us start here, start now, right where we are... where the Divine is waiting.

Make time to just appreciate all that is before you, regardless of the circumstances and to seek ways to move forward, even if you need help to do so. We all need to sing in the rain and help each other through the hard and sad times; only then can we be grateful for the sunrises. Take time to pause and connect. The Divine will always send you a lifeboat. We just need to look for it, climb in, and chart the new course from right where we are.

About the Author

Jules Impiccini is an educator, an author, and an advocate whose life achievements are centred around Secondary and Tertiary teaching spaces and community interactions both face-to-face and online. Creative expression in the classroom, on the stage, and through community projects have always been an integral part of the journey for Jules with both performance and published works being recognised by community audiences.

Jules believes that there is a writer in everyone, just waiting to emerge which prompted her to create *The Clutter Space* and the *Finding Synergies: Clutter Space Writing Course.* Currently, she works in Special Education and the Creative Arts where she dabbles as a creative working with writers, artists, and performers in realising their own creative endeavours. *Finding Synergies* has been Jules' soulful practice and her search for a meaningful existence. Some of the synergies that she specialises in include: aromatherapy, sound therapy, creative writing, oracle readings, visual art and energetic practices.

Jules is passionate about the use of aromatherapy to heighten the senses and support the whole person physically, emotionally, and energetically, and using oracle cards to empower those that seek further guidance and direction.

Over the last 5 years, Jules has also worked in editing texts for publication including the Modern Oracle and Modern Oracle of Essential Oils decks, the Modern Oracle: How to Tap into Your Unique Psychic Powers and the Modern Oracle: Intimate Secrets to Enhance Your Intuitive Gifts books by Katy-K and is open to future work in the editing world.

This is Jules' second chapter publication in a collective work. She first contributed to *Powerful Conversations* published by Samantha Jansen Publishing where she examined the importance of connection and conversations of parents raising children with Down Syndrome. Jules is more than excited to be collaborating with fellow creatives on *Evolving on Purpose: Co-Creating with the Divine* and provides insight into daily practice and interaction with the Divine that leads to an empowered life.

Connect with Jules below:

- Website: findingsynergies.thinkific.com
- Facebook: www.facebook.com/findingsynergies
- Instagram: www.instagram.com/oilsynergies

KARL OLSON

Stepping from the Darkness into the Light

❧

August 1981

It was a beautiful summer's day, and Kessingland Caravan Park was an oasis of fun and adventure for any child. As a typical 11-year-old boy, you would either find me doing backflips in the swimming pool or on the Space Invader or Galaxians machines in the clubhouse, but today was different. I went on a little adventure exploring the pine woods that the site was set in and decided to climb to the top of a tree. This was the turning point in my life.

I'm not quite sure what happened next as I found myself on the ground with people gathered around me. My mum was kneeling by my side comforting me before I blacked out again.

I was driven to Norwich hospital for tests only to be released later after the doctors told me that I'd had a grand mal epileptic fit. I was only 11 years old, and I had no idea what was going on or what this meant or how much my life was going to change.

The fit was triggered by the sun breaking through the branches in the tree, much like the flickering of a strobe. I would continue to have seizures on a regular basis throughout my teenage years. Before this first seizure, I was a good lad. I always did well at school, and I was attentive with a craving to learn.

After the fit, my personality changed. I started to constantly get into trouble at middle school, and when I moved to the upper school, my behaviour became more erratic. I was suspended multiple times before finally being expelled for fighting with a teacher.

Through these early years, my behaviour was fueled by whatever high I could get my hands on to block out the ever-increasing darkness of my thoughts and feelings.

The seizures changed my brain and my personality. I began to find ways to numb the feelings and thoughts I was having of *nobody cares* and *how could anyone love me* with whatever was at hand. This coupled with the seizures started to change me too.

Drugs weren't available so freely back in those days, so you would need to find your high elsewhere in things like bags of Tipp-Ex or glue, a motorbike petrol tank, cans of lighter gas, Tipp-Ex thinner, or raiding the drinks in the family drinks cabinet on a regular basis.

It wasn't long until my addictive personality had been created.

I don't fit in. Why doesn't anybody love me?

I ostracised myself because of the seizures. Somebody who was on the news and programmes like Blue Peter a lot at the time was an author called Joey Deakin who suffered from Cerebral Palsy. The terms Joey and spastic were commonplace banter back then, two things I was called on a regular occurrence, not another "spazzy fit."

I couldn't go to the school or weekly discos at the local community centre or the YMCA for fear of having a fit. The doctors advised me to not be around flashing lights which was almost impossible in the early 80s. I would have a fit tuning in the old style black and white and then colour TV's, which became a game for myself, constantly testing to see how long I could hold on staring at the screen before blacking out and going into a full-blown seizure. This became a regular process, but I was unaware of the damage I was doing.

I was different, and I felt so unlike everyone around me. People used to smile at me, but I began to believe the thoughts that were coming through. Nobody really liked me, or so I started to believe.

Surrounded by people but always feeling alone

I thought I'd become a man overnight as I was able to get into certain pubs and drink instead of sitting at the park with umpteen cans of Special Brew and Tennent's Super. Woohoo! I was practically an adult. Again, that feeling of never fitting in always came back.

What the hell is wrong with me?

Why don't people like me?

Why do I feel so alone?

They say that I'm a good laugh and people appear to like me, but I didn't believe them. Although being surrounded by people, friends I felt so alone. I was smiling, laughing but all the while, there was a hidden disconnection between my external behaviour and my internal feelings and thoughts.

The darkness always felt safer

I started to question myself: "Maybe I'm not a good person. Maybe I'm just pretending. Maybe I'm not a very nice person deep down. Well, I do seem to keep getting in fights. That's not the work of a nice person, so I can't be as nice as I think I am. There you go! It must be true. Let's have another drink anyway."

When I was in my early teens, self-harming was a regular practice. I would sit in the family bathroom surrounded by the old avocado bathroom suite famous in the 1980s, using my dad's old blades from his razor to carve my name and various shapes into my arms. I would feel a sense of relief as the blood began to ooze through my freshly pierced skin. The uneasiness and quiet anger I felt subsided as I pulled the blade through my skin.

I wasn't deserving of the heart and life that I'd been given

Some years later in 1987, at 17 years of age, I laid in my room listening to U2's "The Joshua Tree." Instantly, I was overcome by a compulsion to no longer be here. I quickly nipped to the bathroom to pinch a razor blade and began to draw it across my wrists. I'm not squeamish, so I just started to watch the blood leave both my arms before waking up in the back of an ambulance with my mum in tears.

My poor mum. Since my first fit, I'd made her life so difficult, and there she was in turmoil with tears streaming down her face asking me, "Why?" All I could say - all I knew - was that I wanted to die.

The life she'd lovingly given me I was throwing back in her face.

The lack of light in my thought was blinding

Three years later, mum passed away after losing her battle to cancer. To be fair, everything between The Joshua Tree and burying my mum was a blur, but nothing compared to the next few years of which I have no recollection. After finding newer, stronger drugs, the coping mechanism for losing mum became worse, and I attempted suicide multiple times.

My self-worth and value had very little meaning for the majority of my adult life until 1997 when my life completely bottomed out. I jumped off a multi-story car park over a bus station.

I woke up, looked around, and realised I was lying on the floor. I knew that I had to get out of the way of the buses, because I didn't want to ruin anyone's day by holding them up. My core values of love, caring, and compassion were in place long before I knew they existed.

Of course, I couldn't move. My spine was fractured, and my pelvis was broken. Upon arriving at the hospital, I was told that I had two broken ankles. My knees were shot (years of Sunday league had finally taken their toll), but they were totally gone now. I'd smashed the heel bone in my right foot to pieces. I later found out the heel bone is the thickest bone in the body, so it must have taken the majority of the impact.

I gained consciousness on a ward in Northampton General hospital to the sound of Martine McCutcheon's Perfect Moment song playing on the radio, a strange kind of irony from what I intended. One of my oldest friends, Pop, was the first to visit and he said he'd never seen my eyes look so blue, it's only looking back I believe my eyes were seeing the world through the eyes of love instead of the blackness, I was constantly trapped behind.

I was bed bound for 12 weeks, flat on my back unable to move while they waited to see if the spine and pelvis repaired themselves correctly. After the final scans were complete, I was told I might be able to walk again. My levels of elation grew but so did my level of fear. What if I couldn't walk again?

Learning to walk again is one of the strangest things I've ever gone through. Your brain directs you to put one foot in front of the other as you have done millions of times before, but muscle memory loss and extreme pain are large obstacles to overcome. But I did, and continued to take those steps one after another, until I could walk again, albeit with a slight limp.

Belief was the light that guided me through the darkness

Life improved somewhat, as I had my own flat, holding down work, life seemed ok. I was passed from psychiatrist to counsellor to therapist. The black dog of depression growled, he slept, and he barked. For most people, I can only assume doing so much damage to their body would be enough - the wakeup call that was so desperately needed. For me, unfortunately, it wasn't, and the black dog escaped his leash on several more occasions as I got older.

At the age of 36, I felt like I was at a good point in my life. The blackness didn't appear that often, and I started to make plans to travel. I met the woman who became my wife and then ex-wife. We had two beautiful children - Ben (who is currently 15 years old) and Myla (13). All the time we were together, the darkness crept in from time to time. My moods, behaviour, and thoughts were always skewed due to me having a pain-killer addiction from my previous suicide attempt. My whole body was riddled with arthritis, so every step that I took was a painful reminder of the damage that I had done.

My kids were the glue that kept me in the light

The Co-codamol helped ease the constant agony, but the recommended 8 tablets a day soon became 12, which soon became 20. I could not function without them.

If I had a stressful meeting coming up at work, I'd take some tablets. If my mood was slipping, I'd take some tablets. If I needed to go to the shop for some milk, I'd take some tablets. I had no idea who I was anymore. My mood and my entire day were controlled by Co-codamol. I was on a downward spiral of addiction, loss of self-control and a sense of hopelessness were always present, I felt trapped in a constant cycle of despair.

Then one day, after a row with my wife, she kicked me out of the house for driving the car whilst I was drunk. That moment flicked a switch, and the darkness descended quickly. I didn't want to be here any longer. The constant physical, mental, and emotional pain became too much.

I grabbed all the tablets from the cupboard when the house was empty, jumped on a train to Birmingham then sat in the Bullring watching the world go by and the people scurrying around going about their day. Every minute, the number of tablets I was taking increased. The drowsiness started to kick in. They were working. The pain was lifting, and the darkness was fading. I could see a light. This was it! I was finally at the end of my journey in life.

I woke up in a bed in a Birmingham hospital after taking over 100 tablets, a mix of sleepers, and pain killers. I was placed under the Community Mental Health Team there and then.

The nurse asked me to leave as they needed the bed, but I had no way of getting home. When I collapsed in the shopping area, someone had stolen my wallet. The consultant pulled out his wallet and gave me £20 to get a train ticket home. How did I get home? I don't know to this day.

I arrived home to a lot of tears. My wife had no idea where I'd been or what had happened, she just thought I'd gone missing again. I wish I could forget the look on my children's faces as I walked back into the house, but I can't because that look was the catalyst for the positive changes to come.

My kids always kept me on the good side, no matter how loud the black dog barked or how dark it became. Their smiles, hugs, love, and laughter kept the light inside me burning long enough to fight off any thoughts of pulling me back into the tunnel of darkness.

Time passed, and we tried to make things work after this, but the irreparable damage to the marriage had already been done. This suicide attempt was the final straw, and we both agreed sometime later that we should part, which we did amicably, but leaving the kids was heart-breaking. I was able to find a place to live which was perfect for when they came over to stay. But the loss of routine, not drying and brushing their hair after a bath, not seeing their sleepy faces coming down the stairs in the morning was crippling, and as such, I defaulted to my normal coping mechanisms - drinking by breakfast to numb the pain.

Something had to change, but I had no idea what or how to change. Without knowing, the Universe started showing me a new path to walk.

Light always follows dark

I joined a gym. In the past whenever I joined a gym, I would usually go once or twice before realising that it wasn't for me. But this gym was different. There was a community feel to it.

This gym was full of people of all shapes, sizes, and ages. Each person was fighting their own battles. Attending the classes each week was a huge step for me and helped my mental state no end.

At the same time, I also received a voucher to attend a crystal healing meditation at a beautiful location that I'd only heard about before. I began to explore other holistic therapies and natural ways of supporting and caring for myself without the need for medication.

I found the benefits of cold-water immersion whilst attending two Wim Hoff training sessions. I found the cold water a release for all that I was holding on to because my mind had no time to think about worry, stress, or depression, whilst in the freezing water.

The defining moment in my transformation came when I signed up for a free life coaching weekend. I arrived at the first training session full of excitement armed with my experiences of the past with numerous counsellors and therapists to stand me in a good position. I didn't realise at the time that I should have left them at the door when I walked into the room.

Wow. This is it! I'd found my calling, a way that I can help and support people That missing piece of me that I'd been searching for. I always knew I had a calling for something like this. I'd always been that person that people shared honestly with, eager to help others regardless of the matter. The empath in me was screaming out, but I hadn't been listening.

I walked away that weekend knowing this was the path I was destined to walk. Life got in the way, but the fire was lit! After COVID, I signed up and became an internationally accredited life coach and NLP practitioner. Throughout my training, a great deal came up for me which I had to work on, but I already knew there was more inner work that I had to do. I found the answers I was looking for when I studied and became an Emotional Intelligence (EQ) practitioner.

My parents, teachers, friends always told me I was intelligent, and I knew I was handy to have around in a pub quiz, but emotionally, I was stagnant despite all the inner work I'd done in qualifying as a life coach.

Emotional Intelligence was a whole new way of thinking, feeling, and believing that allowed me to master my emotions. The connections with my children, my family, and my friends all felt the ripple effect of this knowledge and understanding that I had discovered during this part of my journey. The changes within me inspired changes in everything and everyone around me. It was amazing to realise and experience the changes I had made; I was now capable of controlling and regulating my self-esteem and emotional self-awareness to a degree that I had never imagined possible.

Find your purpose, and everything else will fall into place

I started my coaching business in 2022, but I struggled to find a niche that I was comfortable working with. Because of my past, I felt a pull to work with people who were and are suffering with their mental health, but it was a difficult place to be for myself as much as I wanted to help these people, they needed specialist support. The people that I did help bring back from suicidal places, didn't align with me and the people that I truly want to help and support.

I wanted to reach out to people *before* they make that visit to the doctors, *before* they become a slave to antidepressants and other prescriptions, *before* they have to wait months to get the support they need. I've been part of that broken system, and if the doctor had prescribed me a life coach early on, my path through life would have been a completely different story - and much less painful. It may have taken some time, but I have found my place, and I'm now providing the transformations for people that they need to live the life that they were destined to lead, before the clutter of their limiting beliefs and old stories got in their way.

I learnt a long time ago, that I had to respect my depression. But how can you respect something that has made your life hell, ruined relationships, and caused so much damage? Simple. If you don't learn to respect depression, it will drag you down deeper each and every time. You must face it, head on. You must do the inner work - no matter how uncomfortable or painful it may be.

My journey in life until now has had its fair share of twists and turns, from the highest of highs to the lowest of lows. To arrive where I am now has taken a great deal out of me, but I wouldn't change one single step of the path that I've walked in my journey through life to arrive where I am today. Through every broken bone, every drop of blood spilled, I have grown - I have evolved - through every moment with a purpose.

The first part of my life I lived in a world of self-generating despair and self-destruction, but now, I have moved to a place of self-growth, contentment, happiness, and confidence. I'm surrounded by love and abundance, and I know that I am truly blessed - as are you, no matter where you are on your journey.

About the Author

Karl Olson is a Positivity and Mindset Coach, providing insight, clarity, and supporting people to take action to live the future they desire. He has nurtured a deep desire within himself to write and share his story in printed form. This aspiration has been quietly residing until recently when a remarkable opportunity emerged for him to become a valued contributor to a multi-author book. Recognising the significance of this chance, he eagerly and gratefully accepted the invitation. It was a moment of alignment between his aspirations and the universe's abundant offerings.

Karl firmly believes that when we remain open and receptive, the universe always provides. This belief, coupled with his readiness to embrace new possibilities, has set the stage for an exciting chapter in his life journey.

Karl hopes that YOU will read his story and know that there is a way through whatever the challenge you may be experiencing. There is a light in the darkness, and that light is YOU. Shine bright!

Karl is from the UK and has lived in a town called Northampton for all of his 53 years.

Connect with Karl below:

Facebook:

https://www.facebook.com/karljohnolson/

- Business Page:

  https://www.facebook.com/KarlOlsonCoaching/

- Private Facebook Group:

  https://www.facebook.com/groups/shinebrightwithkarlolsoncoaching

KARLA KOPP

Evolving with Purpose

D o you ever wonder if and how you could change your life? Do you ever feel stuck in your circumstances? Does the life that you really want feel too far away to achieve? Have you given up hope thinking, "My dreams will never come true?" Maybe you give it up as "that'll never happen?" I've felt lost, alone, and hopeless at many different times throughout my life.

I entered this world differently than many. I was born with a cleft lip and palate. My life began with multiple surgeries, and I experienced frequent ear infections and sore throats as a result. Despite this, I'm told, and I see in my baby pictures, that I was quite happy and joyful in my early, pre-school years. My sister says I was mischievous, with a glint in my eyes. She says if I didn't get my way, I would put my hands on my hips and march down the hallway saying, "Damn! Damn! Damn!" Funny thing about that is, I don't remember my parents ever cussing! There is another story where I was helping frost a cake and held up my chocolate frosted hands and stated the same!

Once the school years began, I missed out on some of the extracurricular activities in school due to surgeries and illness. More importantly, it was entering school where I learned that I was perceived as "different," possibly "not good enough" because I wasn't like everyone else. I became a "people pleaser" to win friends, and in turn, I lost *me*.

I was very shy and quiet, rarely speaking out of fear of being made fun of. This went on for years and escalated in my teens as I moved from living in the city for 12 years, to a very small farm community where there was one building for Kindergarten to Seniors in high school.

My 7th grade class and graduating class had only 12 students. Before this move, I had dreams of taking photography in high school, of all the variety of courses that would be available, however that was not to be in this new very small school that provided only the basics. The extracurricular activities were all centered around football and basketball. A very different life. Once again, I'm different. I don't belong.

Thankfully, I had a natural belief that once I finished high school, I would go to college. I signed up and took myself to live in the dorm. I met a guy who was from an adjoining small town. We started dating and, in a year, we got married.

Once married, I became more comfortable talking with others. I took a work study job at the boy's dorm at the front desk, and it was so much fun! They were like my brothers! I don't think I would have ever done that before marriage. I continued college towards my Bachelor of Science in Elementary Education degree, and my first son was born three months before my graduation.

My husband worked for a department store and transferred a few times in the next few years. Our second son was born two years later. We moved back to the original city I was born and raised in, and my third son was born. I had a job working in our church day care, and one of the moms who was a foster mom came in with a foster child - a baby girl. I fell in love immediately and adopted her by the time she was a year old.

After 36 years of marriage, I didn't feel part of my marriage. I realized that at 18, my first year in college, my focus was to start a new life, a new family. Since I had not experienced a variety of relationships, at the time I thought this relationship was ok and I said yes to a proposal. Years later, I realized I felt more alone in a marriage than actually being alone. We had been busy raising 4 children, working our jobs, and there seemed to be no joy, no partnership. I wasn't happy, and I decided to divorce and move out on my own. I had finally gotten to the point that I could take care of myself, the kids had grown and moved on. This was the first time in my life that I'd ever been completely on my own. Pretty freaky at first, I was 55 years old and home alone for the first time ever!

I went to a counselor who gave me a CD of Louise Hay. That's what got me moving into more Purpose in my Evolving. I have had so many amazing mentors in the last decade: Abraham Hicks, Mike Dooley, Wayne Dyer, Mary Morrisey, Nick Breau, and many others! I've learned and evolved so much in my life. Besides my LMSW (Licensed Master Social Work) in Social Work, I have coaching certificates with Health Coach Institute and Dream Builder Life Coach Certification with the Brave Thinking Institute as well as Infinite Possibilities trainer certification with Mike Dooley.

I learned that thoughts cause feelings, feelings cause emotions, and emotions cause action. I learned that the Universe, the Divine, is always with me and always wants what I want. I began to work with the Divine in harmony which meant that I began to think and act in my best interest; rather than resistance, which included putting others first, doing the "right" thing-according to other's definition of "right." I began to think thoughts that felt peaceful, happy, excited, joy-filled. Once I felt better, I took more action towards my own desires.

I now know that as my thoughts are towards my desires, my excitement and determination increase which lead me to action steps that include courses that teach me effective ways to change my thoughts towards more of what I want and take me closer to my dreams each day. I know now that as I feel in partnership with the Divine, everything is always working out for me. My dream of living on a cruise ship is becoming my reality. I recently retired and have been on 3 cruises so far, with 3 more scheduled.

What is "evolving"? The definition is "to develop gradually from simple to more complex" or "to change or develop gradually." By this definition, every living being evolves from a seed to birth to a person, animal, or plant. Plants and animals have a completely natural evolution if left in their natural environment. However, a newborn baby requires care and nurturing. Babies grow and change rapidly in their beginning years and learn from their environment, their families, their caregivers, and so many others in their lives. Most kids don't have much more than family or neighbor exposure until school, then they get to know other kids' perspectives that are based on their families' unique beliefs.

There's not really an opportunity for intentional evolution for a baby or a small child. As a small child we are guided by what others tell us. I recall as a child being asked, "what do you want to be when you grow up?" or "what are you going to do with your life?" and thinking, I have no clue! I had no idea, or if I did, I didn't want to say it out of fear they would make fun of it or tell me that's not possible!

Perhaps you've been told "you should do" this or that. Perhaps you've been told "you can't do that because..." Sometimes you hear a bold "you're not good enough!" Or perhaps "you're not good enough" felt like a subtle and ceaseless chipping away at your self-esteem throughout your life. A subtle "you're not good enough" in other ways. When I was growing up as a child, I thought I was the only one that felt the sting of being "not good enough." As I got into the personal development world, I found out it is very common!

Since we know all of us evolve (change and develop) gradually and naturally, then what does it mean to "evolve on purpose?"

Evolving on Purpose: Co-creating with the Divine is intentional evolving, making choices based on your true desires - not the desires of your mom and dad or your friends, but what YOU - the Divine in you, your soul - wants. The desire that lights you up! The more joy you feel in this desire generates more ideas to move you closer to your desire. You then feel the impulses to take action.

I've had smaller desires that happen in a short amount of time such as, I'm really hungry for ice cream and perhaps, I'll get a call from a friend asking if I'd want to go get some ice cream or I go to the store and my favorite ice cream is on sale!

I've had BIG desires that have come true over time. I've had a dream/desire to live on a cruise ship for decades! It's been a process of thinking about what it would be like. Thinking about places I would like to go. Wondering about options of what my life would look like on a ship versus living on land. I talked about it with others at times and each time they had questions, I would think of the answers. It was a gradual evolution of planning my dream over several years. As I've begun living this dream, it continues to evolve! Each cruise I take gives more information about what I prefer and what I don't care for. It's interesting that my thinking about living on a cruise ship, which could be considered "different" by many, others' opinions, didn't matter to me. It has been my highest excitement for years and it doesn't matter to me what anyone else thinks about it! Also interesting is that as I have cruised, I've met many people who have been on many, many cruises just as I have dreamed of. I'm finding that as you move towards what YOU truly want, you find your people, your tribe.

This journey hasn't been super easy and most or maybe all the reason is *ME* getting in my own way. I worried about what others thought, not what I wanted. One thing I've noticed big time is my resistance to change as I tend to prefer comfort of routine and familiarity. Another thing is simply having been a child born in the 1950's when life was very different to what it is now. One huge difference has been the explosion of technology in our lives. We now have access to so much information NOW, with cell phones and computers always available. It's my job when resistance from a limiting belief comes up to get curious. I ask myself:

- Is this true?
- Does this belief continue to serve me?

227

- What could I do to change it?
- What's another way to look at this?

Evolving on Purpose means change; it means moving out of your comfort zone and many times into the unknown. *Evolving on Purpose: Co-creating with the Divine* means facing your fears and moving through them. Trusting in the Divine to guide you on the path of your highest excitement! *Evolving on Purpose* involves changing thoughts to generate new ideas and awareness of infinite possibilities.

As I mentioned earlier, my main resistance has been getting out of my comfort zone. I've begun traveling more which definitely takes me way out of my comfort zone at times! I participated in a zipline adventure excursion recently that included several other activities: waterslides, jungle bridges, mule ride, and repelling down a waterfall. I'm not a fan of heights! I feel safe on a zipline because I'm connected by pulleys and cables. There were other parts that felt really scary!

I've learned a new phrase: "On the other side of fear is excitement." Once we completed that excursion, the excitement was through the roof! It was SO MUCH FUN! So, exhilarating and empowering to have accomplished each of those adventures. I'm still in love with it, and I want to go back!

Along with that new phrase "on the other side of fear is excitement" is a new commitment to step into fear more often to experience more of the excitement and accomplishment on the other side!

EVOLVING ON PURPOSE

What is helping me *Evolve on Purpose: Co-Creating with the Divine* is that I'm connected and co-creating more with the Divine who communicates via intuition, impulses, and downloads of information and feelings of happiness, excitement, clarity. I have a myriad of affirmations in each room of my home. I created a Book of Positive Aspects, per Abraham Hicks' recommendation, which is filled with rampages of appreciation, affirmations, poems, and other inspirations.

I am more aware of my true desires and passions, and I am becoming who I want to be. This has been a big shift, to step into that version of who I want to be. What is that person who I want to be doing differently than what I have been doing? What could I change to get closer to my desire? What is one step I could take today towards my dream? Stepping into that version typically brings up limiting beliefs of "I'm not good enough," "I don't have the time," or "I'll get to it later." In this process, I've learned that the Divine continues to let me know through longings and discontent what is best for me. The longing to step out and take a chance on writing a chapter. I've learned to do what I can with what I have, knowing there's always way more than I'm aware of!

My passion is becoming the most expanded, most source-connected version of me and helping others who want the same. I've helped people in crisis mode for 30+ years, and I would love my retirement to be about helping those who are aware of *Evolving on Purpose* and could use support and guidance in the process.

I am creating an amazing coaching business called Coaching4DreamsComeTrue. I am so excited to be on the journey of *Evolving on Purpose: Co-creating with the Divine.*

About the Author

Karla Kopp, LMSW has had a 30+ year career working with those in crisis. She spent the first 15 years of her career as a social worker in Children's Services supporting children in foster care and their families. The second 15 years of her career, Karla has been working in hospitals, caring for patients and families in their plan of care towards a safe discharge. Working with people in crisis has made Karla passionate about improving her own health and life to Live, Laugh, Love and Learn towards her Dream Come True. While on that journey of *Evolving on Purpose: Co-creating with the Divine*, she has a strong passion to educate and raise awareness to others that the time to take control of your life is NOW.

Karla has witnessed so much pain and despair that could have been avoided by being present, tuning into the Divine within, and working towards the life you would absolutely love, no matter what anyone else tells you, no matter what your current circumstances are.

Karla is more cognizant than ever in listening to her Divine within, her longings and discontents that lead her to fulfilling her dreams. Karla's favorite mantra is: "I am Happy, Healthy, Wealthy, Joy-filled, FUN, and in love with life!"

Karla is the founder and CEO of Coaching4DreamsComeTrue. She believes in creating a healthy mindset because your thoughts create your feelings which create your actions that equal your results. She is excited to guide you in discovering a passion that lights you up and moves you towards your dreams come true.

Karla is a certified Life and Health Coach with The Health Coach Institute and The Brave Thinking Institute as well as a Certified Infinite Possibilities Trainer with Mike Dooley.

Connect with Karla below:

KarlaKopp@gmail.com

KATI LUDWIG

The Path of Beauty

The Divine

S oft, white sand under my feet, turquoise-blue water glistening in the sun, the sound of waves reaching for the shore, the warm sea breeze on my skin, the infinity and depth of the ocean unfolding in front of me. I connect deeply with the Divine as I witness the beauty of this scenery, the balance and harmony in all that surrounds me. The Divine is the secret of all things, the great mystical power and energy that creates, preserves, destroys, and regenerates. This sacred power calms me, soothes me, grounds me, transforms me, and relaxes me deep inside. As I immerse myself in the play of the ocean, I discover so much about the Divine: its infinite wisdom about the cycles of birth-life-death-rebirth as the waves come and go; its sacred connection with Mother Earth and Father Sky; its softness and compassion for all things; and its tremendous, alchemical power of transformation as the ocean changes its surface and the landscape nearby.

The Divine moves through us, surrounds us, is in us and beyond us. The Divine invites us every day to be a creative contributing part of it by expressing our unique creativity and letting it shine. The Divine calls us to notice its beauty, its simplicity, and its authenticity. The Divine teaches us who we really are at the core: spiritual beings with an embodied human experience – a mirror of the Divine. The Divine initiates us into the *Path of Beauty*.

The Path of Beauty shows us how to embrace our human experience here on Mother Earth whilst not losing our connection to Father Sky and the spiritual guidance we can receive if we are open to receiving its wisdom. We are asked to feel our feelings fully, to embody them, and to evolve into the next version of ourselves – just like the caterpillar transforms into a butterfly after retreating inside the cocoon.

Walking the Path of Beauty challenges us to reconcile with our wounded self, our shadows, and the parts we do not like about ourselves. The Path of Beauty brings us closer to the Divine as it guides us to see the sacredness in us, in our life, and in all things. It can be light and playful to walk the Path of Beauty, and it can be painful and weary at the same time – just like the ocean ebbs and flows. The reward of walking this path is the gift of a deep, wholesome, sacred soul connection. This is the most empowering and joyful state of being.

Embodying the Divine – Walking the Path of Beauty

For me, co-creating with the Divine means to walk the Path of Beauty with all its flavours and colours, to not shy away from the challenges it has in store for us, and – equally important – to not hide away from the beauty and gifts it has to offer.

In her podcast series 'Sacred Power,' the wonderful Caroline Myss introduces eight aspects of the Divine. By embodying these aspects, we can take steps on our path of beauty towards embodying the Divine in our life. If we allow ourselves to make choices towards the Divine, we are co-creating with the Divine. These eight aspects are:

1. To not betray yourself or others
2. To live with integrity and truth
3. To know and live your values
4. To have a spiritual (energetic) worldview
5. To practice kindness
6. To be reflective daily
7. To be of service
8. To empower yourself and others

1. To Not Betray Yourself and Others

Self-betrayal has self-suppression at its root. When we feel shame, guilt, and (self) blame about who we are or who we are not, we feel compelled to suppress our true feelings and essentially our nature. In doing so, we are moving away from ourselves until the distance is so great that we have lost reception to our core – our soul. Our soul communicates the Divine all the time; however, if we lose connection to our soul, we cannot hear its messages, nor can we freely co-create with it.

When we betray ourselves, we are at risk of betraying others as we are not in touch with reality anymore. We are not in touch with the present moment and the feelings unfolding within us from moment to moment. We are not honest with ourselves, and we cannot really identify our state of being – sad, alone, abandoned, rejected, unworthy, indecisive, overwhelmed, exhausted, impatient, insecure, stressed, angry, discouraged, inert, sluggish, disillusioned, irritated, frustrated, bored, optimistic, hopeful, accepting, peaceful, enthusiastic, open, content, passionate, secure, grateful, joyful, empowered, whole. How open are you to fully feel all these feelings as they show up? How honest are you with yourself? How have you betrayed yourself by suppressing your truth?

2. To Live with Integrity and Truth

In the Maori language, the word *Mana,* which can be translated as "spiritual power" or "a supernatural force in a person, place, or object," communicates the uniqueness of our soul – its unique signature, essence, and energy. What is the supernatural force within you that wants to bring forth your essence and your energy? How can you share the unique signature of your soul? What is your *Mana?*

In order for us to find or rather to receive the answers to these questions, we need to cultivate integrity and truth within us. Ask yourself: *Am I in alignment with my thoughts, feelings, and words? And do my thoughts, feelings, and words align?* Most likely the answer to these questions is: no.

As life happens, we reinforce our patterns and ways of being, and they become habits. Not all our habits are of integrity and reflect our inner truth. All too often, we say things in a rush that we actually do not mean, or we hold our innermost longings back out of fear to be judged or rejected. That is the opposite of living with *Mana.*

This way of being disempowers us and makes us feel less connected to our soul. The word integrity is connected with the word integration. In order for us to live with integrity and truth, we are called to integrate all aspects of us – the good, the bad, and the ugly.

Only through the process of honest, compassionate self-inquiry can we get to know our unique soul essence and learn how to wield our supernatural forces. For some of us, this is the road less travelled as we come into touch with our vulnerability – that challenging feeling we get the moment we step out of our comfort zone or do something that invites us to let go of control. And the thought of losing control evokes fear and stress in most of us. So how can we find the balance between feeling vulnerable and navigating our fear of being vulnerable so that we feel empowered to live with integrity and truth? We need to remember and connect with our internal resources: *our values*.

3. To Know and Live Your Values

What do you want to do with your time on this planet?

What sort of person do you want to be?

What personal strengths or qualities do you want to develop?

We can argue about all sorts of things with ourselves, with loved ones, or with other people. But we cannot argue about or suppress our true core values without long-term consequences. Values are the commitments that truly matter deep within our hearts. These are the parts of our life we cannot live without; and if we do live without them for a prolonged period of time, we will feel this inconsistency in the form of inner emptiness, discontentment, feeling unmotivated or spiritless.

Values translate themselves into being as needs which, in turn, we sense through our feelings. For example, if you often feel disregarded, you may have the value of respect or recognition. If you feel triggered when someone is a blabbermouth without much substance, you may appreciate competence or integrity. If you do not like people throwing away food or leaving the lights on, you may feel strongly about sustainability. If it irritates you when someone ALWAYS asks for help, you may find self-reliance very important.

Our feelings carry the messages of our needs which are informed by our values. Increasing our awareness about our needs and values will also empower us to set clear boundaries within ourselves and with the world around us. Once we identify our values, we will be able to determine our "YES" and "NO." This is the antidote for self-betrayal and a guide on the path towards integrity and truth.

4. To have a Spiritual (Energetic) Worldview

Everything is connected through an energetic web of synergy, collaboration, and balance. And everything follows its unique cycles. Just like Mother Nature does not remain in a never-ending summer, we will experience all the emotional seasons within us, and we can learn to harvest and integrate the fruits of winter as well as the bliss of summer.

Recognizing and deeply accepting the cyclical nature of ourselves and life itself is the portal to developing a spiritual worldview. As we begin to view life as a balance between ebb and flow, summer and winter, inspiration and integration, expression and reflection, we open ourselves to the Divine, and the Divine can move freely through us.

On the other hand, when we prefer a certain state at the cost of denying the other, we resist this profound truth, and we prevent our initiation into a spiritual worldview. However, we need to be spiritually tuned in for the purpose of co-creating with the Divine.

5. To Practice Kindness

As we move forward on the Path of Beauty, we need a genuine, humble self-care practice that is rooted in compassion, acceptance, and gratitude. This is the step that looks after our heart: its openness, courage, and wholeheartedness. "If your kindness does not include yourself, it is not complete," Jack Kornfield said, and I wholeheartedly agree. I would add that if your kindness does not include yourself, your kindness towards others cannot be fully authentic either. Practicing kindness and self-compassion is the medicine for shame, blame, guilt, and betrayal. It has the power to shift our focus to something nurturing that fills our heart and soul with the healing essence of love.

The moment we truly allow ourselves to value and nurture ourselves, we feel a deep sense of peace, harmony, and calm. We recognize that we all are trying to find our way back to this natural state of being. This is the moment we connect with our compassion towards others. By looking after ourselves in an authentic way, we create more space and increase our capacity for being loving, kind, accepting, and grateful to the people around us.

The need for changing others into a version that would be a better fit for our needs loses its importance, as the capacity for holding space for ourselves increases. And so, we become witnesses for the great release of our 'mind energy' that we used to focus on manipulating or judging others now that energy is available to us again in its full potential. I truly believe by making friends with ourselves in a deeper, meaningful way, we also transform into more loving partners, parents, friends, work colleagues, etc.

6. To Be Reflective Daily

Finding balance between external inspiration and internal integration can be a challenge in our modern, busy lives. However, if we lack this balance, we end up feeling overwhelmed, scattered, and exhausted. We lose touch with our heart and soul; and we lose touch with the Divine.

When was the last time that you asked yourself one of these essential questions?

- What inspires ME to let ideas flow?
- What sparks up MY desire to create?

- Where is MY balance between external focus and internal reflection and integration?

You will feel so empowered and energized to explore the sources of your connection with the Divine. And you will feel even more empowered to know your limits and boundaries: when it is time to be still, to rest, and to let the external inspiration marinate until it is ready to be birthed into *being*.

This process requires us to be courageous and comfortable with creating space for inner stillness and emptiness to receive our messages and insights from the Divine. The emptier we are – as opposed to 'being all over the show' – the more space we must create the things we truly want in life and the more discerning we will be to make choices in alignment with our needs and life purpose.

Becoming empty does not mean becoming nothing. It means to become calm and neutral so we can connect with our inner world – our inner stillness. This can be associated with fear and resistance, as many of us are not used to being in this state anymore. We have been taught to fear feeling our authentic feelings as they show up from moment to moment. The more we focus on external things, the more we distract ourselves from ourselves, and the more fear we have to reconnect with this realm. Nevertheless, it is only in reflection and stillness we are capable of receiving guidance and messages from the Divine.

7. To Be of Service

Practicing kindness (see above) is to be of service for the Path of Beauty towards the Divine. Everything we infuse with the essence of love, gratitude, and kindness is of service to us and to others. Have you ever asked yourself what your true gifts to the world are? And what are the catalysts for this gift? Oftentimes, the answer to these questions will bring us to a state of flow and joy, or what feels easy and light.

We have been taught many ways that we need to show up in the world to be successful, valued, and acknowledged. Be strong, be perfect, hurry up, try hard(er), please others... These are a few examples of our inner 'drivers' – the sub- or unconscious programmes driving our behaviour in certain directions. While we might *think* we are of service by engaging in these drivers, we *feel* more and more exhausted and burned out when our actions are only being driven by these inner mandates. This is because they are coping strategies helping us to feel valued, accepted, and accomplished. However, allowing these drivers to dictate our lives is not sustainable. We are losing touch with our natural gifts and skills – a realm we can only access via the pathway of feeling rather than thinking.

So, to be of service means to engage in beneficial, nurturing actions that are good for us and for others. This is a new inner programme for many of us and it will require lots of reflection, self-compassion, and repetition to transform.

8. To Empower Yourself and Others

Empowerment is the degree of autonomy and self-determination that enables us to represent our interests in a responsible and authentic way. Self-empowerment is a natural consequence of connecting with ourselves at a deeper, honest level. The more clarity we have about ourselves, our needs, our feelings, and our boundaries, the more confident, trustful, and self-empowered we feel. And the more courage we have to feel our feelings, the more wisdom we embody for ourselves and for others.

Rather than directing or manipulating others into a certain way of being, they can choose to be inspired by you as you stand in your own sacred space and power. A person who emanates their purpose, wisdom, and intuition simply by being themselves has so much more potency to empower others than a person who is leaning on artificial guidance and concepts to manipulate others in a certain way.

The bridge to self-empowerment is to be willing and courageous to feel vulnerability. Brené Brown describes vulnerability as 'uncertainty, risk, and emotional exposure.' It's that unstable feeling that we get when we step out of our comfort zone or do something that forces us to loosen control. Daring to be vulnerable takes us into the depths of our feelings to acknowledge our pain, our helplessness, and our wounds.

The more willing we are to connect with these aspects of our self, the more capable we become in navigating and processing them. In other words, the less fear we have to hold space for all of our parts and feelings. This is where our power lies. This is true empowerment – the moment when we realize we can allow ourselves to stop running away from ourselves, and just be with what is.

The reward for this practice is feeling whole, clear, at peace, and in alignment – that is what true empowerment feels like. The need to hide away diminishes, and we have more energy and vitality available to invest in our potential. This is a highly contagious state: by giving yourself permission to be vulnerable, you also inspire others to step into their full potential and power to be who they are. This is the Path of Beauty – the embodiment of sacred power and humbleness.

Practicing the Path of Beauty in Your Day-to-Day Life

We all have different lessons to learn and life experiences to integrate into our lives. I invite you to reflect about the eight aspects of the Divine Sacred Power:

What areas are you strong at?
What needs further focus?

Walking the Path of Beauty is not about getting overwhelmed by perfectionism or anxiety if we realize we have work to do – and we all do have work to do. Living in alignment with the Divine is about taking one step at a time and then feeling what is coming up, and what is changing in your life. I recommend picking one or two aspects to be your focus before moving on to the next one. Some of these areas might very well be the greatest lesson of your life.

We all carry a unique essence of the Divine Source within us like a seed. Our journey through life is to plant this seed, embody and manifest it within our capacity and capabilities. This is the Path of Beauty. This is co-creating with the Divine. Our purpose is to discover, fulfill, and express this essence so we can live in an authentic, intentional way.

About the Author

Kati Ludwig is a hybrid-healer who weaves spirit and energy medicine through her scientific background of clinical psychology. She transforms her clients' lives to be hopeful, stable, and empowered.

You are your own guru. Be inspired by your own story.

Your answers lie within you; you only need the tools to access them.

Kati's mission is to help people to hold space for themselves and to achieve steadfast inner peace. She approaches biology and the hardened industry of clinical dis-ease with a maternal, soulful presence.

Kati has mastered traditional cognitive therapy, but her piercing eyes and understanding reach into one's body, far surpassing the limits of the mind, in order to meet the soul exactly where it is and coax it back into its full vitality.

Connect with Kati below

www.kati-ludwig.com

www.mindyourkarmaonline.com

KATIE CAREY

I Surrender

This is our Divine calling: to let go of all of the heavy emotional baggage that has weighed us down and that we have carried our whole lifetime - or perhaps several lifetimes.

But so often, instead of letting go, we choose to hold on tightly to our past childhood trauma. Then as we carry our trauma into adulthood, we become resentful and judgmental which causes even more trauma in our adult relationships. And thus, the torturous cycle begins.

As children, we became the chameleon to keep ourselves safe. We learned when to stay out of the way of our parents (whose last nerve we always seemed to get on). We've taken on board childhood stories about ourselves that we've been told or have, most likely, made up in our heads. The story we often tell ourselves is that we are not good enough, not lovable enough, not clever enough, not talented enough. We will never amount to anything because back then, when we were children, our brains were still developing, and we could not properly process everything that was happening around us.

We have learned to be constantly productive and almost machine-like because we learned that we were useless to anyone within mainstream societal models unless we were producing in a workplace. But we forgot… *we are not machines*. We are human 'beings' – not human 'doings.' We were not designed for the constant push and uphill struggle of a productivity-driven society.

As an adult, I went on to attract partners similar to - but seemingly better people than - my father. After I had my children, I began to reflect on the trauma of my own childhood which reinforced the belief that my parents could not possibly have loved me since they had mistreated me so effortlessly - something I could not imagine doing to my own children whom I loved.

I found myself getting caught up in a cycle of negative thinking where resentment was continually building, and when I understood how the law of attraction and other laws of the universe worked, I began to piece together how my perspectives had potentially ruined past relationships and went on to lead me to attract the very things that I did not want in my world.

Worse still, attracting these experiences into the lives of my children. The judgment cycle was perpetuated. First blaming others for my never-ending cycle of suffering. Then, turning that blame inwards on myself and the guilt and shame soon became relentless. Realising that my actions created a spiral for my own pain and suffering hit me like a ton of bricks when I understood that I may have passed these patterns on to my children.

I had so many unhealthy generational patterns going on and I had no idea. As a teenager, I went through a phase of wanting to die because it felt so unbearably painful not to be loved, not to be liked, not to feel good enough. I started seeking love outside of myself. My quest for love began at an early age when I started singing in front of audiences as a five-year-old in the school playground.

I loved people's attention and adoration when they heard me sing. Singing before an audience made me feel seen, heard, and acknowledged. I loved all the beautiful emotions that came along with performing. I grew to love music. So much so that I later wrote a song about it in my thirties called "I've got it in my heart." (My song is on my website if you want to listen to that). Here's a snippet of the lyrics:

I've got it in my heart; I've got it in my head.
It's what I'm all about; I'll feel it til I'm dead.
I wanna scream and shout for all the world to hear:
Music is my love. It's what I hold so dear.

You can hear my passion for singing in those lyrics and the sadness and pain that I felt about those who hated and were jealous of me. I have been on the receiving end of standing ovations and the opposite, hatred, jealousy, and anger. And I was even physically attacked and bullied in my teens, because the people surrounding me did not like show-offs. And that was their perception of me.

Now that I understand the laws of the Universe, I can reflect on past events from that perspective. Understanding that the opposite energy exists for each energy, my biggest realisation was to be content with it all: the good and the bad, the love and the hate, the happiness and the sadness, for all of these emotions are just a natural part of our human experience.

As children, we learned to label things as 'good' and 'bad.' I have reflected on the so-called 'bad' events, going way back in time to my grandparents meeting during the second world war in Coventry, when they had initially lived opposite ends of the country, or looking at my parents going through the tragedy of having a stillborn baby just before me. If these 'bad' events had not occurred, I would not be here now to share my stories.

If my father had not given me the life experiences he did, I would not have gone on to found and create the mental health charity that I did. I would not be here now sharing my life stories through my podcast or with my books and my poetry. I would not have been the teenage performer because my father was the person I grew up singing with.

Being a parent can be so difficult, and more so these days than ever before. Because we understand more about how our actions and behaviours affect our children. But our biggest downfall is judging others and ourselves. Judgment keeps us locked in the past, and from that place, we are only ruining the gratitude that we can have now. We remain oblivious to the joys that life is attempting to put on our path. I have had evidence of the spirit realm supporting me since I was 9 years old. But back then, I did not understand any of this.

In my early twenties, my dad passed away, and I became interested in psychic parties where a psychic would come along and give us readings. My first experience at age 24, my dad came through. And I remembered that I was sitting on the man's knee, and he was singing to me. That didn't actually happen; it was my dad coming through, I was remembering sitting on my dad's knee as a little girl. The man sang songs that my dad had sung to me, describing things that no one could have known. Because then, in my 20s, when I was a young army wife, I was very private about my past. People did not know about my history as an actress and a singer or the chaos in my childhood. However, at psychic parties, some of my friends learned the truth about some of the pieces of my past that I was holding and hiding.

As the years went on, those readings became more private. I had fantastic evidence of the afterlife. I will skip my teenage years for now. You can read that in some of my previous chapters in *Intuitive: Knowing Her Truth, Soul Warrior,* or *Entangled No More.*

In 2015, I trained as a mindfulness coach, alongside studying for an open degree whilst running my mental health charity STAGES and local GPs, and the local NHS mental health teams referred people to my projects. We were even the Mayor's chosen charity to support in 2018. But while I was studying, I was still working in the job I hated until I was ill-health retired in 2017.

I was learning more about psychology, the science of the mind, consciousness, and all the exciting things that lit me up. My spiritual awakening began in 2010. When I first started to meditate, I went down lots of conspiracy theory rabbit holes. Many of my service users at my charity had also become aware of them and they certainly did not have the mental capacity to cope with any of that.

Most people get angry and start spewing hatred, whether it is true or not. There's also a lot of messed up, crazy stuff online created to disturb us. Usually, of course, this comes from politics. A mixture of truth and fiction is enough to confuse anyone to the point that you don't understand how to perceive anything. "It becomes nearly impossible to distinguish fact from fiction. There is evidence of everything when you go looking for it."

"Observation disturbs the phenomenon observed."
-Werner Heisenberg

The double-slit experiment was a physics experiment that demonstrated the wave-particle, duality of matter, and the phenomenon of interference. In this experiment, a beam of particles, electrons, and photons was directed towards a barrier with two narrow slits. The particles then passed through the slits and created an interference pattern on the screen behind the barrier.

Richard Feynman, a renowned physicist, spoke about the double-slit experiment stating:

> It has been found that the behaviour of particles like electrons and photons is in agreement with what is observed when waves pass through two slits. They produce an interference pattern on the screen, which suggests that particles behave as waves." (The Feynman Lectures on Physics, Volume III: Quantum Mechanics).

I have learned that I lead a much more peaceful and rewarding life since I became more of a neutral observer. Instead of judging things as good or bad, I discovered discernment which cuts off the charge of the negative energy of judgment. By releasing all judgment, I feel more aligned and connected to Source energy. I ask myself if this is for me or not. My intuition is accurate these days.

People often judge people like me for being a 'snowflake,' but in reality, we are the badass Lightworkers going deep into our messed-up programming to heal because we have learned the way the world works. Pushing against what you hate gives more energy to that thing, and you make that thing you hate a million times more powerful. Because of this vital energy transfer, my mission is no longer to save the world and everyone around me but to heal myself and understand that I am responsible for the energetic frequency that I emit into the world. If we all took responsibility for our own energy, there would be no wars, no suffering, no disease. If enough of us were focused on self-responsibility, we would shift the trajectory of this planet from negativity to positivity and from hatred to loving care for one other.

On my path, I've been called to release five and a half decades of abuse, trauma, neglect, pain, and suffering. I have let go of the hustle and the chaos that was no longer serving me. I have been called to remember my authentic identity. I do have plenty of evidence of myself. I have experienced times as a teenager when I was living out my dreams as an actress between the ages of 14 and 18. Life was easy and carefree. Being around my family living in poverty with terrible negative beliefs was the hardest to cope with. I felt like I had one foot in two different realities even back then!

I realised I couldn't follow my dreams; I had to return to the real world and get a job to pay my way, because I needed money to get to auditions on the other side of the country and our family were unable to provide me with financial support. I took on a job with the idea that I would save up and later go to drama school. That did not happen, but I don't regret the route my life took.

Marrying husband number one, took me on a journey of travelling, living in Germany, and co-creating our three beautiful children. But I recognise that I was filled with self-hatred around the changes that occurred in my body during and after my pregnancies. I resented my military husband because we kept having to up sticks and move every year. I had no say in anything. He chose to stay in the military for his career, (which was not the original plan when we married) and in those environments it was almost impossible for me to build a career of my own.

As a stay-at-home mum, I was always doing something to feel like I was contributing to our family. I never felt safe and supported, which showed up as lack consciousness because of a childhood growing up living in poverty. I gave up on my creative gifts and dreams because of that poverty and later chased my tail to make ends meet financially to keep our heads above water...until I came across a spiritual coach in April 2020. There began a journey of self-love, rescuing myself, and being open to listening to my intuition.

My understanding of "inner work" has gone deeper this year, and my spiritual business has given me the most significant insights into the areas that I sabotage myself with my energy. I have had to learn to trust myself and the Universe so profoundly, constantly being nudged to surrender control... a difficult task – especially when running a business with deadlines and client expectations, I constantly felt that I needed to meet. But the call for me to surrender got louder.

Life and business get easier as I surrender control and ask for support from spirit guides, the Universe, and the goddess within. I've witnessed the pressure that appears with every launch, and it's my job to let go and trust that everything – regardless of the way things go – is always working out in my favour.

With hindsight, every single event – good and bad – has led to this moment right now. And at this moment, I am so grateful for the life I am living. The future will be bright because I am present NOW.

Everything comes back to my teachings from 2015: mindfulness, connection to nature, trust, and faith. We must know that everything is divinely orchestrated and that our only job is to love ourselves even more profoundly. Creating boundaries, recognising the things that feel out of alignment and disconnecting from that pessimistic spiral of energy while simultaneously moving towards positive thoughts and emotions.

Don't get this confused with the instant gratification dopamine hits. That's another chapter... And you can learn more about that if you go and listen to Mark Styles's episode on my podcast or read Aileen's chapter in the first *Evolving on Purpose* book.

For now, I will leave you with this message: *"You've gotta love yourself with all your heart. If you don't already, it's time to start cos nothing's gonna to work out til you do." (Soulfulvalley Podcast theme tune written and performed by Katie Carey)*

Let go of your preconceived ideas. You CAN change your limiting beliefs and allow love, joy, and abundance into your life. You CAN create a life that you are madly in love with. If you surrender all control and allow your Higher Self to lead, your intuition will guide you. You are more powerful than you know, and powerful people leading from their souls will serve this world. By serving ourselves first, we will operate more efficiently.

Understand that your first loyalty must be to yourself. Our triggers are our most prominent teachers. There is a root cause for those triggers, and it is usually a negative story that we are running on repeat in our subconscious minds. The next time you feel triggered by something that someone else says or does, ask yourself these questions and journal on whatever comes up for you:

- What am I making this mean?
- Where can I love myself even more?
- What is the kindest thing I can do for myself right now?

Here's a poem from my book, *Soulful Poems: Heal the Heart and Soul*, which I published last year.

What If

By: Katie Carey

What if you could see that you're more than a label?
What if your difference is really your gift?
What if you knew how to connect to your spirit?
What if hearing your soul could lead to your shift?

What if the work was about your connection
To the Source that gives you the power?
What if believing is not in the seeing?
What if love's the connection with your own heart?

What if allowing yourself just to be you,
without all the masks that hide who you are?
What if all there is to know is within you?
What if you could access all of your power?

What if you realised your energy is everything
And you learned how to prioritise that?
What if you let go of the thoughts that consume you
And allowed yourself to dream… think about that?

What if you trusted the guidance within you?
What if that led you to where you should be?

What if you knew that you're already worthy?
What if you're healed and there's nothing to fix?

What if abundance was all that surrounds you?
What if you're keeping yourself stuck in lack?
What if one little change revealed it all for you
And you felt that weight shift when you understood that?

What if you tapped into higher intelligence?
What if you stopped yourself blocking your soul?
What if your ancestors are all stood around you
Trying to guide you out of your hole?

What if you remembered you are loved and supported
All you need is to breathe deep and connect.
What if you remembered you're a miraculous being,
a star in this universe? How magical is that?

As I move deeper into surrender, I trust that this chapter that I have written is enough... until the next book, the next podcast episode, or when we meet again in one of my coaching, mentorship, or healing sessions.

About the Author

Katie Carey, an International Best-Selling Author, is the CEO of Katie Carey Media LTD and the founder of Soulful Valley Publishing House. She is also the host of the Soulful Valley podcast, a globally ranked podcast in the Top 0.5%. Through her podcast and multi-author books, Katie provides a platform for spiritual entrepreneurs, visionary artists, coaches, energy healers, authors, and conscious creators to elevate their work and connect with the people they are here to serve.

Previously, Katie founded STAGES, an alternative mental health charity, and strongly advocates for mental health, disability, and emotional well-being. Having experienced health issues that led to her retirement due to disabilities at the age of 48, Katie is particularly passionate about supporting individuals in these areas, drawing from her journey.

With a love for blending science and spirituality, Katie collaborates with like-minded individuals in her multi-author books. Many authors have shared stories of synchronicities that led to their collaboration with Katie. She aims to bring these concepts and ideas to a broader audience, supporting mental, spiritual, emotional, and physical well-being.

Katie's background includes work in TV, Radio, and Theatre as an actress and singer, which she pursued from a young age. She resides in a Northamptonshire Village in the UK and is a proud mother of three adult children and a loving grandmother.

Katie is dedicated to educating and empowering people to find healthier solutions and break free from ancestral, toxic, and generational patterns of lack and trauma. She actively raises consciousness through her roles as a mentor, coach, podcaster, author, publisher and through her songs and poetry.

If you want to collaborate with Katie on one of her multi-author books, write your own solo book, or to learn more about her 1:1 coaching, healing, or mentoring services,

Connect with Katie below:
- Website: https://www.soulfulvalley.com
- Linktree: https://bit.ly/KatieBioLinks
- Podcast: https://apple.co/3BkJdkn

LALITHA DONATELLA RIBACK

You Came from the Stars

In the Beginning

At the time of creation, a magnificent bounty of supernormal powers was placed within you, gently hidden from curious eyes.

This priceless inheritance catapulted you into millions of incarnations throughout many galaxies and planets with the noble intention of realizing your true divine identity, your true divine self.

You're now in this lifetime on Earth as a direct descendant of the divine Father-Mother, who filled your DNA with unlimited possibilities for joy, abundance, and growth.

In the beginning, the Father-Mother of the cosmos said:

"Let us make mankind in our image, in our likeness…"
(Genesis 1:26)

The divine act of your creation happened in such a glorious, mesmerizing way that it was mentioned three times:

"God created mankind in his [and her] own image,
in the image of God,
he [she] created them;
male and female he [she] created them."
(Genesis 1:27)

And so the divine Father-Mother created you in their own image through much love and intensity throughout the birthing. Later, they observed your magnificence and rejoiced deeply.

"And the Divine Father-Mother *saw*
everything that they had made,
and behold, it was very good."
(Genesis 1:31)

The Goddess Archetype Will Heal You

If you are wondering why we are talking of Father and Mother and not just "Father," it's because, according to scholar Neil Douglas-Klotz, the Aramaic word used by Jesus translates into the meaning of a Being who is both Father and Mother. So, we are talking about the Infinite Creator and Infinite Creatress, or the Almighty God-Goddess.

In the Vedas too, Lord Shiva was originally half-male and half-female. Then later his female part became his consort, Goddess Parvati. Goddess Parvati, in her erotic, playful form as consort of Shiva is called Lalita Tripura Sundari, meaning "the most beautiful in three worlds and states of consciousness."

This is, indeed, the time of the return of the Goddess archetype in all her glory, who will help you heal both yourself and the world. Lalita holds a powerful energy and represents three stages of our awareness:

- the waking state
- the dreaming state
- the deep sleep state

Your Divine Inheritance

Your divine origins entitle you to a heavenly inheritance that includes a sacred identity, and a celestial kingdom that belongs to you forever.

You could never lose your noble origins and divine realm. But the only obstacles on your path to claiming these precious gifts are forgetfulness, doubt, and fear. You, however, own all the tools to remove these obstructions.

And the choice of claiming your inheritance is entirely yours. Your freedom of choice, or free will, came as a perfect gift from your loving Source which allowed you to grow at your unique pace.

But collectively we need to conquer our forgetfulness which runs deep. Our true history, too, has become lost in the eons of time. Our formerly perfect lives filled with omniscience, omnipotence, and omnipresence are now in the grips of a shorter lifespan that was not originally in our DNA.

The consequences of this loss brought us to ignorance and forgetfulness which have contributed to poisoning the Earth Goddess. In this process, we have neglected our divine potential. These unwise choices have resulted in a mediocre lifestyle and willful choices without true power or hope.

The Time of Ascension is Now

We are now receiving an invitation to take action – and join a new consciousness where greater awareness and deeper love await you. We are being called one by one to help with a great cause that will lead us to a collective rebirth. Some people are calling this the *Great Awakening.*

EVOLVING ON PURPOSE

We could spend some more time thinking about our life purpose, even if clarity on how to proceed is still missing. Kali Yuga, our current era, is filled with much darkness, which descends cyclically when the consciousness on Earth drops to lower levels, due to changes in the Sun. The Sun is, in fact, a generator of consciousness on Earth.

Also, in Kali Yuga humanity's great longevity is lost. In other yugas, our ancestors lived for thousands of years, and others were immortal.

Of course, confusion can be a stumbling block during this time of transition as we leave the dark era of *Kali* and enter the *Golden Age* of crystal clarity and higher truth. And the good news is you already have a purpose – the highest of all – which is remembering that you are divine.

The ancient sages have called your sacred purpose and act of remembering: *God realization*. This realization will help both you and the earth plane rise to a higher dimension.

From this empowered state, you can also tap into the vast knowledge of the ancient Indian yogis, who used their entire brain, reached higher states of consciousness, traveled to other galaxies in higher dimensions, and met beings millions of years more evolved than humans. The yogis have revealed the technologies for you to activate your advanced powers of creation and manifesting. You will regain your immortality.

"We have drunk the Soma; we have become immortal;
we have gone to the light; we have found the gods.
What can the hostility of a mere mortal do to us,
O immortal one?"

Rig-Veda, Book 8: HYMN XLVIII. Soma.

Today's Problems Will Lead Us to a Better Future

Today's challenges will lead us to a new consciousness, spiritual solutions, and a better future. As humanity reaches the threshold of the era of light and higher evolution, you will receive the key to your full divine inheritance.

Then evil will be destroyed, as it cannot sustain itself when the energy on Earth becomes entirely positive. Even the planets in our solar system will become auspiciously aligned in the sky.

The new era will be a time of dharma or righteousness and evolution, which will bring the end of suffering. Many wisdom traditions have called this transformation by different names:

- Satya Yuga
- Golden Age
- Return of Krishna
- Arrival of Kalki Avatar
- Return of Jesus
- Great Awakening
- Return of the Messiah

- Arrival of the Messiah
- Ascension to the 5th Dimension
- And more

The upcoming Golden Age signifies the time when we will collectively engage in divine activities. In fact, Kali Yuga, or the time of suffering that we have experienced in the past 5,000 years, is now shockingly apparent as the energy of the Sun increases.

So, as the light grows on Earth and in our consciousness, we become more aware of our current reality in all its tragic details. As we remove our collective blindfold, we notice the devastation of our beautiful, blue planet, the Earth Goddess who has been neglected, exploited, and abused.

In this emptiness of the soul, our young offspring feel much angst and often numb themselves through cruel video games filled with blood and destruction. The internet has replaced much parental love and guidance. The *metaverse* is lurking. Diseases old and new now weaken our bodies and resolve, and our divine creativity is under the attack of insidious meaninglessness.

Soul-utions

Despite the tragic events transpiring during this last leg of Kali Yuga, it is not a time for fear, but a time to rejoice for the immense opportunities for leaps in consciousness.

Notice the *siddhis* or supernormal powers that are surfacing in millions of souls incarnated at this time for a rare opportunity to experience heaven on earth. Perhaps, you have noticed that your intuition has made a leap. You might also realize that you have been dreaming prophetic dreams, or a mysterious power has brought you unexpected solutions to long-standing problems.

As you consider these facts, you may begin to fully understand the power of prayer. Your sacred conversations with the Divine can now help you manifest what you want. You may also realize a sense of unity with all of creation. You will learn that your life on this planet was a mere interval from your true divine light state. Satya Yuga or era of light will make this whole planet a 5th dimensional plane.

As you join this grand, divine party, you will soon celebrate. This is the reason global interests in astrology, past-life regressions, readings of ancient palm leaves, numerology, and meditation have reached an all-time high. These ancient sciences and the Ascended Masters have returned to aid us in this important transition.

Vedic astrology, the ancient science of light and time that is connected to your soul, points to your divine origins, and is attracting more students than ever before.

Divine archetypes or the *Devas* are coming into people's dreams and meditations. These extraterrestrial light beings of love and dharma are returning to our consciousness because they will play a pivotal role in protecting humanity and the Earth in the upcoming ascension into the higher dimensions.

You are God and Can Do Anything

You appear to be a material being of flesh and blood only in a tridimensional world. You are not even a solid being: you are *really* made of photon light. The yogis saw that the physical world of matter that seems so real is actually made of sounds. And this "persistent illusion," as Einstein called it, keeps us stuck in a simulation in the three *left-right, back-forth, up-down dimensions*.

Like the yogis, physicists of the *superstring theory* suggest that there are infinite dimensions. When you consider that you are not just matter and you are not limited to a 3D reality, then what defines you? According to both superstring theory and the yogis, everything in the universe is made of sounds and vibrations. So are you.

So, particles in the universe are actually one-dimensional strings vibrating at different frequencies. Similarly, different thoughts vibrate at different frequencies. Your thoughts, too, can vibrate either at a low frequency or in a higher, divine frequency.

Take Control Over Your Life

When you will become completely conscious of your creations and harness your powers through the use of intentional sounds, your life will reflect your divine nature and authentic desires.

More importantly, when you use the *mantras* revealed by the yogis – great experts of consciousness who received these sounds from heaven or other galaxies – your creations will bring you very desirable outcomes.

The Divine Can Change Your Brain

Perhaps one of the most important books written in recent times is "How God Changes Your Brain" written by two pioneer neuroscientists, Dr. Andrew Newberg, M.D., and Mark Waldman. In their extensive studies, they proved that God and images of divine beings activated significant parts of the brain connected with higher intelligence, compassion, harmony, peace, creativity, and productivity. Also, behavioral changes brought more love and even slowed aging.

We then wonder why this book has not catalyzed massive changes in school systems and among government officials. In the USA, only courts of law can allow the display of divine or religious imagery in public buildings and public schools.

There is power in prayer, say the yogis. And you are very, very powerful. Divine symbols, in fact, act as effective reminders of your own divinity and bring about a deep connection with the Divine.

5 Powerful Ways to Co-Create the Life of your Dreams
1. Believe, Believe, Believe

In a world that demands to be rational to a fault, to be "scientific" in all our expressions, it is no surprise that we find so many individuals who choose to focus on the bottom line and stick to being pragmatic, secular, and skeptical.

In this context, those who live by faith in a higher power and hold beliefs in the existence of celestial beings, angels, otherworldly spirits, and extraterrestrials might appear as hopelessly naïve.

Considering the incredible number of studies of parapsychology run by medical schools and governments that observe paranormal phenomena, and how quickly the results of these studies become classified – failing to reach the larger public – those who believe in otherworldly phenomena and supernormal power could have an advantage.

We often get stuck in a rationalistic perspective. Let's examine the viewpoint of an atheist, for example: there is no God, and we have evolved from a chimpanzee.

Yet no scientist has been able to prove with definite evidence that God does not exist, that we have evolved from an animal, and that the universe did not originate from a divine creation. Atheism is, in fact, another belief system.

As another example, most disbelievers affirm, "I only believe in what I can see with my eyes." But our eyes can only perceive colors and objects within a certain frequency range, and most of us can only detect wavelengths from 380 to 700 nanometers. Yet birds can see light frequencies that the human eye cannot perceive and can detect a color spectrum that is invisible to us.

I have witnessed studies on young children who, wearing a double blindfold and in the presence of researchers, could read clearly a page of a newspaper, a written note, and a banknote. The children read word for word by just touching the page with their fingertips. A 9-year-old little Indian girl was also able to "read" with her naked feet. Sitting at a desk, she simply rubbed the front page of a newspaper with the sole of her foot. During the experiment, the newspaper was placed under the desk. She could also read small, printed letters and identify tiny images. Is this not an observable and repeatable experiment, which is the basis of our scientific model? It is. Linear thinking can often lead us astray and curtail our truths, blocking positive outcomes in our lives.

An example of outstanding healing capabilities can be found in the incredible effectiveness of placebo in reducing pain just like – or even better than – common pain relievers. This shows that we can *believe* ourselves into creating better health and even reduce our biological age.

In 1979, Harvard psychologist Ellen Langer, a mind-body researcher, conducted a study on eight elderly men who were 80 years old or older. The men were asked to live in a retreat in a simulated 1959 environment. The men were exposed to songs from their younger years, their clothes were from the 1950s, the radio played programs from that era, and newspapers and magazines were also from 1959.

Gradually, the men undergoing the study showed signs that their aging process had stopped, and a new process of rejuvenation of all their biological systems had occurred. Their hearing improved. Their blood pressure and cholesterol were reduced. Their hearts were healthier, and their appetite returned.

Also, their depression disappeared. Their moods were more positive, and they seemed to live each day with anticipation, curiosity, excitement, and optimism. Two months into the study, medical tests showed that the men were biologically 15 to 20 years younger than their chronological age.

Try telling yourself that you are 15 years younger than your actual age. Dress as if you really were that younger age. Believe it, think it, and repeat it to yourself often: *I am ___ years old.* Put reminders around your living and working spaces to reflect this new biological age that you wish to be.

Say out loud every day, "I believe, I believe, I believe that I can do anything." It is a mantra.

Remember that your consciousness is superior to any physical phenomenon, and you have the power to create your own reality. Even your body will respond to these new positive beliefs and state of consciousness.

When you understand that there is only a physical and mental world based on consciousness, and that you have the power to live your dream life, then raising your consciousness through changing your belief system becomes paramount for you to create a joyful, satisfying, loving, and abundant life.

2. Choose Your Sounds and Thoughts Very Carefully

According to harmonic mathematician, Randy Masters, the thoughts we think create sounds that affect both our organs and other people's bodies. These sounds create vibrations that cause consciousness effects that influence their health. This is why thoughts of unconditional love can help heal yourself and others.

Moreover, when you engage in prayer through words of love and praise for the Divine, you are changed mentally and even physically. You acquire well-being and can attract more of what you desire. You and the Divine are one, and it is to your benefit to show gratitude, devotion, and respect to the Divine.

In Sanskrit, the attention you shower on celestial beings through your love, devotion, and offerings is called *Parasparam*, or a reciprocal, equal relationship in which they will return your love and offerings by fulfilling your wishes.

Through this special connection, prayer and sounds become a technology that you can use to receive what you want. For this methodology to work, though, you will need to become aware of your thoughts and speech and learn the sounds that invoke different beings. For example, if you want wealth, the mantra *"Shreem"* is believed to represent the vibrations for wealth. In fact, *Shreem* is wealth itself, because this mantra's frequencies match the vibrational frequencies of prosperity.

Instead, the sound *"Kleem"* activates the parts of the brain connected with love and attraction. So *"Kleem"* is love itself. Additionally, these yogic sounds represent and vibrate at the same

276

frequency of certain celestial beings. In this case, "*Shreem*" is connected with the Vedic Goddess of wealth, Lakshmi, and "*Kleem*" with the Goddess of love, Parvati. Another powerful mantra that you can use to purify your consciousness and attract a new and better reality is "*OM*" or the primordial sound of creation.

So, keeping the right thoughts and using the right mantras can help you create the life you want.

3. Set Emotional Goals

The yogis have revealed that to manifest, your thoughts need to be both passionate and emotionally satisfying. In fact, these seers said that we cannot create an object through the intellect but only through desire, deep emotion, and focused passion.

And it does not matter whether the thoughts appear to be too grandiose to your logic. That's because your logic is not your most powerful way of thinking. For example, if you want a house, a technique to emotionalize your thoughts is by using your imagination, joyful visualization, and words of deep desire. The powerful emotions brought by your desires and imaginings will grant you the necessary sound waves and thoughts of a much higher frequency. So, bring love into your imagined new reality. Affirm that you will not accept anything less.

After using your emotions to create your wanted outcome, you may want to test and add a measure of realism according to your beliefs. Do you believe you can have it? Ask yourself if your wish is realistic. A realistic goal can still be grandiose. But your sacred work is believing that it is truly attainable. If you strongly believe that you can have it, then you will.

4. Commit and Connect

Since mantras match the object they represent – be it prosperity, health, love, or spiritual enlightenment – you must commit to this new reality. Now you know that the whole universe is nothing but vibrations, so it is your responsibility to commit to your practice of manifesting and connecting with divine archetypes.

Planets are divine beings. Through their vibrations they bring you different thought forms, both good and bad.

The Rishis or intuitive sages traveling within different levels of reality, saw that the planets emit powerful sound waves, and heard their planetary mantras in the cosmos.

Moreover, as we have seen earlier, the sounds contain the energy and vibrations of different celestial beings who rule these planets.

For example, there are mantras for spiritual enlightenment and Shiva, the Vedic supreme God, and the planet Jupiter is associated with Shiva. The Goddess of wealth, Lakshmi, corresponds to the planet Venus.

There are also mantras for love, relationship and attraction, and Goddess Parvati or Lalita Tripura Sundari brings you loving relationships. The planet connected with this aspect of the Divine Feminine is the Moon. So the sounds from the mantras will allow you to reach all the layers of your mind and consciousness, helping you overcome doubt and slow time.

The mantras of the planets and stars can be considered a seed, just as a seed can contain a huge sequoia tree. The mantras will help grow your supernormal powers. For example, once I chanted a mantra in a sacred temple in India that was considered to be a power vortex, and I had an out-of-body experience that changed me. The next day, a long-standing financial problem vanished.

Mantras are super thoughts that can:

- act as powerful thought forms that bring you your desired object (for example, *a private plane*)
- replace weak thoughts that could cause undesirable outcomes
- help you transcend your limitations
- rewire your mind to experience a miracle
- and much more

5. Surrender Your Ego to the Divine

The ego is both a necessary structure to function in the world and a limited reality. The ego can also be defined as an enemy of our happiness, which blocks our joyous creations. In fact, the yogis considered the ego a false identity that originates in lack of love, as the ego will use all kinds of tricks to defend itself and separate us from others, hiding the Divine, and blocking our intuition.

Holding the intention of surrendering your ego to the Divine frees you from automatic thoughts and *karma*. Karma is your habitual thought process, which is usually a blockage to the grandiose and beautiful life you want to create. Also, karmic thoughts can include memories of past failures that still haunt you, and block your capacity to accept a new, wondrous reality.

In the Vedic tradition there are many technologies for karma removal. The easiest are:

- Meditation on different forms of the Divine
- Doing charity to alleviate the suffering of others
- Offering humble prayers that include kneeling and sincere crying to the Divine for help

This latter method works because when we cry, our ego is subdued, and when we kneel, the ego loses its self-importance, surrenders its resistance, and you become open to miracles. Also, when you let go of karmic limitations, you can tap into your divine identity, which is your true nature.

Planets are Both Responsible and Responsive

Another powerful way to surrender your ego is by "*looking*" at your planets. For example, if you are in the period of Saturn, it may be difficult for you to believe that you can fulfill your wishes. So an astrologer can help you identify your planetary period and give you some effective remedies to improve your Saturn.

If you are in the Venus period, and your Venus is well placed in your birth chart, this planet will help you fulfill your desires. A badly placed Venus may harm your relationship and block you from forming a loving bond with your loved one. And so on.

The planets make a great impact on our lives, and traditional remedies can turn difficult planetary influence into auspicious energy for our creations.

Take Loving Care of Your Divine Self

In closing, I want to remind you to be gentle with yourself as you begin to dive deeply into your creative process. Ignore small setbacks and trust with all your heart that what you want will come to you.

If you can, dedicate yourself for a month each time that you want to create something – and if possible, reduce your contact with naysayers and the media. Comparison, frustration, and fear can stifle your creativity.

If you don't mind solitude, choose to be away from the mainstream world for one month, or even better, for 45 days, while writing and chanting mantras. Enjoy your wonderful transformation.

Know that as a child of God, you are entitled to all His-Her treasures. You are one with the Divine, and there is no separation at all. Be unconditionally loving with others and share your good fortune. You will be enlightened.

About the Author

Lalitha Donatella Riback is an Author, a Multi-certified Life Coach, Spiritual Mentor, and Vedic Astrologer. Her business, ShreemLab, helps women entrepreneurs create a successful life filled with abundance, love and spiritual transformation. Since 2004, she's helped thousands of people experience spiritual growth through her programs, blogs, videos, and speaking engagements.

Lalitha holds a B.A. in Vedic arts and science from the Academy of Vedic Art and Science, Sam Geppi, in San Francisco, and certifications as a Yoga teacher, Reiki master, and Ayurveda consultant. She has studied with Deepak Chopra and Dr. Baskaran Pillai (Wayne Dyer's guru). After living in India for five years, she wrote a book on spiritual transformation, Bliss Lab: How the Ancient Yogis Acquired Supernormal Powers and How You Can Too, which was #1 in Amazon New Releases in Eastern Astrology and #2 in Astrology categories.

She is now a regular contributor at *The Astrological Magazine*, one of the most prestigious publications of Vedic

Astrology in the world. She has taught masterclasses on Vedic Astrology for the Dr. Raman & Rajeshwari Research Foundation, along with world renowned astrologers and scientists.

She has traveled the world as a freelance journalist, worked as vice-director at the Italian Consulate General in Chicago, and chaired cultural committees for the International Women Associates, connecting professional women with diplomatic affiliations.

Lalitha has also studied classical, modern and contemporary art for over 15 years, and was a women's board member of the Museum of Contemporary Art in Chicago.

In Italy, her birthplace, Lalitha has studied several foreign languages and literature at Università di Bergamo, and she holds a child psychology major. She has contributed to different Italian magazines as a freelance writer on travel and business. When she is not working or meditating, Lalitha loves practicing Yoga and classical Indian Odissi dance.

Connect with Lalitha below:

: https://shreemlab.com/

LIDIA KULESHNYK

The Divinity of Horses

When Two Great Beings
Humans and Horses
Unite in Love
The Soul of the Universe is Healed

A Sister of Horses

Y*ou are a Sister of Horses,*" echoed through the vast
landscape of open plains, as my spirit weaved through a
herd of wild horses. The whispers of my soul were calling. I was
silent… observing from a distance, indulging in the presence of

my power. I forgot all will and human resistance. I flowed, free and whole, with the kinship of my soul.

And in a flash, I jolted back to a once familiar place. The walls of my room loomed tall and stern. At first, unaware of this strange place, I returned in human form. I could feel the constriction of time and space, where just before, there had been none. I could feel the weight of my body return, where just before, I had been One.

And so, my relationship with horses began – not in a barn or a stable but in the world of spirit. As I fell asleep, I would leave my body spontaneously. I never had a thought or desire to do so. These experiences unfolded naturally as my energy strengthened, cleared, and aligned. Through my dedication to my own healing, I became an empty vessel, a pure channel of energy. In these out-of-body experiences, I travelled to many realms. I appeared in many guises, and I met many friends. I began to remember who I was and how I was meant to live.

One of the great gifts of connecting with the divine is that you reunite with your soul, your true purpose and mission. You begin to see your vision and understand your calling. At first, my only mission was my own survival with the will to heal myself and return to the life I once had. But just like the butterfly cannot return to the life of a caterpillar, I could never return to who I was. I had evolved. I was ready to create more energy and space. I had expanded my capacity to be more, do more and live more. I stepped into my power and became the conscious leader of my life.

Since those out-of-body experiences, horses have continued to come to me in dreams. They appear as pillars of light – powerful and serene – guiding me and asking me for help. While I love all animals, I had no desire to be with horses. The horses recognized me before I recognized myself. This is the power of co-creating with the divine. You access the certainty of who you are and why you must do what you are guided to do. In this certainty is a feeling of connection, a security deep within. This connection grounds you in your knowing that no matter what happens, you are strong in your power. You begin to feel relief from the stressors of the world. You feel the flow, freedom, and security of your essence, of being centered, connected and conscious.

When you are on a path of healing and growth, you remember key moments that changed your life. One of these moments was when I was guided to a horse named Trigger who would forever change me, connect me with the divine and set me on my path of healing with horses.

In A Dream, He Did Arrive. In His Heart, I Came Alive

On a beautiful autumn afternoon in Toronto, I received a spiritual message telling me to go on a trail ride with horses.

I thought I must have heard this incorrectly, as I hadn't been with horses since I was a child.

Nevertheless, I listened. I found a horse ranch with public trail rides one hour out of the city. I called, "Hello? Do you have any horses available for a ride today?"

A woman replied, "The last trail ride of the year starts at 5 pm." It was Friday rush hour, and the traffic was jammed. I felt this sudden life-or-death urgency to get to the ranch. I had no idea how I would get there on time. I sat in my car in the eight lanes of highway traffic and visualized myself floating to the ranch. While my vehicle didn't move, I felt energy flowing, connecting my heart to the ranch. Something – someone – was drawing me near.

I arrived at 4:57 PM - just a few minutes before the last ride. I was assigned to a horse who looked tired, sad, and sore. Trigger had been waiting for me. The heavy saddle and riding gear seemed like lead weights that would break his back.

I followed the instructions of the riding guide and gently climbed on Trigger's swayed back.

I should ask for another horse. I thought. *But if I ask for another horse, then someone else will probably be assigned to him and inadvertently cause him more discomfort.*

We began our ride together. Then an interesting thing happened. I started to feel immense joy. A lightness and happiness moved through me as a feeling of deep connection and fulfillment. *"Was this my joy or the joy from my horse?"* I wondered.

My awakening had begun.

When the trail ride was over, and it was time to leave, I felt a strong sensation to stay. I watched as the staff took my exhausted horse away. I was filled with deep emotions, frozen in a trance. I felt angry that they would make him carry people on trail rides. I felt guilt and shame that I was one such person. I felt joy and love, wanting to stay with him, as he disappeared around the barn. Unbeknownst to me, I had been reunited with one of my soul mates, from the divine realm.

I had listened to the messages. I honoured the urgency of my spirit and took aligned actions. I felt the fullness of my emotions. I centered in my power. I embraced faith and inner knowing. And in so doing, I was guided to the high spiritual being who would heal me, as much as I would heal him.

After that first fateful meeting, Trigger came to me every night in my dreams. Even in my yoga class, his spirit would fill my heart with a visceral pulsing, pulling me to visit him at the ranch. His calling was urgent. I soon discovered why.

Getting back to Trigger was difficult. I did not have a car. I was still frail from my own healing. But "where there is a will, there is a way," and I found a way to visit Trigger as often as I could. To my great shock and distress, I discovered that my beloved Trigger was about to be shipped to slaughter. I had no idea horse slaughter still existed and was a big business. Trigger knew. Trigger knew the horrific intentions of the ranch one year before. It all started to make sense. I understood why he came to me in dreams every night and why I felt our connection was life and death. My intuition and guidance had been validated.

One night, Trigger came to me in an especially powerful dream. He had been standing by himself, ignored, and neglected. Tears streamed down his face. In utter desperation, Trigger struggled to say, *"I hear you have a farm. Take me to your farm."* He was as exhausted in the dream as he was in real life. Alone and afraid, Trigger used his last ounce of energy to urge me into immediate action. He knew he had to do everything in his power to escape torture and death. His spirit called out to the one human who could save him: *me.*

At the time, I was returning to the world and creating a new life as a butterfly fresh out of the cocoon. My resources were limited. I decided to use a new credit card that the bank had just offered. Trigger was my first purchase on my new line of credit! While the small debt of purchasing, transporting, and boarding him, and upgrading the barn at my family farm, was a big stretch for me at the time, it saved Trigger's life. Soon enough, I saw how my faith in the divine started turning lead into gold. Saving one horse created a stream of events that soon brought me the greatest abundance, happiness, and purpose of my life. I realized Trigger was the gateway to my soul.

Trigger eventually arrived home at my family farm. He began to heal. I had been told he was 36, but horse dealers often give the age of horses as ten years younger, so he was more likely 46. After a vet exam, I was told Trigger was crippled with arthritis, had painful hoof issues, was blind from cataracts, and was dying of organ failure from the toxic anti-inflammatory drugs given to horses to keep them working beyond their capacity. "How would I ever help him?" my soul cried out.

Trigger wanted to live, so I tried. I started healing him with what I knew and understood: reiki and macrobiotic healing foods. I brought in the support of a farrier and others who would honour our mission. One year later, Trigger had regained his vision. His organs, hooves and arthritis had healed. He reveled in his new body and freedom, running at full speed, bucking, inhaling the fresh clear winds and enjoying deep sleeps of pure peace. By using his spiritual powers, sending out an SOS for help, Trigger saved his life. He took a chance on a young woman he had never met and who had no clue about horses. He saved my life, too. I am forever grateful that I heard his call.

Trigger lived out his days with purpose and passion, priding himself in being the protector of the farm and me. When we welcomed a companion horse for him, our Lady Maggie, their eyes met, and it was love at first sight! Lord Trigger and Lady Maggie lived happily ever after, in green pastures, under star-filled skies, beaming their love as great pillars of light.

Icons of Love and Peace

Throughout history, horses have been the greatest guide, protector, ally, and companion to humans. Horses have supported our epic journey to connect to our soul and find our way home.

Horses have played a pivotal role in creating the lifestyles we take for granted today, including the freedoms we have gained from fighting in wars, the development of agriculture, transportation and land, the creation of sports and recreation, and the advancement of our healing and personal growth.

If there is one species who has suffered and sacrificed the most to help the planet and humans evolve on purpose, it is horses. It is time horses are recognized and honoured for who they truly are: Divine Icons of Love and Peace on Earth.

Equine Assisted Therapy: Uniting Humans and Horses For Healing

We are in a time of great healing and transformation. The incredible love and light of horses is needed now more than any time in history. And horses need our love and light now more than any time in history.

At my horse rescue sanctuary, Apona Healing Ranch, in beautiful Rideau Lakes, Ontario, Canada, we rescue horses from slaughter and provide a forever home where they shine their light as healers. We recognize horses as sentient, spiritual beings who help us heal, grow, and evolve.

With my degrees in Animal Behaviour, Psychology, and Environmental Science, combined with my spiritual relationship with horses and holistic healing with humans, offering Equine Assisted Therapy and Equine Healing Retreats was a natural progression in my evolution.

Equine-Assisted Therapy (EAT) has the power to change lives in the moment and create a lasting connection of inner strength and peace. EAT is an approach to healing and personal development that incorporates the presence of horses with clients who are on a healing path, facilitated by a therapist. The therapist, skilled in psychology and horse behavior, supports clients through individual or group sessions with the horses. Clients have time before, during, and after their sessions with the horses to understand their own transformational experience in achieving goals unique to their individual healing journey.

At Apona Healing Ranch, Equine Healing Retreats focus on healing through stillness with the horses, allowing for the deepest energetic connection and transformation by becoming the "empty vessel." The Taoist expression "from nothingness, all is created" is a founding principle of Oneness within oneself and the Universe.

The power of horses to heal has been scientifically studied by the Heart-Math Institute, revealing the electromagnetic field of a horse's heart is five times greater than that of a human's heart. Simply standing beside a horse may help one feel rejuvenated, centered, and bring many documented health benefits, including relief from stress, anxiety, and trauma.

Accordingly, every horse that is saved from slaughter and is given an opportunity to heal, has the ability to heal 5 humans. So, 10 horses saved, means 50 humans healed; 100 horses saved, 500 humans healed; 100,000 horses saved, 500,000 humans healed; 1,000,000 horses saved, 5,000,000 humans healed. From the simple act of saving horses from slaughter and offering heart-centered healing, horses can help humans and the planet heal and evolve.

If humans loved horses, the way horses love humans, there would be peace on earth.

Divinity Lost: Humanity's Fall from Grace

Where do all the old and unwanted horses go,
When they no longer have a home?
Where do the blind and injured rest
After they have given humans their very best?
After the trophies and shows,
After "best friend forever" is forgotten and sold,
Where do all the old and unwanted horses go?

I wrote this poem to show the hidden plight of horses. In their majesty and grace, horses do not complain. As the true angels they are, they endure silently, hoping, praying that they will awaken the souls of the humans they deeply love, and in so doing, they will no longer be abused and killed.

Millions of horses are needlessly tortured and slaughtered every year worldwide. Horses everywhere on the planet are at risk of being sent to slaughter, horses who:

- were once a special family member and friend

- have brought money, fame, and glory to their owners in sports, recreation, and rodeos
- have brought pleasure and healing to children and adults in summer camps, riding lessons, and trail rides
- were born wild and free and have been captured against their will
- were raised for meat, endure daily pain and suffering, and live with deep loneliness and despair in the knowing they will be slaughtered.

How has our world come to this? How have humans fallen so low that we kill the divine beings who are here to help us? How has humanity allowed their greatest guide, protector, and ally – their beloved companions and pets – to be treated worse than a widget in a factory?

Our treatment of horses reveals how we feel about ourselves. If you do not honour the divinity within you, you will destroy the divinity in all of life. One cannot escape the ancient principles of the Universe:

"Everything That Has a Front, Has a Back. The Bigger the Front, the Bigger the Back."

This ancient principle is evident in the cruel way that we treat our horses and, therefore, ourselves.

We are no longer living in the Dark Ages of medieval times with a low light frequency. Today, no one anywhere needs to eat horse meat. It is time for humans to return to their true role and responsibility as humane conscious stewards who honour life. It is time to evolve and end horse abuse and slaughter.

Ask Not What Horses Can Do for You, But What You Can Do for Horses

Horses need our help.

Just like Trigger, every horse wants to live their life in health, happiness, and peace and in divine service to humans and the planet.

Just like Trigger, horses do not want to be abused, abandoned, betrayed, tortured, or slaughtered.

Just like Trigger's desperate SOS calls, horses are beaming messages daily to the humans who can save them and who they are here to heal. This is how co-creating with the divine works. It is expansive, limitless, inclusive, mutually abundant, and beneficial. Co-creating with the divine is always a win-win.

Never underestimate the intelligence or spiritual power of a horse. They are telepathic and always know. They meet you where you are at. Horses will dumb down when they have to, and they will share their magnificent glory with you when they know you are ready.

We are all brothers and sisters of horses. We are here to unite in love with horses. When you hear their cries for help, when you see their abuse and betrayal, when you feel their love calling you, what will you do? Will you deny the divinity within you and turn away? Or will you embrace your light and choose to love a horse?

To be loved by a horse is to enter into a holy realm, a great honour and privilege of deep union with the divine. Few have experienced the ecstatic sensation of being enveloped in the angelic wings of a horse who trusts you and loves you. It is truly life changing. To be loved by a horse is to be initiated into the greatest unconditional love of the Universe and liberate yourself from the separation, confusion, and sadness of your soul.

The time is now for humans to evolve on purpose. We are moving through one of the greatest paradigm shifts in human history. You are needed. The time is now for you to remember the high spiritual being you are, to reclaim your sovereignty, and to honour the divine beings of Planet Earth. The time is *now* to place horses on altars of reverence and to show gratitude for their great sacrifices and eternal love.

It is time… time to acknowledge and celebrate the Divinity of Horses.

About the Author

Lidia Kuleshynyk As a Renaissance woman and the founder of AponaHealing.com, Lidia (also known as "Lady Apona") brings together 30 years of passion, expertise, and wisdom in pathways for every stage of personal development, to help you live a Centered, Connected, and Conscious™ Life. Lidia's Apona Healing Ranch offers Equine-Assisted Therapy (EAT) and Equine Healing Retreats to help you return to wholeness through heart-centered, transformational relationships with horses. Equine Healing Retreats are a powerful pathway to reclaim your health, regain your energy and refine your power.

As a High-Performance Wellness Coach, Lidia helps overworked, stressed-out, high-achieving men and women master their inner power, manage their energy and stress, and create their highest state of health. Spending time with horses in nature helps you de-stress and return to your center, allowing you to step into your power and become the conscious leader of your life and a conscious leader of the world. At Apona Healing Ranch, retreats are designed for your unique goals and needs, including private, group and corporate retreats.

Through her own incredible journey, starting at the age of 10, Lidia developed a deep relationship with horses, animals, and nature. This connection helped her heal her chronic health conditions, master her inner power, and reclaim her sovereignty. Lidia now loves sharing her passion, vision, and mission as a Thought Leader, 3 x Best-Selling Author, Columnist with Expert Profile Magazine, and Executive Contributor to Brainz Magazine.

Lidia is honoured to be a recipient of the Global Super Minds Award by Expert Profile Magazine, Global Women Leaders Award by Passion Vista Magazine and to be featured in Who's Who Of The World Industries by Unified Brainz Group.

Connect with Lidia below:

www.AponaHealing.com

MICHELLE GRANT

HeART Connections and Healing

❧

When was the last time you desired something so strongly that you were willing to work through all the doubt, fear and procrastination to achieve your goals? My journey through this lifetime has produced many hurdles to overcome. I could have chosen to curl up in a ball and given up or numb the pain with alcohol or any other distraction. Instead, I chose to take responsibility for the outcome of my life and not let trauma keep me trapped in an unhappy ending.

My story starts as a happy little girl growing up on a grain and cattle property in Central Queensland, Australia, with many animals, including horses, cattle, and other wildlife. I was born in Clermont, Queensland in 1971. Before I started school, we moved further away to a large remote cattle station in Central Queensland. There were no schools close by so when I started Year One at the age of 5. I had to leave home to go and live with family friends in town. Here, my happy memories seem to fade. I had to grow up very fast as I was given a lot of responsibility for a 5-year-old. I would have to get myself ready for school in the mornings as they had both left for work before 7am. I then had to walk down the road to their relatives to wait for school to start. Then walk a further mile down the road to school and back on my own each day. I had a lot of alone time to entertain myself in these early years.

I don't remember when the grooming and the abuse started. The wife was like my second mum. She worked a night job which left me alone with him a lot. At night, he would come into my bedroom when I was asleep. At first, I didn't know anything was wrong. It was not until I was older that I was more aware that this wasn't right. The abuse went on for years. The older I got, the more he would threaten me to stay silent. I was never able to stand up for myself. I was silenced and had my voice taken away. I still struggle with speaking up to this day.

On weekends I would get some reprieve at my grandparents' property. It was always my safe place filled with unconditional love. Growing up away from home from the ages of

5 to 9, I didn't realise that I had developed the deep-seated feeling that I was sent away in the first place because I had done something wrong. In so many situations in my life, I believed that I had "done something wrong", "I was always at the wrong time", or "said the wrong words". This feeling of being wrong has stayed with me my whole life.

I spent much of my childhood in and out of hospitals with respiratory illnesses, appendicitis, and Bell's palsy. I had a lot of trauma around getting blood tests or putting cannulas in, as needles never worked on the first go due to my super-small veins.

Halfway through year four, a mining camp and a temporary school opened closer to our cattle property. I was nine before I lived back home full-time.

Throughout school, I was the quiet country kid who didn't seem to fit in. I never felt like I belonged anywhere. My teen years were spent always seeking approval and desperately wanting to be liked. I constantly felt rejected, excluded, and made fun of. I was very easily embarrassed. From age ten to fifteen, I attended a school in Middlemount, a small coal mining town about forty minutes away from home. Then I went to boarding school in Rockhampton for Year 11 in 1987. I spent much time in and out of the hospital that year with asthma.

My relationship with my parents was not easy. I felt like nothing was ever good enough for them and that I was useless. There was always something wrong with everything I did.

I grew up confused and angry and mourning the person I never got to be. My self-confidence was non-existent. My thoughts were always: *Would I be right if the abuse hadn't happened to me? Would I be worth it if the abuse hadn't occurred?*

I never told my parents what had happened to me, so I always felt like an invisible wall kept me at arm's length.

The moments that gave me a reprieve from the pain growing up were my love of animals, drawing, creating, and escaping to the beach with my grandparents. These were the moments that I would hold onto when I felt whole and good enough.

I was drawn to creative things from an early age. My earliest creative memory was winning a Blinky Bill hardcover book for something I drew in Year One that went into the local show. I still treasure that book to this day. I was always drawing, colouring, or designing little outfits for my Barbie Dolls. I have many special memories with my grandma, where I would draw up little dress designs for her to sew for me. I loved creating with my grandma. She taught me to sew and cook and to always have a creative outlet in your life.

In 1988 I studied Hairdressing at TAFE in Emerald, Queensland. I continued my Hairdressing Apprenticeship and Beauty in Middlemount. Working with hair colours gave me a good foundation and understanding of colours, which has helped me with colour choices in my art.

EVOLVING ON PURPOSE

I met my husband at 17 in 1988, but I felt like I had already lived a lifetime by then. Everything felt natural and safe with him. Safe enough to tell him what had happened to me. We moved to Middlemount where I had the best time playing all the team sports I missed out on living on a property, including Rep Netball.

I was so in love and happy. We had two children: a daughter in 1993 and a son in 1995. As many mothers may relate, my children became my world. I knew I wanted to make the world a better place for them. I knew I had to learn to find my confidence so I could in turn, then teach them to be confident.

My life felt whole and complete for the first time. I cherished being able to re-experience the world through the eyes of a child. I strived to give them the childhood that I never had. They have always been the driving force behind my desire to be a better person they could respect and look up to.

However, my self-confidence struggled again as my children got older and started going to school. I worried I was passing on my lack of confidence by proxy to the kids.

Doing something creative would always come back to the forefront throughout my life. I discovered Scrapbooking in 2002. Scrapbooking was a creative art form that allowed me to show the beauty of preserving precious memories through art. I loved that I could combine memory-keeping with making art. I was hooked.

My scrapbooking journey would continue for many years and became a big part of my life. It started with a few Creative

Memories classes. Then my world opened up when I attended my first Inspiration Scrapbook Convention (ISC) on the Gold Coast. Here we learnt that we could sew, tear, paint, stamp, and so much more on our pages. I loved every minute of it.

This was the first time I felt the true power of a connection with my tribe; I found my people. Being with so many like-minded creatives was electric. I have made many friendships and connections worldwide through scrapbooking, which I truly appreciate and treasure to this day.

In the early 2000s, I owned a small beauty salon, and it wasn't long before I had set up a little Scrapbooking shop in the salon and hired the local hall to teach scrapbooking classes and workshops.

At one of the ISC conventions, one of our tutors saw my album and told me I should submit my work to magazines. This was a sliding doors moment in my life because someone had believed in me and my work. That person changed the course of my life. Wherever I can, I try to pay it forward and give encouragement and belief to all those that I can. You never know how much of an impact you can have on someone's life by being kind and passing on a bit of belief. Had I not gotten that nudge to submit that day, I don't know if I would have had the courage to do it alone. I often wonder if I would have chosen this creative path without that timely advice.

I had my first publication within a month of submitting it to Australian magazines. The first couple of rejections were the hardest, but I quickly learnt not to place the value of my work on one- or two-people's personal opinions. I started treating submitting for publications more like a lotto ticket. It really was the luck of the draw, not my work's value. Wondering if what you have created is good enough in someone else's eyes will quickly stop you from growing and sharing. I was able to submit my work without any attachment to the outcome. As long as I loved it, it was a winner. I had many publications over the next fifteen years. I also wrote articles and was featured on the covers of several magazines.

When I was 35 in 2006, we moved from our small mining town to the outskirts of Mackay near the coast, just before my son was to start high school. We wanted to give our kids more opportunities than a small mining town could provide, and I selfishly couldn't send them off to boarding school. I wanted to cherish as much time as I had with them before they inevitably left home.

After we moved to Mackay, I was fortunate enough to teach at a local scrapbook store, where I met a beautiful friend who introduced me to metaphysical healing. This opened up a whole new world for me. I no longer had to continue living with all the guilt, shame, pain, and anger from my past.

To that point, I had spent my life running away from my emotions and keeping super busy, so I didn't have to process my feelings. I kept busy working all day and looking after the kids, helping friends and family, and then creating scrapbook pages or art and mixed media all night before collapsing into bed early morning. I never sat still long enough for my emotions to catch up and feel them.

When I started with the energy healing, I learnt that every emotion I had ever felt had been locked away in my heart, and I had thrown away the key. After the first session, I had a week of extreme emotions. I didn't know if I wanted to laugh, cry or scream from one minute to the next. It took a while for me to learn to trust my judgment. I often felt confused and disconnected from my feelings, not knowing how I should feel.

In 2009, my grandad passed away. This was the first significant loss in my life. Going to see him to say goodbye when he was in a coma was one of the hardest things I have had to do. Then a couple of years later, in 2011 my beautiful grandma joined him, just in time for them to be back together for their 65th Wedding Anniversary. Losing my grandparents was hard. It felt like I had lost my safe haven of unconditional love.

Around this time my daughter was creating unique art in high school and painting incredible faces. She inspired me to want to learn to draw faces. This was when my desire to create art pieces beyond the page and onto canvases started.

While on the journey of healing my childhood trauma with Metaphysical healing, I discovered art journaling. At first, I couldn't see sense in putting anything in a sketchbook to play with paint, inks, and papers with no purpose. That was until I started creating in my art journal. It was a way to process the pain in my heart and express my thoughts and feelings while playing and experimenting with different mediums. There were no rules. Art journaling allows you the freedom to create what is in your heart with your art.

In 2013, at 42 years old, my first art journal helped me to find the courage to tell my parents about the abuse I suffered when I left home all those years ago. I did a lot of art journaling around my feelings while trying to find the words and the courage to tell my parents what had happened to me. The words are not always visible in my journal for everyone to read, but I immediately know the meaning behind the page when I look at it. As soon as I told my parents, it was like this giant wall had come down. I spent a lot of time healing my trauma, and art was there every step of the way.

Teaching scrapbooking gave me such a sense of accomplishment. Helping people to record and relive special memories was truly a privilege. You can't beat the feeling of seeing the light flick on for someone when they realise they could create something beautiful.

In 2015, I reached the pinnacle of my scrapbooking career by becoming a "Scrapbooking Memories Master," a yearly Masters competition for the Magazine. After this, I taught Scrapbooking at expos, events, and scrapbook stores all around the country.

I was fortunate to travel, share my passion, and plant the seed in others "that they can create anything they desire". Everyone is creative; it is just a matter of finding and tapping into what lights you up. Anyone can do what I do. You need the desire to do so and then decide to pursue it. Everything can be learned and fine-tuned with practice. Your desire needs to be strong enough to make you start. Then keep pursuing and creating what makes you happy, the secret missing ingredient - it is not the end result that truly matters. It is how it makes you feel in the process. Getting lost in the flow of creativity is such a beautiful and peaceful place to be.

The past seven years have probably been the hardest so far in my life. 2017- 2018 was a year of highs and lows. I got to teach on a cruise. It was a great experience. Not long into the cruise, we got the devastating news that our nephew had passed away in a car accident. It just didn't seem real. How can I continue to have a good time while our family is hurting so much? Then six months later, I lost a dear friend who had been like a sister to me in another accident. The grief just seemed to be all too consuming. In total, I knew nine people who had passed in a 12-month period which took me to a dark place where I was waiting for the next bad thing to happen. I couldn't help feeling who was next. I again turned to metaphysical and spiritual healing and my art journals to get me through.

During this time, I was also dealing with my marriage falling apart. I was heartbroken that my husband didn't want me anymore, which completely crushed my soul. All I ever wanted was a long and happy marriage like my grandparents, whose only regret in life was not marrying each other sooner. We have worked through a lot to get back to the same page. It hasn't been easy. Thirty-two years of marriage is a rollercoaster. But we both agree, it is worth fighting for.

Around this time, my health also took a turn for the worse. I went from walking every day to not being able to walk at all with a bad knee for the next three years. Living with the constant pain and inflammation quickly wore me down. Over the last seven years, I have cried so many tears over pain, loss, betrayal, and grief.

The only thing that has got me through is my art and metaphysical healing. I could have easily given up, but my tribe and helping others kept me going. Going for a walk every day out in nature always helped me to deal with life's hurdles and helped to keep me sane, but now I couldn't even do that. I felt so trapped in my pain and misery. Some days I couldn't even walk from one end of the house to the other.

After two years of going back and forth from the hospital for my knee and other health issues, I was at my lowest of lows. I was getting conflicting advice from different doctors each week and given more drugs to counteract the side effects of the last ones I knew this was not the life I wanted to live. I had had so many tests, scans and injections during this time that I lost count. After avoiding hospitals for nearly 20 years, all the decades of playing polocrosse and competitive sports finally caught up with me. The surgeons finally decided that I would need a complete knee replacement on my right knee.

The medication my doctor put me on for my knee pain contributed to many side effects and health issues. I gained over 25 kg of weight in this time and suffered from all the known side effects. I was so uncomfortable in my own skin, and the medication that was supposed to help with the pain did very little for the pain and only caused more problems.

In January 2021, I had a hernia operation, leading to an internal bleed a few months later. I was so ill during that period and had lost half my blood and needed a double blood transfusion; my iron count was zero. After this stint in the hospital, I had had enough of doctors and hospitals and feeling like shit and in pain. I was even given a date to get a full knee replacement on my knee; by now I had no confidence in the doctors or hospital.

I decided it was time to seek alternative therapies and started focussing on wellness rather than illness. I decided then and there that I wanted to be 100% drug-free, including the asthma medication I had been on my whole life.

With the help of alkaline water, essential oils, deep tissue massages, and books, I am finally drug-free! I have discovered new strategies to incorporate into my life that promote wellness instead of simply medicating [and masking] illness.

I learned breathing techniques to help me naturally manage an asthma attack from the book *Breath* by James Nestor. Drinking a bottle of Alkaline water and learning how to Alkalise my body with foods helped heal the inflammation in my body. The deep tissue massages and reflexology helped me regain my movement and flexibility, allowing me to cancel my knee replacement operation. I can walk again and get around without the inflammation and swelling. I will hold out on getting it replaced for as long as I can. I finally feel like I am in control of my health for the first time. Essential oils have also been my saviour.

There have been key moments in my art journey, like the magical art pieces that just emerged or the ones that challenged every inch of my soul. These are the special projects that uplevel you as a creative. It is the best feeling in the world when you surprise yourself with a breakthrough and what you are capable of. Every time I have achieved a goal, I strengthen my self-belief muscle.

I was commissioned to paint a surfboard in 2016. That was a stressful experience at first. I had to overcome my self-doubt as I was being paid to do this project, so the pressure was immense. This project presented many challenges. The hardest thing was saying yes in the first place and having the courage to back myself to have a go. To feel the fear and do it anyway. After I finished it, the feeling of accomplishment gave me a sense that there was nothing I couldn't do artistically.

Art, mixed media, and scrapbooking gave me a sense of community and belonging that I never truly felt before. Teaching over the years has connected me with many beautiful souls. I have been truly blessed to have made many friends worldwide on this journey.

Sharing my work on social media and teaching around the country also led to an opportunity to design collections for an Australian manufacturer, Colour Blast, now known as "Bee Arty." I design artwork for stamps, stencils, metal dies, and scrapbook paper collections.

I didn't know how to create these before I accepted them. I just said, "Yes!" and then learnt how. You can learn anything as you go.

My art has helped me to improve my inner dialogue. MY INNER CRITIC IS SILENCED when I am in the flow of art. I have spent many years with a bitch of an inner critic. She was great at tearing me down, reminding me I was not good enough and a useless and dumb bitch. My inner critic was never short on harsh comments. I never felt genuinely confident; yet another voice deep down was stubborn enough to keep telling me, "You can do this." That little voice is the very faint one in the background. Sometimes you need to silence all the external noise to hear it but trust it when you do. At the end of the day, even that small part of you believes in you.

Reading the books *Playing Big* by Tarah Mor and *Big Magic* by Elizabeth Gilbert taught me to silence the inner critic. Little did I know that the inner voice cheering me on was my inner mentor. Knowing that I have the answers within me has given me more confidence to trust myself in decision-making and taking chances to back myself. I don't doubt myself nearly as much now.

The year 2020 was a year that changed for so many. The world was introduced to the COVID-19 pandemic and lockdowns. So many worldwide were affected with loss, uncertainty, isolation and, sadly death for some. I was teaching in Brisbane in Queensland when my classes were cut short with our first lockdown. The creative arena also changed with so many things going online. I did my first Facebook Live when I was asked to teach at a Cyber Crop. I was super nervous doing the Live, especially teaching alongside some of the biggest names in the art industry. What an honour! This Live was the start of a new journey for me. Three years later, I am still doing regular Facebook Lives.

In 2020 I also challenged myself to do the 100-Day Project, where you create something every day for 100 days. I could see the potential for growth by creating something consistently. I chose to draw faces on Procreate on the iPad, which inspired me to turn them into digital images for people to buy and print them out to use in their art journals.

I then started weekly free Facebook Lives on my *"Michelle Grant desiGns"* Facebook page. I was showing people how to use the printed digital images in their journals. I also have free Live videos in *"Michelle's Creative Warriors"* Facebook Group. I started this group so our creative community can connect, grow, learn, and be inspired by our team and each other.

I now have a team of artists designing digital *"Art Image Packs,"* and it all started with one person seeing something in me when I couldn't see it myself, which is what drives me to teach and inspire others and to instil that seed of belief that you can do it too. Art has helped me process my emotions, so I don't have to carry the weight and heaviness within me.

Everyone starts somewhere. Writing this chapter for the *Evolving on Purpose* book has been another challenge that I didn't think I could do. The self-belief that I even belonged here was a huge hurdle to overcome. I still don't know if I do. I am not great with words or spelling, but I am doing it anyway. So much fear came up for me about sharing my story or that my journey was even something worth sharing – another example of feeling fear, jumping in, and doing it anyway. Just say "Yes!" and then find your way through. I have found that generally, once you have decided to go in one direction, the answers and solutions will present themselves to you.

Nothing can stand in your way if you have a goal in mind and are determined to get there. If your excuses are bigger than your goals and commitments, they will always win. Anyone can do anything if they desire to do so. Desire and determination can take you anywhere. You only need the tiniest bit of belief in yourself to start. If you are not quite there, find someone to help you get there. I believe in you. You have got this!

I can now see that I am a better person because of my experiences. I can look back now and be proud of all I have achieved despite not feeling confident.

I am stronger now after working through all the pain and trauma I have endured.

My confidence still wavers, but I have learnt on this journey that the bigger and scarier the challenge, the more I learn, and the more my confidence grows.

I love seeing the light turn on for people as they catch that first flicker of belief. I will always continue to grow and evolve while inspiring creative journeys; this is my purpose for being here.

I always strive to find my confidence and do it anyway to show my kids and everyone out there what is possible and that they, too, can chase any dream. After all, we can only truly ever lead by example. I am proof that it is possible to overcome life's hurdles, trauma, and heartache, strive to be better, and put more love out in the world.

About the Author

Michelle Grant is a Mixed Media Artist whose passion is connecting with other creatives through art, community, and self-belief. Michelle has turned trauma into triumph through a journey of creative expression and self-reflection.

Michelle is the founder and CEO of Michelle Grant desiGns and Michelle's Creative Warriors offering online classes, retreats, challenges, and creative communities for over 20 years. Michelle is passionate about creatives connecting and feeling supported and encouraged, instilling the belief that anything is possible.

Michelle has been teaching and exploring all forms of Mixed Media and Art for over 20 years and continues to grow and develop her artistic skills, techniques, and product knowledge to provide a complete learning experience when teaching Mixed Media Art and Healing.

EVOLVING ON PURPOSE

Her art designs and products are found at:
https://www.MichelleGrantdesiGns.com and at
https://www.BeeArty.com.au, an Australian Art
Manufacturer.

Connect with Michelle below:

https://linktr.ee/michellegrantdesigns

SARAH BRIGID BROWN

Honouring the Knowings of my Soul

❧

Dedicated to my great grandmother,
Daisy Elizabeth Kendrick,
who I never got to meet,
but who was present at my birth.

According to the book *Earth Angel Realms* by Doreen Virtue, I am a Wise One, a co-creator with the Universe, able to manifest anytime I use my magical powers.

However, until I was in my 40s, I had not been able to see myself as a wise woman and definitely did not think that I could manifest anything. I believed that major events in my life were due to outside circumstances over which I had no control. Despite being highly sensitive and intuitive, I did not give myself the credit I deserved and ignored the many talents that I have.

Before we go any further, I want to share with you how difficult I found it to actually write this chapter. Each time I sat down to write, I could feel my throat tighten and anxiety rise in my chest. I resisted writing it for months, and I finally understood the reason for this after revisiting some of the things I had written in my journal.

Here's the journal entry that seemed to sum up everything that I had been feeling:

> *"I woke up, breathing very shallowly, and was reminded of something on Facebook last night. An invitation to open the nearest book to you, go to page 18 and read line 4. So, I picked up Rise Sister Rise and OMG! Those words! They deeply, deeply speak to me even after all the work I've done on myself... 'Persecuted for speaking out and trusting my innate wisdom and power.' I've definitely carried this, called the witch wound, through to this lifetime. This is apparent in women who identify as medicine women, healers, shamans, and priestesses according to Kairos Healers Academy."*

You see, maybe like you, I feel the witch wound really deeply in my body, my cells, and my womb. I know that I was a witch in past lives, a beautiful, wise witch who minded her own business, lived in the woods, and healed anybody who ventured to see her. I can feel it in my bones and sometimes see the scene when meditating.

I was also tortured, locked up, and killed on more than one occasion because of the magical powers that I possessed. How do I know this? Because I have had a few past-life regressions that took me back to those troubled times where I did not feel safe to speak my truth or to share my wisdom and knowledge with others. As a collective, we are remembering a lot of shared trauma right now, and many women are identifying with this particular wound. Connecting to the Universe, tapping into our innate power, and trusting our intuition still does not feel safe, yet we feel this longing in our belly to claim it all, loud and clear.

So, with the help and encouragement of a dear friend, I decided to share this part of my story and the resistance I was feeling about writing my chapter, in the hope that you will feel safer about honouring the knowledge of your own soul and maybe even give yourself permission to speak your truth.

At times, it is very easy for me to consciously co-create with the Universe, through meditation, setting intentions and practicing gratitude. These are three activities that help me to gain clarity, to focus on my desires, and to maintain a high energy level.

EVOLVING ON PURPOSE

On other occasions, I realise that I have been co-creating on a more subtle, subconscious level. As a child, I was absolutely fascinated by France and the French language which was extremely uncommon in the 1970s. Whenever I heard someone speaking French, something felt so familiar to me, as if I was coming home. When I first set foot on French soil at the age of ten, I knew deep down that I would live there one day, and my dream became a reality after I left university.

I would also spend time doodling in class as a lot of children do. My doodles were always the same – just the face of a man with a big grin, short hair, and long visage. Although my doodles looked like cartoon characters, I did not realise until years later that I was actually drawing the face of my future French husband.

Our meeting was nothing other than Divine intervention! The minute I saw him, I recognised him. My whole body came alive as if it was remembering some sort of pact that had been made a long time before that day. I was unaware of soul contracts then, yet felt an immediate 'other-worldly' connection to this man. I was fascinated to learn that he had also been drawing since a child, drawings of the Union Jack and men in bowler hats. This was proof for me that we had both been co-creating our future together from a very early age.

The more comfortable I have become with my powers of manifesting, the quicker results have come. A few months ago, my husband and I were waiting for the delivery of the personal development diaries that we had created to sell as Christmas presents in France. Their delivery had been postponed a few times, and I needed one of them to take on a journey with me to give to someone who had ordered a copy. Despite our emails and phone calls asking the publishers to speed things up, nothing happened... until one morning when I openly asked for help from the Universe. I remember asking for the diaries to be delivered before I left two days later, and after just four hours, a delivery van pulled up outside with the boxes!

Another example of quick manifestation is when we had sold our house and were looking for somewhere to rent. I had already visited several properties, but there was not much available that satisfied our needs and wishes. So, I sat down in front of my computer and asked the angels for help. I typed in the same words that I had been using beforehand and was surprised to see an offer that I had not seen before. I phoned the agency, booked a visit for the following day, and one hour after the visit, the house was ours to rent.

What is also really amazing about this particular story is that a couple of weeks before we signed the rental agreement, I had remarked to my best friend, *"I would love to live in this neighbourhood!"* Little did I know, just a few weeks later, we would be moving in! We were out walking along the river surrounded by some very old, wise trees and enjoying the gentle summer breeze on our skin. Everything felt so perfect. As soon as

I saw our house, I just knew it was the one for me and my family, and we are still living there today.

The year 2016 was a major turning point for me. That was the year I made the conscious commitment to change my life. I decided that I needed to finally do something for *myself* and get my life back on track after several years of soul-searching and self-doubting. Early in the year, I had journaled about three questions which I share with you now, as they may well help you on your journey:

1.   What do you want to experience?
2.   How do you want to grow?
3.   What do you want to contribute?

As I thought about the first question, I wrote about my desire to travel to lots of faraway places. I wrote down the names of many countries that I wanted to visit – some of which I have yet to go to, but the rest of my answer about future experiences gave me chills as I read my notebook again. All the experiences I wanted to have - writing books, interviewing people, helping people, leading workshops, and conferences - have come true for me, although not necessarily as I had imagined at the time.

This is part of the beauty of co-creating with the Divine – the 'how' is not for us to work out. We simply need to set a crystal-clear intention and then trust ourselves enough to follow the signs along the way.

One of the ways to set a clear intention is to create a vision board. You may be no stranger to this but allow me to share my own way of creating a vision board which may be different from any other way that you have heard of before. First, we begin by grounding ourselves and getting clear on our desires for our future.

We also focus on our priorities and visualise the actions that we need to take to bring harmony back into our life. A short, guided meditation follows, before we start the intuitive phase of choosing the words and pictures that we want to include on our vision board. The final phase is obviously pasting these words and pictures onto our blank piece of paper and letting the magic happen. By taking the time to be still and listen to our intuition, we can be guided by the Divine and create a vision that is in service to our Higher Self rather than our ego Self.

Back in 2018, my vision board turned out to be the one that most reflects the power of co-creating with the Universe. Here are some of the words that I pasted on my vision board: '*the other side of the world*,' '*listen to your body*,' '*family*,' '*summer training*,' '*energy*,' and '*conferences*.' The pictures included the Grand Canyon, a woman smiling, branches of a tree, golden leaves, a woman sitting and meditating in a circle, and a drawing of a body showing the main chakras and energetic fields.

I listened to my body and worked on my energy throughout the year, thanks to salsa dancing and leading chakra workshops. I went to the other side of the world when I accepted an invitation to take part in a women-only spiritual development retreat just outside of San Francisco. We meditated in a circle every day in some of the most beautiful surroundings I have ever seen – trees and bushes everywhere plus a labyrinth that was very energetically charged. I attended several conferences – both on and offline – and delivered my first conference on stage at a local wellbeing festival.

Family has always been very important to me, and in 2018, I travelled back to England to see mine, as well as spend several long weekends with my family-in-law in France. The summer training turned out to be in July of that year when I became a certified emotional freedom technique practitioner.

For question two, I wrote: "*I want to grow by inspiring others through my writing, workshops, and conferences, meeting more spiritual guides, spending more time in nature, stopping procrastinating* (this is still a work in progress!) *and getting over my fear of not being where I should be to grow spiritually.*" I love my answer! I have been blessed to receive everything I wrote for the second question. I have already met several of my spiritual guides in person in England, France, and the USA, all through listening to my heart, to the excitement welling up in my chest, to the heady feeling as I pressed 'Pay' for their workshops and retreats.

In my experience, we get to embody everything our heart desires by leaning into the whole process, even and especially on the days when it feels like the whole Universe is against us. Those are the days we are invited to stop, breathe, and go within. To calm our anxious mind which is sending out panic signals to our body and messing about with our emotions and feelings. To get curious about our feelings, to ask the questions that will lead us to more self-discovery, and to uncover another layer of 'stuff,' hence improving our connection to the Divine.

The third question was a little more difficult for me to answer. What do I want to contribute to the world? At the time, I was not exactly sure that I had something meaningful to contribute. I used to feel like an imposter and seriously doubted myself on more than one occasion. I have since worked through all those feelings and now guide other women to do the same. You can find more information about how I can help you to do this at the end of my chapter.

In 2016, this was my answer to the third question: "*I want to grow a community of (self) compassion, sharing, and caring. I would like to be a reference for people who are soul-searching and who need that extra nudge, to help them accept, welcome, and overcome their fears.*" While my vision for contribution is clearer and more refined today than it was years ago, I know that my initial answer allowed me to co-create my contribution to the world – a contribution that I create and re-create daily.

When I sat down to answer those three questions, I had no idea if or how anything would manifest in my life. Yet I had faith. I knew that if those words had come through me, there was a reason. This is now how I live my life on a daily basis, tuning into the voice of the Universe through journaling, meditating, and oracle card reading. There are days when I feel like there is a much greater presence in and around me, and those are the days when I channel some absolutely beautiful messages either for myself or for others.

I now choose to share two very intimate channellings with you – not so much for me, but for *you*. I am being guided to invite you to replace my name with yours and to read it out loud. I am being reassured that those who need to do this will and that this message will forever change your life.

These words are in one of my journals and were written on two different days in 2022, the year my dad passed away. The second excerpt was channelled on September 16th, 2022, the day I joined the group of authors in this book, the day I became the eleventh author to sign up. The number eleven in numerology is a master number, relating to the spiritual teacher, and that is who I am.

> *Dearest Sarah (or should I say Brigid),*
>
> *I see everything that you've done since the day you were born. All the love, kindness, and compassion that is in your heart, and all the hurt, pain, and grief that you're also carrying here.*
>
> *This tends to overshadow your true essence and stop you from shining brightly. You feel the hurt, pain, and grief because you don't understand why certain people are so horrible, unfair, judgmental, and uncaring, and in your*

quest to help them, you succumb to these feelings.

Your job is not to take on their pain. Your job is to help them move with and through it. Please let go of everything that isn't yours to carry, to lighten yourself, and be in a better position to help the world transition into what is called the Golden Age.

Signed, Your Loving Higher Self

Dear Sarah,

I have seen you struggle so much this year with your feelings, your memories of the past, and your hesitancy to move forwards. I seen you question your path, your motives, and your very presence on this Earth.

One of the reasons for your struggle is that you're still holding on to your past. Let it go! So much has changed since you incarnated, and it's not helping you to hang on to the past.

Trust that you can let it go. Trust that by doing this, you won't lose your real Soul identity. Trust that you will find the exact place, people, and support to help you be fully aligned with your Soul. Let go, trust, and shine. You are already connected with some of your

tribe here on Earth, and the rest are just
waiting for you to fully step up and step out.
Signed, Your Higher Self

When I am feeling unsure or overwhelmed, I will also call on my spirit guides and guardian angels. In April 2016, I went on an amazing spiritual journey in the form of training to become a practitioner in New Paradigm MDT13D®. I know that we often say that some things blow our mind but let me tell you that this training really did. During one of the guided meditations to meet our higher Self, I saw her as a beautiful little fairy just like Tinkerbell in Peter Pan, a luminescent being who was dancing and swirling above me. My heart was filled with so much love and awe at the time, and I knew that my life would never be the same after that.

I decided to become a vegetarian, step out of the mould, and follow the whisperings of my heart – even if they made no sense to anyone else or to myself. I had been an English translator and teacher to adults in France for twenty-five years and had been feeling the itch to do something different. I still wanted to help people to become comfortable in communicating with others, to express themselves freely, and to live their lives fully.

Becoming a coach had never crossed my mind until the day when one of my students came to talk to me during the break. She shared this with me: *"Ms. Brown, I'm sorry that I didn't do my homework. I've just been going through a lot at home."* Although her story was not uncommon, there was something about her energy that inspired me to *really* listen to her.

After I got home that night, I could not stop thinking about my students. I really knew very little about them and wondered how many others were just suffering in silence. But what could I do?

Angels and my computer are often good friends, as I have already said. When I am consciously looking for something, I always sit down and ask them to guide my search, even if it means going down those infamous rabbit holes.

One day in May 2016, I sat down in front of my computer and again asked the angels to help me find a job or career that would really make the most of my listening skills, empathy, and resilience. It was not too long before the word 'coaching' came up in the search results. After looking into it and deciding that I would love to train, I then needed to find the perfect company for me.

After quite a lot of research into online coaching programs, similar to the story of Goldilocks and the Three Bears, I finally found the company that was just right for me. This coaching program offered online training for those who lived too far away to attend in person and an intensive six-month course that was due to start only three weeks later. I signed up and graduated just in time for Christmas that same year.

As part of our end-of-training written work, we were asked to write a dissertation recounting the journey we had been on to become certified. I ended it with my mission statement which, at the time, was *"helping you to create a bright future by releasing the positive light within and letting you shine."* Even back then, I was focusing on the light in and around me, so it makes sense that I attract people looking for this.

At the beginning of this chapter, I mentioned that I can also co-create with the Divine on a more subconscious level, and this sometimes happens when I am in a one-on-one session with a client. I tend to receive messages from clients' Higher Selves during an energy healing session, for example, whether we are in the same room or not.

These messages very often come in the form of speech, but I have also experienced strong smells or seen vivid images. I believe that my role is to share these messages with my clients as they always provide deeper understanding of any past pain, fear, or trauma. Working with the Universe on this level has brought me a feeling of loving support, greater satisfaction, and more meaningful connections with my clients.

If I was to sum up my experience of co-creating with the Divine, I would say that it all comes back to the heart: living from our heart, listening to our heart, and following our heart. As Sonia Choquette said: *"A clear heart is a self-loving heart because only a clear heart can see and guide you to creative expression and solution."*

May you be guided by your heart to a place of inner peace, love, and harmony. May you find the way back to your SOUL (Self, Others, Universe, Life) and reconnect to your Divine power.

331

About the Author

Sarah Brigid Brown is your SOUL (Self, Others, Universe, Life) Connection Healer and Mentor and a teacher, coach, author, and speaker. Sarah specialises in creating and nurturing a safe and empathetic space for sensitive women who feel like outsiders, to show them the way to get to the root of their imbalance, disconnection, and misalignment.

She is passionate about helping women who identify as people pleasers, perfectionists, and high achievers to understand themselves, be kinder to themselves, and transform their way of thinking, so that they can have healthy relationships with themselves and with others.

Since training back in 2016, Sarah has inspired hundreds of women to connect to the Universe and live a life free of guilt, judgement, and fear. She does this by accompanying them on a journey to shift their past narrative, release their pain, and awaken to their truth. This leads them to put an end to the toxic relationships they have, especially with their mother, get clear on their true desire, and be brave enough to connect to their own wisdom, inner strength, and power to finally become leaders of their best lives.

Sarah knows exactly how they feel, as she went from being a people pleaser, always wanting to control everything, afraid to speak up, and totally disconnected from the powerful woman she *really* is, to a passionate coach, teacher, and guide. She is completely in love with life and her life, following her calling to help as many people as possible, embracing all her imperfections, and believing in a future where love and community reign.

Her approach is very holistic, as she is trained in neuro-linguistic, emotional, and energy healing techniques. More than anything else, Sarah loves to let her intuition guide her towards the modalities that would best serve each individual person and hold space for people to learn to rely on their own power and resources.

She is one of the co-authors of the Amazon international best-selling books, *Evolving on Purpose* and *Entangled No More*, published by Soulful Valley Publishing. She is also the creator and producer of guided meditations and visualisations, as well as EFT (tapping) sequences which are available for free on her YouTube channel.

Currently, she lives in the south of France with her husband and two cats, close to her three adult children.

Connect with Sarah below:

: SOUL-Based Healing & Mentoring to Empower Empathetic Women: www.sbhmentoring.com

- Start on your journey back to your SOUL by purchasing Sarah's *From Imposter to Authentically You* bundle here: https://sarah-hate.ck.page/products/from-imposter-to-authentically-you-bundle
- Book a SOUL call today: https://tidycal.com/sbhmentoring/book-your-soul-call

STEPH DARMANIN

The Goddess Within

In the beginning, it was dark. The snow fell silently, weighing down the treetops and blanketing the ground. The light from the full moon filled her room. She sat up wide-eyed, peering out the window. Many nights, she wondered where her father was, why her mother cried, and how her brother was always getting into trouble at school.

She felt alone with endless thoughts circling her mind. She pressed play on a familiar ocean soundtrack and laid her head down to rest. The sound of waves soothed her. They swelled and crashed as she drifted in and out of sleep.

"Surely, this can't be it," she thought impatiently. She watched as headlight bent around her room as a car drove past in the distance. "I'm destined for an extraordinary life. Surrounded by people who understand and appreciate me. Where the air is warm, sky is blue, and ocean is near. I'll create a life of magic and show others they can do it too!"

A fire burned deep in her soul. She refused to let the pain and anger of those around her make her feel small or forgotten. Little did she know, expansive forces of immeasurable strength were ever-present, sowing seeds in her heart to grow an important message she was destined to deliver.

"I'm going to break the cycle. I'll show everyone how powerful I am and make the world feel more like home." She wiped tears from her eyes and a promise was made.

12 years later, that promise came true…

In 2015, I was in a healthy, loving relationship with a beautiful young man. We had two blissful years together until suddenly, they weren't blissful anymore. Something was off. Even though our lives seemed perfect from the outside, I felt like I had lost my way.

Once again, I was playing a role to escape my circumstances, adapting in survival mode so others would see me in a certain way. I always felt so proud telling others that I was a chameleon. "I can fit in anywhere," I would say. Then, as I got older, I realised how much I had been sacrificing and what a disservice to myself and others it was to be anything except the real me.

For years and years, I repeated the same patterns on autopilot simply to feel like I belonged. Like I was finally safe at home in a normal family. But I knew this story wasn't mine to tell.

It was the first time I had loved someone so much, yet I knew the best thing for both of us was to leave. Besides, who's to say what's "normal" anyway? If I didn't leave, I would have always wondered what my true sense of normality was instead of trying to fit into someone else's definition.

At the time, my reason for leaving Mississauga was an innate pull to see the world. I longed to trek Bali's rice fields and visit the countless temples in Thailand, to scale glaciers and surf tropical and shimmering coastlines. I craved my Eat, Pray, Love moment and needed to backpack off the beaten path while I still had energy, two feet and a heartbeat.

Long before iPhones, I was enchanted by Lonely Planet, my mother's encyclopedias, travel shows like Departures and The Amazing Race, and anything involving National Geographic. I was hooked by the uncertainty travelers faced with each new day, having to make do with tiny budgets, and how calmly they dealt with obstacles and detours. Then, there were the magical moments when they reached their destination or discovered a new place they weren't even searching for, and for a moment, time stood still.

I was 23 and working at the bank. I looked around at my beige office, the beige folders, and couldn't help but laugh, noticing the beige pants that I wore that day. "How the hell did I end up here? I used to be living it up in Fratland, performing at bars, hosted a radio show, worked the coolest promo gigs, and met new people every day. I refuse to die drowning in beige!" I saw an old friend who said she was taking a trip to Australia and my heart skipped a beat.

The next day, I applied for my working holiday visa, and it was approved almost instantly. I couldn't believe it! I told my mom and brother, then everyone else I knew, and felt on top of the world. Before long I quit my job, sold my car, and left my white-picket-fence life behind. My epic life was about to begin.

The first 3 months in Australia were wild. I fell in love with the freedom, glorious weather, exotic plants and animals, and of course, the cruisy sexy lifestyle. The backpackers I met from all over the world were fascinating. I couldn't get enough! Decoding accents, listening to origin and travel stories, admiring their playful banter over pints, and defending unshakeable opinions about things I couldn't care less about. I had no idea young people outside of Canada were so passionate about politics, history, and their favourite sport teams. I often wondered how much was rooted in their own beliefs compared to what they inherited from family and friends.

I was also shocked at how young some of them were. Fresh out of high school, mostly German and Dutch, encouraged by their parents to explore the great beyond. At the time, I was 24 and sure, a 6 year gap is nothing in the grand scheme of things. But for me, it was mind-boggling to see young women with such confidence, backed by their families to leave the nest.

My personal experience was the polar opposite. I was made to feel like I was doing something wrong, abandoning my tribe and everything I had worked for.

"You're being selfish. How could you throw it all away?"

It was this backwards way of thinking that I hoped to escape. Unfortunately, as you may have guessed, shame and guilt were just as keen to tag along and stayed with me 14,000 kilometers from home.

It was hard for me to grasp how these young women appeared to navigate life so effortlessly, because it took me 18 years to "know that I know nothing," which was one of the most valuable pieces of information I had ever learned. To this day, that paradox continues to drive my curiosity and humility.

My most significant self-discovery began in university, when my brain underwent massive expansion and my liver took a hit. After a year, I withdrew from philosophy because my days were overshadowed by existential dread. During periods of intense transformation, with unstable friendship groups, unhealed family traumas, and deteriorating health, I looked to my doctor for help. She suggested a few herbal remedies as well as Eckhart Tolle's

The Power of Now and John Kabat-Zinn's *Full Catastrophe Living*. And so began my foray into spirituality and the expanded consciousness.

Sadly, the dark and heavy cloud resurfaced in 2017 when I found myself in a trauma-bonded, codependent relationship. Staying in Sydney with this person was the lesser of two evils, but the pain was intolerable. Every day I was brimming with emotion, about to explode or collapse into myself. I had zero confidence, was living in a share house with six people and one bathroom, worked numerous jobs to keep myself afloat, and was 50 grand in debt.

I had no energy to look after my body, did my best to enjoy life in the slivers of time I had in between shifts, assignments, and bawling my eyes out. For the most part, I had terrible friends and a shitty mindset. Multi-day arguments became the norm, and everyone told us we should split.

I didn't listen because our connection was unlike anything I had felt before. I saw amazing potential in him and dreamt of a beautiful life together. All the ingredients seemed right, and yet it just wouldn't click. Our entire relationship was like forcing two puzzle pieces to fit, except when we were intimate.

For 4 and a half years, I mistook our codependency for love and commitment even though my gut literally told me our situation was unsustainable. We concluded relationships take work. "We just need to try harder. We can't quit."

Eventually I realised love is the greatest, most energising and empowering feeling in the world. It isn't supposed to hurt, bring out the worst in you, or make your stomach feel like a pit.

We both brought immense trauma to the relationship, projected our abandonment issues and consequent lack of self-worth onto each other, and every time I wanted us to get closer, I pushed him away. He did the same and resentment ensued.

We trained ourselves to be addicted to the pain. I couldn't understand why he wouldn't leave me and why I couldn't leave him. It was the closest thing I felt to family, which had always been a rollercoaster of love and chaos.

Our on-and-off again pain parade drove away many of my friends. This resulted in me being even more dependent on him until I finally broke free for an entire year in 2019.

You know the funny thing about rock bottom? Before it gets better, it always gets worse. When the pandemic hit, I achieved a new personal low. I chose to stay in Sydney and found myself more alone than ever before.

The few friends I had left stopped returning my calls. I lived with 3 roommates who all lost their jobs while I kept mine and got to work from home. This made them resentful and in turn, they made me feel unwanted and small. "Let's bond over a shared enemy. We've got nothing else to do and it makes us feel like we have some control." I found no relief in calling home as there was nothing but worry and fear to absorb from the other end of the phone, and my bedroom was slightly bigger than a double bed with an angry neighbour below. The only relief I felt came from morning runs and solo evening walks, having my mind blown by the works of Dr. Joe Dispenza and cuddles from Cleo, a Godsend in kitten form.

After countless nights of talking my anxiety off the metaphorical ledge, I had to make a serious call. Would I allow the darkness to overcome me, or take a stand and choose happiness instead? I prayed for strength. Then God sent me a lifeline in the form of incredible new friends.

At the time, everyone was in desperate need of community, but I also wanted to challenge myself physically and reconnect with my spiritual side. As local restrictions eased, we met more frequently, exercising at dawn by the beach, sharing book and podcast recommendations, going to self-development workshops, and relaying genuine bursts of love and encouragement to each other.

I still get emotional thinking about those days because it was the first time in a long while that I felt truly accepted for who I was, rather than someone I was trying to be. Those friendships allowed me to meet myself again, outside of the context of my upbringing. I peeled back the layers of fear and anger and rediscovered the old me.

Looking back, I went to a high school where most people came from well-off families. They drove their parent's luxury cars, had all of the name brand clothes, and enjoyed summers in cottage country.

EVOLVING ON PURPOSE

Unlike my classmates, I came from humble beginnings. We didn't have much and though my dad was around, we were largely raised by our mom who was single for the majority of my teens. She busted her ass and sacrificed a lot to make sure we were safe, well-fed and could enjoy being kids. She took me to soccer practice, piano and dance lessons, girl guides, air cadets - you name it. I spent my weekends going on long bike rides, dancing in my bedroom, and flipping through my favourite magazines. I also enjoyed watching shows like *America's Next Top Model* and *Sex and the City*. The models' confidence and eccentric outfits sparked something in me.

In our household, allowance wasn't a thing. When I needed money and weighed the guaranteed outburst with the movie ticket or clothes I wanted, the juice wasn't worth the squeeze. So I got my first job at 13. Not surprisingly, minimum wage in the early 2000's didn't stretch very far, so most of my wardrobe came from Goodwill and Vinnies. I loved digging through racks and finding one-of-a-kind gems. Sadly, the cool kids weren't impressed and it sucked feeling like I couldn't compete.

For years, I convinced myself that I didn't have style because I wasn't wearing what everyone else was. I hated feeling like an outcast for looking and acting differently from my peers and family. "I must be an alien," I thought. "I don't belong here." This false sense of separation got me down and made me feel lost and empty. It wasn't until my 30's when I realised my uniqueness was a blessing and my ultimate superpower.

When it comes to memory, our brains can be so unreliable for useful things and yet, the cringiest moments live rent-free in our minds indefinitely. Why do these uncomfortable interactions haunt us before we go on a date or try to sleep? This is because, without the practice of mindfulness, the brain tends to operate in survival mode and when you feel anxious, it replays worst case scenarios to help you avoid making the same mistakes that led to discomfort or pain.

While it seems inconceivable to live in a world without it, the construct of time is absent within our brain. So next time you're reliving an encounter that makes you wince, it will seem like bad timing, but shake it off and thank your brain for the warning.

On other occasions, our brains treat us to pleasant memories of life-changing conversations. One in particular was a chat I had with my dad's partner around the age of 15. I remember frantically explaining how I couldn't decide who I was because I never knew what to wear, as if there was some deadline that I had to have it all figured out by. I felt embarrassed and behind since everyone else seemed so sure of who they were. One day I was sporty, and the next, a rocker chick. Today a tomboy, and tomorrow I'm pretty in pink. "What do I do? I don't know who I am or where I belong!"

She laughed and took a long drag of her cigarette. I hated that they smoked inside. "Why do you have to choose? You can do or be anything."

Woah. Wait a minute. I was so concerned with fitting into a box that I didn't realise how much joy and excitement existed outside of it! From that day on, I stopped obsessing over the clothes I wore and just had fun.

Consider this. Does what we wear determine our identity? Are other people's perceptions of us a good judgment of our own personality? The answer seems obvious, but I wonder how much thought and money was invested into your wardrobe over the years with the underlying thought of fitting in. How much time and energy are invested into protecting the persona we've built for others to see?

This desire for validation is evident in the jobs we have, cars we drive, houses we live in, and places we go to be seen. It's more prevalent now with social media – everyone splices and dices their lives into highlight reels.

In my opinion, this only becomes a problem if you view other people's happiness and success as taking away from yours in some way. This is living in a scarcity mindset. If you explore the law of abundance, you will see there is no limit to the amount of love, wealth and beauty any one person can experience. Use other people's highlights as inspiration and stepping stones in your own life story.

To review, the way you present yourself is important but not inextricably tied to your personality. This lesson became ingrained in me after 17 years of working in experiential marketing. In this job, I approached random people at stores, concerts and in the streets, to tell them about some amazing new product they have to try. After a few hundred times, it became clear that most people are equally as nice and non-threatening. No matter how snobby, shabby, or disgruntled they appeared, they typically welcomed small talk and connected with me.

These experiences helped me learn that regardless of clothes, hairstyle, skin colour, weight, age, tattoos or piercings - nothing matters as much as what is underneath. You can't judge a book by its cover and life will surprise you when you approach it from love, service and curiosity.

In my last year of university, I was headhunted into a strategic sales role and became fascinated with psychology. As emotional beings, our purchases are determined by how we feel. My reading pivoted towards mindset and persuasion, notably *The 18 Laws of Power* by Robert Greene, and I became very good at my job winning salesperson of the year at RBC. The experience allowed me to connect with people from all walks of life and showed me how beautiful people are, especially when they expose vulnerabilities. We all just want someone who cares and can help us make better decisions. And so began my career in sales and the advertising industry.

Flashforward to 2022. The year of balance, faith, manifesting miracles and new opportunities. Life was good. I was making cash money at a global media agency, renting my own place without housemates, and in peak physical shape. Yet I couldn't shake a gut feeling of loneliness. The world was moving at hyper speed around me and I was just along for the ride. Most of my life was spent in the driver's seat, but in this season I wasn't feeling main character energy.

Then out of nowhere, I received a call from an old friend – the one who helped me rediscover myself and my passion for fitness and personal development.

"We're heading to the blue mountains next month and have one space left in our cabin. Would love to see you. You in?" As if I had to think about it.

"Hell yeah, I'm in!"

I heard him laugh, "Okay cool, one more thing. Have you heard about sound healing?"

I paused, connecting the dots. "Are we talking Tibetan bowl meditations or...?"

He chimed in, "Ayahuasca. I've done it a few times before and it was life changing."

I smiled and shook my head. I couldn't deny the calling. They say the best things in life are on the other side of fear. I took a deep breath in and said, "What time do we leave?"

My first experience of the sacred medicine was undeniably pivotal and very hard to explain. It moved through my body with precision, intention, ferocity and care, shining a light in every crevice, treating me to vibrance in every language, with colours and shapes I had never seen before. It sifted through every atom of my being, tore me apart, and after weeks and months, brought me back together again.

There I was, an infant in the womb of a tree. Surrounded by the vines, mist and sun rays snaking through the branches and leaves, warming my soul, hearing a faint heartbeat. The petals and pollen wisped around and through my body. Then my dad appeared. His face was carved into the bark and animated, as he always is. In that place, everything we needed to say was communicated without words – purely through the energy flowing through the roots and soil around the tree.

The blissful and terrifying parts of the journey passed, and I purged extensively. My earth body could hear how awful it sounded while my astral body felt a tremendous release. The purge definitely did not come from my belly. It was much deeper than that, breaking through the sediment of the earth like a roaring volcano, bubbling up after lying dormant for centuries. It reconnected me to my ancestors and was very humbling.

My second journey with the grandmother was even more beautiful and challenging. That night, I saw my mom. We were so close yet so far, reaching out for each other yet unable to touch. We stared into each other's eyes, communicating every thought and emotion for what felt like an eternity.

Her image and connection were so strong; I honestly believe we actually met and were together in those moments, in a place where there is no space or time. When she started to fade, my heart was bursting with love and tears streamed down my face.

The medicine gifted me with an infinite number of stunning visuals, showing how everything is One and birthed from

Love. Simple and complex, beautiful and grotesque. Then in a flash, everything disappeared.

Pitch black. I was alone, drifting in space. Lightyears from any sign of life. I floated for eons in silence and my hands were heavy like concrete. At times they resembled lobster claws which felt so real and scared the shit out of me. I saw the others awaken to consciousness and desperately wanted to join them, but I couldn't rush my journey. So I waited, straddling consciousness, with no end in sight. Every time I fought the medicine to let me out, it pulled me back in. It felt like I was being punished, though oddly, my sentence was peace.

I didn't realise until months later that it was forging my patience and reminding me that feeling lonely does not mean that you are alone. Only you can bring yourself back to center and find peace. We are not to take solitude for granted and should instead use this gift to reconnect with our Inner Being.

After two nights, my body was depleted and I felt like an empty shell. At first, I was woeful, anxious and scared, which is typical having lived my entire life associating emptiness with a sense of lack. In the events that followed, my perspective completely changed.

Before parting, we concluded our journey with a group meditation, sitting cross-legged in a circle, close enough for our knees to barely touch. Our shaman invited us to close our eyes and raise our hands to our sides, palms facing inward. We followed her lead chanting the word *Om*, gradually increasing in volume and vibrato. It was unfamiliar and took us a minute to find our groove, especially after feeling so raw, but eventually we found ourselves in a rhythm.

Once I let go of the desire to make sense of the sensations and allowed myself to be present, I felt a wave of safety, euphoria and relief wash over me. Instantly my body was recharged, and I felt deeply connected to the group, to the past, present and future versions of me, to my roots on this earth, to my family and ancestors, to the energy flowing through and around me, to sound and breath. Everything was connected and time did not exist.

The emptiness I felt that morning transformed from a burden into a gift. A space to fill with as much pure love as I could find and create. And the most beautiful thing I discovered in the next 9 months and beyond was that the void was actually a revolving door and could never be filled, meaning there was just as much value in finding and creating love to experience for myself as there was to pass onto others.

It reminded me of a Toaist analogy. Thirty spokes are joined in the hub of the wheel, but it is the center hole – where it is empty – that makes the wheel useful. We make a clay pot, but it is the emptiness inside that makes the pot useful. We cut windows and doors to make a room, but it is the inner emptiness that makes the room useful. We seek to take advantage of what is, but we also find much use for what is not. Emptiness is an opportunity, and it is often the catalyst that drives connection.

Recently I was sitting on a bench, visibly frustrated. I was looking down and noticed an elderly woman stopped in front of me. I looked up into her kind eyes and took notice of her small frame and thin, white hair. I was about to stand up to offer her my seat, startled with the unexpected eye contact, assuming I was at a bus stop. She quickly motioned for me not to stand and said, "I only wanted to stop and admire your hair. I've always wanted big, curly hair. Do you have any to spare?" She smiled softly, and I couldn't contain mine. It was such a selfless, genuine compliment, clearly intended to ease my pain. My heart opened like a floodgate.

It was 40 degrees and 80% humidity, so I replied, "In this heat, I'd be happy for you to take some." While no hairs were exchanged, I felt that revolving door at work again, and the energy passing through it was unmistakable.

Simple, unconditional, infinite love. It stopped me in my tracks. The thing I was mad about completely vanished. I thanked her multiple times for brightening my day and wished her well.

As we waved goodbye, I thanked the Universe for that reminder. Things aren't as serious as we make them out to be. If there's anything you should make more time for in your life, it's joy. We aren't getting any younger. Don't get so busy stressing yourself out that you forget to play.

Since my experience in the mountains, life flowed beautifully. The day after I got back, I meditated and received an intuitive calling to write my dad a letter. I put pen to paper and wrote for an hour straight.

That evening, my dad texted, and I replied with a few of the thoughts I had journaled earlier. His responses are typically short and indifferent, but this time, his response brought me to tears. He said he was proud that I made it on my own and evolved into such a sensible young woman. He acknowledged that he doesn't say much but always knew I would find a way because I was tough. He called me stubborn and said he was glad I inherited it from him since it meant I wouldn't settle for anything less than Greatness. It was exactly what I needed to hear. 30 years of disconnect and with one message, love overflowed in me. I was so grateful and in disbelief.

The next day, something even more incredible happened. After 6 years of disapproval and guilt, my mom called to ask for my advice. She was searching for flights to come visit me. I broke down in the grocery store and kept asking, "Is this for real?" I have never been so convinced as I was in that moment of the cause-and-effect relationship between my sound healing and reconciled family trauma.

Within two days of my journey, I experienced a gigantic shift from feeling lost and detached, to safe, centered and reconnected with Source. Of course, my experience hadn't completely healed every part of my relationships, but it was a pivotal step in the right direction.

EVOLVING ON PURPOSE

In the months that followed, my connection to Source continued to expand. Anytime I saw a butterfly, dragonfly, angel number or feather, a light flickering or flame, I paused and looked around me, became in tune with what I felt in my body, and thanked the Universe.

Your angels, ancestors and spirit guides will always try to communicate with you, but we must move slowly to receive the messages they are channelling to us. If you ask for help, make sure to listen and look for the answers you sought. They're usually right in front of you.

I've learned that when you focus on the powerful, magical and synchronistic parts of life, the Universe will keep giving them to you. Everything is a reflection – as above, so below. Like a tree whose roots extend just as far underground as the branches reach towards the sky, you are not limited to your body.

However deep you are willing to go within your Self will determine the depth of the relationships you have with others. Conversely, if there is something you are resisting or fear, that will be shown to you repeatedly in others. The vibration you let out instantly ripples back towards you. Call it karma or physics. It is written and recorded. You don't get what you want, you get who you are.

As a child, I prayed for my situation and the people around me to change without realising *the power within*. As a woman, I strive to be 1% better every day. That's it. Do the best you can with what you've got, and dream big, baby!

I focus on showing up as best as I can for myself and the ones I love. I refused to let my circumstances determine my fate. I transformed my pain into power and now I have the honor of helping others do the same. By trusting in God and the Universe, my guides and ancestors, there is no room for uncertainty.

This is my story, and its intention is to remind you that you can have and feel anything you want. By co-creating with the Divine, I stopped begging and chasing, and instead attracted everything that I had dreamt of for the last 12 years.

My mom visited and we had a marvelous time with luck at our beck and call. She said she finally understood why I didn't come home to Canada and would love to retire in Australia.

This week, I bought a car with cash, booked a girls trip to Queensland, went on a fabulous first date and obtained my Australian permanent residency. I quit a job that was not aligned with my soul purpose and got back into modeling and experiential marketing. When you honour yourself by living authentically, you emanate love and magnetise abundance with ease.

Dr. Joe Dispenza speaks about brain and heart coherence. When we align how we think and feel, we emit a magnetic field up to two meters which affects how things outside of our bodies respond to us.

With every thought and every word, you adjust the dials. You decide your mood, your mindset, and your frequency. If you want to speed up and achieve great things, I invite you to first slow down. Look around. See how every bit of life is miraculous. Every moment is full of beauty and synchronicities. It is a gift to make mistakes and age.

If you're lucky enough to stick around for another decade, you will realise how cyclical our human experience is. We live through seasons and cycles. What goes around comes around. So be kind and do the things that make you smile.

May your life be filled with struggles that are worthwhile. May you see the absolute necessity of pain for joy and discomfort for peace. Surround yourself with people who believe in you, and always speak your truth. It's the only way to get exactly where you want to

About the Author

Steph Darmanin is a Maltese Canadian living in Australia. She graduated from the University of Toronto with an Honours Bachelor of Arts in English literature paired with a minor in women and gender studies. She also earned a marketing and communications diploma from Australian Pacific College and has worked in sales, marketing and events for 17 years.

Steph is an international life coach and certifed NLP (neuro-linguistic programming) practitioner. Her soul purpose is to help women step into confidence, reach their full potential, and leave a fabulous legacy behind.

She is currently in pursuit of her dream role within the corporate sphere while expanding her qualifications as a coach, writer and speaker. Her ambitions are to host transformational destination retreats, give an official TED talk, guide thousands of women to conquer their fears and self-limiting beliefs, write a personal development book, and one day soon, start a family.

In her spare time, Steph loves to sing, travel, get into nature and spend quality time with her loved ones and beloved cat, Harry.

Connect with Steph below:

- Website: https://www.legacysoulcoaching.com
- Business Instagram: @legacylifecoach
- Personal Instagram & Tiktok: @stephdarmanin

SUSANNE KURZ

Moving Beyond Loss of Purpose

It was in summer 2014, around my 38th birthday, when the devastating realisation struck me: *the joy was gone.*

After eighteen years as an academic, I was close to achieving my big dream: becoming a professor of Islamic Studies for lifetime at a German university with my text-based focus on the cultural history of the Persian-speaking world. The past six years I had spent in a rather well-paid research position, preparing my second book that would formally qualify me to apply for lifetime professorships. And here I was working in my dream job with some nine months of contract ahead, yet having to beat myself to the desk. What had happened?

My Intuitive Youth

For a long time, I used to say that I have never made a decision in the full sense of the word. I did not have to, as decisions came naturally to me: by the time one was due, the right choice would already be evident – one hundred percent certain, no question about it, without a shadow of a doubt. Well, at least for big life decisions: which school to go to, which subject to study at university, who my partner for life would be. Once I knew in which direction to go, I would follow that path with complete dedication, not looking right or left. No plan B was in place as anything else was out of the question, and I had no interest in wasting energy on deviating from the right path.

It worked like a charm into my thirties, and I have never regretted any of my "decisions," even if, in hindsight, I might have adjusted some with the knowledge gained later. Looking back, I was naturally good at mindset too. When others said: "Why should *I* of all people succeed?" I used to counter: "***Someone*** will, so why ***not*** me?" When I was gifted a calendar with inspirational quotes in my teens, I selected my favourite quotes and looked at one daily - an example of intuitive mindset self-hypnosis before I had consciously learned about those concepts.

At the time I finished school, I had high aspirations: I wanted to become a professor, making great contributions to my field, and also a famous writer. As for money, I assumed that I would earn decently as a professor eventually and, until then, be able to fund my modest living standards – I was intelligent and talented, after all.

My confidence suffered a severe blow after finishing my degree when I set out on my PhD journey, in the early 2000s now having to provide for myself. Soon, I realised that the economy was tough: everyone was struggling not to lay employees off rather than hiring new ones, mini jobs spread, and in Germany, they refrain from hiring someone overqualified for a job, so my hard-earned degree actually became an obstacle for making a living! Thus began my money struggles at the very moment I had to find a source of income. Nothing has caused me as much stress ever since.

Yet for a while, I retained my blessed way of intuitive decision-making. I had clear desires and purpose and was on the way to my dream.

The Joys of Academia

My passion was learning how people in distant times and places brought order and meaning to their world, how their reasoning worked, and how they felt. I relished diving into these worlds, gaining insights, and widening my horizons of understanding. I used my talents and honed my skills by translating and interpreting ancient texts, solving their puzzles, marvelling over the stories and tragedies of people long gone and how they could enrich our contemporary world. I got to travel, to learn from some of the greatest minds in my field, to give talks and some interviews.

My work as a cultural interpreter felt important for our globalised world as we need to understand not only our human commonality but also our different approaches towards life and their right to exist. Embedded in my fascination with the other, there was a growing conviction that, to create a more peaceful world, we have to accept other ways and to acknowledge that everything has a reason.

This was my purpose: unfolding my abilities, transcending limitations, and thereby contributing to building a brighter world. It was the perfect mix. But now, I suddenly found myself pondering how to escape academia. I had lost something on the way. Hence, I started to evaluate my journey so far and to learn how to get back in touch with my intuition and discover what I now wanted from life.

Up to this point, I had wanted a lifetime professorship: an economically safe, financially comfortable, highly respected position, and the highest qualification available on the globe – something to be proud of, to make my family proud. This position would grant me the ease and space to revel in expanding my mind, my understanding, and my creativity with the carefree delight that

I was longing for and that would allow me to realise my full potential by coming up with groundbreaking insights – finally!

I still remember one of my happiest moments as a researcher, alone at my desk at the university, leisurely reading the beautifully edited pages of a Persian text written a thousand years earlier, thousands of kilometres away. The inner peace and the joyful sensation of gentle intellectual stimulation when I discovered a piece of new information will never fade from my memory.

Then, there were moments of sheer delight about a new insight, that sudden spark of understanding, illuminating my mind like a lightning bolt, and the subsequent rush of excitement reverberating through my whole body each time I explained it to others. I also liked giving talks and teaching, the excitement of being on a "stage" and sharing my enthusiasm.

But I did *not* like the constant inner hurry and haste created not by my work, but by the permanent pressure of existential dread attached to the fact that all contracts were always temporary, and I might not get another job afterwards. No matter how well you perform, after this contract, the position will expire or *must* be given to someone else.

This insecurity and existential dread to lose my income, my beautiful home, my comfort, and to drag my partner into the abyss with me created extreme stress. Although it was only a half-conscious undercurrent during my luxurious three-year contracts, eventually it had killed the joy.

Looking back, I realised that this same stress was the reason why I had lost the connection to my unfailing intuition: it was buried under a huge pile of fear of a financial apocalypse.

Whenever my intuitive feeling shyly raised its head to point me in the direction of my desire to be my own boss, it was instantly crushed by the all-important question: *"And how will you provide the income you need?!"* I felt hopelessly trapped.

When my crisis reached its peak in summer 2015, I finally noticed that the fire of my passion had burned down too. Maybe it first was a form of burnout as I felt completely drained even several months into unemployment. But I also had not felt much personal progress anymore. After some twenty years of passionate dedication, I had lost my purpose.

Death and the Meaning of Life

At that point, my midlife crisis had been well underway for some years. I would have liked to have a child but that did not happen, and the instability of my economic situation played a big part in it. As a woman, I was keenly aware of the limited time I had left to become a mother once I hit my mid-thirties. Around that time, my midlife crisis reached its peak.

This crisis brought my attention back to the big puzzle: do we dissolve into nothing when our brains stop working? What is the meaning of life then? The fragility of life and the threat of death have accompanied me since childhood as losing relatives was a frequent experience, but the materialist paradigm of my intellectual upbringing suggested the answer: you have to create any meaning yourself because we are accidental products of our brains, hence we dissolve with them.

As the evidence seemed persuasive, I feared that it might be the truth. That made everything feel terrifyingly hollow and pointless. After a quest from my teens to my early twenties which included reading about Near Death Experiences, I decided that this life was all I could be certain about, so I should strive for happiness. That meant to stop questing since my inability to find satisfying answers made me feel anxious, depressed, and miserable. I focused on doing the things I loved: studying, then research, writing and teaching, and that felt meaningful for a while. But I overlooked that the crux for me was metaphysical meaning.

When my dear grandmother, my last grandparent, died in 2007, I experienced another intense fit of desperation which remained. The most devastating experience was sorting her belongings. When we opened her cupboard, all that she had kept of the little gifts we had made for her as children came to light - and was returned to us one by one.

It felt as if she had completely vanished, like all our love had become unstuck and was roaming space without purpose, sense, or meaning. I have rarely felt so lost.

It was a turbulent time in my life; I had just submitted my doctoral dissertation, then had to look for a new job and, shortly after gaining my PhD, started working in a research project over four hundred kilometres away. I got distracted again. Besides, I already knew it was pointless anyway.

Our tiny human brains, I thought, would not be able to grasp – much less to provide proof for – anything like the divine or an afterlife. So, I labelled myself an agnostic, someone who acknowledges not to know, since I believed it was impossible to **know** anything about these matters. Despite a lifelong fascination with PSI phenomena, I also had a deep distrust of anything "esoteric." Yet for my inquisitive researcher mind, being unable to know was unsatisfying.

For a few years, re-focusing on enjoyment of my work, life, and income worked. But eventually, I wanted more: more expansion and more meaning. I wanted to make a difference. Yet I never reached the breakthrough I was longing for, the eruption of whatever it was that I had been feeling locked up inside myself since my teenage years, that waited to be unleashed: the thing that would be my unique contribution to the world.

I had also tried in vain to find a creative form to combine my love for the fantastic and fabulous with my academic skills and knowledge. But there was just so little space for unfolding all parts of myself.

When my struggle with not being a mother triggered my midlife crisis, the crucial questions popped up again in a more personal form: What sense did life make in the face of being eradicated by death? What would be my legacy to the world? What is the meaning of my life? To find an answer, I had to revisit the possibility of an afterlife. I returned to my quest for meaning and to my experiments with meditation and self-hypnosis.

Towards Spirituality

First, I resumed studying Near Death Experiences (NDEs) in 2011. The first book I read was by the physician Pim van Lommel who concluded that we are part of an endless consciousness. I will never forget the first days of integrating this idea into my world view: how much brighter the world suddenly looked, how much more beautiful, warm, and welcoming. I felt relieved, as if iron bonds around my chest had been burst open. Sometimes you only realise the compression you have felt once it dissolves.

Naturally, as a researcher with an obnoxiously inquisitive and sceptical mind, I did not fully trust one book alone. I also looked for scientific explanations inside the materialistic paradigm, reading on the brain and on physics. Yet no materialistic explanation fully accounted for NDEs.

Admittedly, it still boils down to considerations of plausibility. There are no scientifically proven facts at our current level of knowledge. But the widespread opinion that our consciousness is a product of our brains, hence will dissolve with them, is exactly the same: a belief, not a proven fact. Hence, we can choose between these equally unproven beliefs.

Curiously, I extended the scope of my reading to various other phenomena and slowly started to accommodate the possibility that there is, in fact, a background reality that we usually do not easily perceive with our five senses. But I still had difficulty to fully trust my findings, hence I looked for personal experiences. None of my experiments with meditation and self-hypnosis had achieved that over the years. The utmost experience I reached was discovering the joy that resides at the centre of my chest. I did some courses on "energy healing" and experienced unexpected perceptions that convinced me that there is more than science has proven. Yet these experiences did not answer my big question: Is there an afterlife or not?

Therefore, I was delighted when I discovered Michael Newton's method of inducing a journey to the "life between lives" in a hypnotic trance. I had reluctantly accepted that reincarnation probably exists although the concept never appealed to me since I have always felt privileged and lucky in this life and the idea of forgetting everything and starting over from scratch felt horrifying.

In early 2017, I finally set out on my journey to the "life between lives." It was the first time that I was hypnotised by another person and a stunning experience. While experimenting with self-hypnosis, I had never felt like I was in a trance state. Now I learned that my idea of trance had been entirely wrong and that I had experienced it often. In fact, I realised that I have always loved trance states.

The first amazing thing was that I recalled a so far unknown memory of baby Me – and then my thoughts when entering this body. I will not lie, there were also elements that could have come from my conscious mind, so I am still sceptical about them. But two aspects completely convinced me of the reality of the experience:

1. the utterly unspectacular prior life that I visited since my vivid imagination would never have made this up,

2. meeting unexpected people in my soul group while some I had expected were missing.

And when I made the acquaintance of my soul guide, he touched my soul-self in a surprising way. It also seemed that the practitioner could directly perceive some of the things that I experienced. She did not ask suggestive questions about the core elements, but she told me afterwards that writing, mediation, and coaching would suit me.

This journey made me much more confident that death is not the end - a conviction that I have further consolidated ever since. Between the first writing of this chapter and its publication, death struck our family again. Although it was even closer this time, I am coping much better with it now than last time.

Another lasting effect of this journey was that I now could connect to my inner guidance securely by entering a trance state.

Beyond Loss of Purpose

As I felt lost with the entirely new challenge of not knowing what to do with my life after my bitter realisation that I had lost my purpose, I had started to work on getting back in touch with my "inner compass" back then.

Maybe for the first time in my life I fully realised that I wanted not just economic stability but financial abundance. It was not only about safety and peace of mind. I also wanted the means, freedom, and energy for the creative life I envisioned. And I wanted to be able to teach the children of my family how to get there too. Ever since that realisation, I have wished to cover my expenses through passive income.

But I still lacked that when my contract ended in spring 2015. I felt constantly exhausted, yet it took me a while to notice that I was still doing the exact same thing as before: Pushing myself to *do* something, feverishly trying to find a solution before my money would run out. That only drained my energy further.

Eventually, I realised that I had to allow myself "holidays at home" with lots of sleep and doing only what I wanted. After a week in which I once even felt well-rested at waking for the first time in ages, my state had improved greatly. Thankfully, as I was offered an interim professorship from 2016 to 2017. By early 2016, I was drowning in work again. This job allowed me to save more money, but it also demanded my full energy and attention as I was travelling some nine hundred kilometres per week and teaching four classes.

At the end of it, I had opened up to doing something completely different for a living: I had broken free from my mental cage. But what could this completely different thing be? It was a strange experience to enter my fifth decade clueless like a nineteen-year-old after finishing school.

Becoming a coach was an obvious option since I had always listened to other people's problems and tried to find solutions. A few years later, one of my friends said I had been coaching her for ages. And coaching did fit with two of my big passions: learning about human beings and transcending current limits. Although coaching still was not perfect, I decided in mid-2017 to prepare myself with a psychology education at a private school.

Yet, when you lose a strong purpose, it is hard to retrieve that level of excitement and enthusiasm. The other big problem that I had underestimated was how crushing the loss of identity was. Academics identify with their work to an insane degree, usually accompanied by great pride since it is all but easy to make your way into the ranks of academia.

Halfway through a new interim professorship in 2018-2019 that had come along just in time to pay for my school, I realised that I had transitioned to feeling out of place at the university, yet I did not feel as though I belonged anywhere else either. If I was not a researcher anymore, then what was I?

Although I soon understood that being a researcher is part of my personality, I experienced an uncomfortable period of feeling "in-between" that reminded me of the time shortly before my first degree when I felt done being "nothing."

When time passed, this feeling started to shrink all by itself. I began to feel better and defining my identity in professional terms became less important. Perhaps my loss had given me the freedom to resume my personal development without the limits of a fixed social identity, but something else had shown up that soothed the pain and absorbed my now homeless passion and enthusiasm. It also created the most powerful shift I have experienced since my teens and even led me to writing this chapter. Once more, it came through what I currently regard as the most powerful medium on earth: video streaming.

Escaping the Big Black Hole and More Miracles

In late 2015, I was pointed to the option of streaming films and shows to my phone. One show that I discovered in early 2016 was going to change my life. While I spent many hours in trains and hotel rooms for a year, I used part of the time to watch downloaded episodes on my phone. In early February 2017, I arrived at the last episode on my journey home after my last class.

To go into the depth of my experience while watching an epic show on the smallest possible screen on that evening on the train would lead too far and this experience would be hard to describe anyway. I have always used fiction to extend my experience of life, and my emotional engagement with film and TV characters has often been something to work through, sometimes in writing. This time, the emotions were unusually strong, deep, and persistent.

Hence, I started, once more, to search the internet for people to talk to. To my delight, I found a huge fandom on social media – and the actor whose performance had left such a mark. Impressed by his versatility in a range of roles and genres and by his kindness towards the fans, I started interacting, eventually building a friendship with him.

By July 2017, I had ended up not only with wonderful new friends, but also running the actor's fan pages across platforms with his blessing. Over the years, as I began to understand some mechanisms better, our collaboration evolved to include other PR activities. In the process, I experienced an explosion of creativity that changed my self-perception as I learned to edit pictures and videos and even started to practice drawing and 3D sculpting.

Obviously, I thought that I would rather spend my time sorting my own life. But this hobby was incredibly rewarding, and after a few months, I realised in hindsight that it had filled the big black hole that had started to open in my life after my teaching duties had ended.

In late spring, I received a clear message in alpha state: that it was okay, and I was planting seeds, emphasised by a plant bulb appearing in my mind's eye. Back then, I assumed that meant acquiring skills for a future business. How much bigger the picture looks now! And who knows what I cannot see yet?

One example is my journey to this book: I had connected with Katie Carey on Instagram through my actor fan page prior to my business journey. Later, it turned out that she had first thought my account was run by the man himself (I used his image as a profile photo). They had performed together as students. When Katie posted about a coaching course in 2020 and I signed up through her link, we connected on Facebook. It was the start of a beautiful friendship.

"Evolving on Purpose" could label a central driving force of my life, and during the past two years, it has become increasingly clear that I have been unconsciously "co-creating with the divine", or: with forces of the background reality. I had some mind-blowing experiences – from a feeling of indestructibility and a deep, peaceful love at my very core in late 2021 to a dream client, promising investment opportunities, and a miraculous unexpected profit showing up throughout 2022 whenever I managed to relax fully.

But there is another reason why this seemed the perfect time to join this book: I have resumed working on a dream that had been waiting in my drawer for over a decade.

A New Vision

I had written part of a high fantasy novel that somehow evolved by itself until I got stuck in conceptual problems, not least because I wanted to shape the magic of my fantasy world according to real-life spiritual concepts and felt I could not do them justice yet. But I dreamt of seeing it on screen one day.

It was my work on the actor fan pages that eventually triggered the idea to shortcut the process by turning it into a script right away. Meanwhile, I also felt ready for the spiritual aspects. Hence, I took the leap to approach my dream cast for the main character in summer 2019 and received a positive reaction. I hoped to generate enough income with my business to free up part of my savings for funding the initial steps of the project. That, however, did not work out.

In autumn 2019, I finished my last term as an interim professor and prepared my coaching business in an intuitive flow. But due to delays, I ended up starting in the middle of a pandemic and struggled to generate clients right away. That curbed my enthusiasm. My flow eroded as I entered the next year with several zero-income months.

While testing various kinds of paid ads, I also spent part of my savings on coaching that gave me more clarity about my passion for my fantasy project which combines my expertise and experience from academia, hypnotism, and personal spiritual growth.

As the pandemic had given me the opportunity to gain more insights into the entertainment industry, my appreciation for the enormous creative contributions that actors can make had risen. A broader vision emerged: the power of plot and characters to build empathy in a worldwide audience for the benefit of our fractioned world combined with a transparent, fan-friendly production process in which everyone feels appreciated and actors are treated as co-creators of their characters (since they get much deeper into them than the writer).

Meanwhile, I had rendered my story outline into English and realised that its scope calls for a series – a format that I prefer over movies because it offers more space for character development. Rich characters are at the core of this story about the quest for purpose and belonging of a man lost between two cultures: a tale about the meaning of life and death, about identity and prejudice, about maturing and family and the pitfalls of desire, fuelled by the power of magic that is connected to the core of the universe.

Perspective is key, hence there are no small parts when the power of cross-cultural belief systems is being shattered, paving the way to even more monumental repercussions. In this enthralling adventure, *Prince of Persia* meets *Game of Thrones* – but with flying carpets and a vision for a brighter world. This project combines all I have learned in this life and it will continue to evolve along with myself.

At the time of writing, all we need to start working on a proof-of-concept pilot short are far-sighted sponsors who love the project's vision and provide funding in exchange for the publicity they can gain for their own business through their support.

The Bigger Picture

I do not know yet if this project is what will finally unleash the force of my full potential. But I do know that it is one of my biggest dreams that has matured even more through personal breakthroughs. When I spiralled into a rough place as my income was not covering my expenses and my savings decreased, I finally found the key to reducing worries: enjoying life regardless as I learned to regulate my emotions more efficiently than ever.

An important step to feeling as happy as possible right where I am and increasing my serenity despite rapidly deteriorating circumstances was, yet again, a thorough personal experience.

In October 2021, I discovered heart coherence meditation and found an easy and powerful way to have more presence in everyday life. I started to keep part of my consciousness focused on the feeling at the centre of my chest while reading, watching TV, going for a walk, or listening to others.

One day, I was sitting on the balcony in the warm, autumn sunshine and reading in this state of presence. Suddenly, warmth, joy, and strength arose inside me. I felt truly indestructible, since I carry the source of happiness right inside me, always at my disposal.

Before 2022, I had two more big experiences of joy and warmth, calmness and love for life filling my chest which stayed for hours. In this bliss, I did not feel like engaging with anything that was not aligned to it. Can you imagine what our world would look like if that was a common everyday experience?

My theory has always been that people who are mainly happy or content – not stressed-out by existential dread, competition, or other pressures – are least likely to harm others. Therefore, I thought lifting material worries off everyone's back would address this sufficiently and create a much better world. I still believe that is crucial. So many people would instantly become happier and more relaxed, hence healthier. So much energy, time, and creativity are locked up in worries and hectic action and could be unleashed to serve our world. Everyone would win.

But since there are enough people without material worries who are still unhappy, there is another important ingredient of a brighter world: a strong connection with our own inner strength, guidance, and indestructibility. My core mission as a coach is to facilitate that through trance journeys to the power within while my bigger mission aims at a wider audience, utilizing the most powerful medium on earth for spreading my vision through the visual storytelling of my fantasy series.

Since we can never see the full picture in advance, I now work on *trusting* that I am always "co-creating with the Divine" on my life journey of "evolving on purpose." The part of me that longs for material security is still freaking out frequently, but my inner adventurer loves the ride.

About the Author

Dr. Susanne Kurz is a German scholar and life coach. She has worked for almost 20 years as a university researcher and teacher on the History of the Persianate Culture in Iran, Middle Asia and India before embarking on a new adventure.

In her "second life" as a coach and hypnotist, she supports people who feel stuck or caged, who want to reconnect with their inner compass (intuition) or simply to feel calmer and happier where they are. One thing that has never changed is her eager interest in people and their stories.

Susanne's favourite coaching tools are the hypnotic trance and her own training process for more inner peace and happiness. Based on the experience she has gained through a hobby, she also offers coaching on IMDb, Wikipedia and social media to actors.

Her most exciting project in the making is an original high fantasy TV series that combines her unique experiences and skills to form a vision for a brighter world embedded in the story of a gripping adventure.

EVOLVING ON PURPOSE

Connect with Susanne below::

- https://www.susannekurz-coaching.de
- https://www.susanne-kurz.com

TAMI ROACH

Spirit Rescue

Have you ever wondered what happens when we pass from this physical life? Pondered if there was life after death, or do we simply cease to exist? Is Heaven, or Home or the Other Side real? (I'll use these terms interchangeably). Does everyone go to Heaven? If not, where do they go? We all have contemplated some, if not all, of these questions at one time during our lives.

I have had Spirit around me since the mid-1980's, during my teen years, although I didn't understand why. It wasn't abnormal for me to hear my name being called when I was home alone. However, it wasn't an acceptable, or normal, topic of conversation to inquire about so I didn't speak of it. I realized a bit later in life that I was an empath, which is more than being overly sensitive, which is what I was told many times. I didn't realize that as an empath I soaked up the good – and bad – energy and emotions around me and took them on as my own. I didn't know that my sensitivity would draw spirit to me and that was the reason the door to the unseen was ajar. The moment I realized I was an empath was when my sensitivities and paranormal experiences suddenly made sense.

Fast forward several decades, and countless paranormal experiences, to the Fall of 2017 and two unforgettable experiences that took place in a hotel suite in Pennsylvania. I was exhausted but could not fall asleep. My attention kept being drawn toward the bedroom door, which I believed was because the living room light was shining bright beneath the door.

After several hours, I finally fell asleep, and in my dream state, I saw a young man with short, sandy-blonde hair and contemporary clothing standing on the side of my bed looking down at me. I looked over at my son sleeping in his bed. As I rolled over to look at my husband sleeping behind me, I saw two tall shadow figures standing at the foot of the bed – one standing behind the young man but in front of the door on my side and the other at the end of the bed on my husband's side.

I calmly turned back over to look at this young man. We stared at one another for a moment, neither speaking nor moving, and then I woke up feeling slightly perplexed as I looked around a dark, empty room.

The second experience began when I fell asleep again, and then two young women were in the room – one sitting on my husband's side of the bed and the other standing in front of the window next to her. I got up out of bed and began arguing – and then physically fighting – with the blonde-haired woman sitting on the bed. The woman by the window kept trying to get between us.

My husband woke up due to all the commotion. As the woman lay across his legs, my husband sat up, turned her face toward me, and yelled, "You killed her!"

Her lifeless eyes and the blue coloring of her face confirmed the same. I yelled back, "Good!" and immediately woke up.

That morning, when getting into the shower, I noticed a quarter-sized bruise on my right forearm that was not present the night before. That was validation that I was not just dreaming, but something paranormal, in fact, had occurred.

I call myself a Spirit Rescuer, but what is that? I am a Medium, although not in the traditional sense of the title as one would expect. Other than my loved ones in spirit, I have mostly communicated with earthbound souls, via pendulum, as well as with my Spirit Team.

After some time using the pendulum, I began feeling the tingling of energy in my hands, which led me to reiki energy healing. Unbeknownst to me at that time, learning and practicing reiki self-treatments would thrust the door to the spirit realm wide open. As I continue to heal from a challenging childhood, finally embrace my authentic self and the abilities I have ignored for far too long to be "normal," my gifts continue to evolve and grow. I find myself decreasing the use of the pendulum as I've begun conducting my crossing ceremony with the Masters, Teachers and Loved Ones through my Akashic records.

My Spirit Team requested many months ago that I "help mediums know that Earthbounds exist," and they have guided me here in beautiful synchronicity to share a fraction of my experiences and practice so that other mediums may have some tools, if needed, should they decide to begin assisting Earthbound souls to cross over into the Light to continue positive, forward momentum on their souls' journeys. The information I will share here is from my own experiences and not intended to discredit anyone else's practices and experiences as we are all uniquely gifted.

That being said, my experience with the Earthbound is that these are souls who, for a variety of reasons personal to them, consciously decided not to cross over into the Light at the time of their last physical passing. My understanding is that when a soul decides to stay earthbound, all positive, forward movement on that soul's journey becomes stagnant for the length of time he/she is earthbound. For simplification, God/Creator/Source decides when these souls will cross over and sends them to the medium who will assist them in doing so as they are unable to cross into the Light on their own.

We live in a world of polarity: day and night, good and bad, light and dark, love and hate. During communication with one of my Ascended Master guides, he defined darkness as the "absence of light" and the longer souls stay in the earthbound realm away from Divine Light, the darker/more negative they become. I have crossed souls passing as recently as four years ago to several thousand years ago, and the longer they remained earthbound, the darker they projected themselves to be.

Many Earthbounds have told me, "Death favors no one." By this, they do not refer to their physical death but instead to their existence in the earthbound realm, which they describe as all-enveloping darkness, ripe with pervasive fear, with no glimmer of hope, love, or life. Their main purpose becomes to instill fear amongst themselves and the living as well. You can liken these souls as "ghosts" that cause the paranormal phenomena that the living consider hauntings.

While some of these souls do whatever they can to create fear, others wish only to let you know they are present and need your help. The Earthbound let me know they're present in a variety of ways:

1. Clairvoyantly – I see the person (or part of them) in my mind's eye.

2. Clairaudiently – someone will telepathically tell me their name, what happened to them, or I hear growling with my physical ears.

3. Clairsentiently – I can feel the energy in the room or receive information through my physical body.

4. In my dream state, or

5. Through physical phenomenon, such as opening doors.

When communicating with the Earthbound, I inquire as to how they passed, i.e., murder, sudden death, or illness and what transpired immediately thereafter. They have all stated that upon their physical deaths, their guides gave them a choice: (1) cross over into the Light to the Other Side, or (2) remain in the earth realm.

Upon their decision to remain earthbound, their guides gave them what the Departed termed as "heart light." This "heart light" (or what I call "God Spark") is a spark of Divine Light placed into their heart space. In my experience with the Earthbound, no matter how dark they portray themselves to be, they still possess their heart light but have either forgotten it, or it has severely diminished over time. Because there is a level of "darkness" that the Earthbound can harbor as many were not what society would have considered "good" people in life, it is important that mediums keep themselves protected whether communicating with them or not.

You do not have to communicate with them to draw them in as I have had a few souls follow me home when running errands. Implement protection practices and tools if you do not already do so. I clear, ground, and protect myself several times a day, including reiki self-treatment. I also carry crystals/stones with me for these purposes. Most importantly, I invoke Source Light protection. (I do this as well for my family, pets, home, and property).

After cleansing my sacred space, crystals, stones, other tools, and myself with white sage and palo santo, I place my crystals or stones in a circle around me when conducting my ceremony. Follow your intuition for what is the best practice for you. I also invoke Archangel Michael, our divine protector, for shielding and removal of any energies (or entities) back to the earthbound realm.

Earthbounds thrive upon the fear that they evoke from you if you allow it. I opine that is one reason mediums may not consider communicating or crossing them. It is important in dealing with the Earthbound that you have released your fear, stand in your power, and use your discernment. Once you have shown that you are unafraid, simply command them to unmask and their façade should fall away.

It's imperative that you have faith and trust that your Spirit Team, your higher power, the Angelic realm, the Ascended Masters, and the Universe will protect you. God (or Creator or

Source – I will use these terms interchangeably), all involved Spirit Teams, and the Beings of Light of the Higher Realms are present at every crossing that I and all other mediums perform. Call upon them for guidance and follow your intuition when performing your own ceremony.

I have asked the Departed to look around and describe to me everything that they see. They see light so bright that it hurts their eyes. They see God, Jesus, Angels, Ascended Masters, thousands of Beings of Light, as well as their guides. It serves the highest good of all to remember that the Earthbound are wounded souls who harbor their own fears. To best assist these souls, it is important that your space be judgment-free and that you treat them with compassion despite their misdeeds in life.

For these souls, the darkness is a façade behind which they keep their own fears, faults, traumas, and misdeeds hidden from those of us who possess the ability to see, feel, and intuit all that they wish to keep secret. I surmise that part of the reason they attempt to instill fear is to deter us from determining their truth.

They have imparted to me that they fear God's judgment, Divine Light, and they will fear you as they, initially, fear me at the beginning of each crossing. Surprised by this, I have asked many why they fear me, and it is always the same response – because of the brightness of my Light. I remind them that they, too, are children of God, which the darker Earthbound will deny. The final part of my healing work with the Departed is an exercise in assisting them in increasing their God Spark hidden within the recesses of their hearts to allow them to remember their divinity and God's promise that they can return Home should they so choose differently for another chance at "life" in the Light on the Other Side.

As we have free will, so do they as well. It is still their decision to stay, or to cross. After this healing exercise, however, most souls experience a profound shift, release their fear, and are then ready to cross over to be reunited with their loved ones on the Other Side.

I have had a few darker Earthbounds that did not cross over immediately, with one elderly man asking me to send him to Hell instead. He was an ornery soul who was an alcoholic in life. His anger festered and became more pronounced in death. After listening to him spew a few expletives at me, he told me he never experienced love.

Knowing this to be untrue, I asked if he had been married. He hesitated momentarily before remembering that he had left behind a wife and adult children. I asked him to go back to the moments before his physical death and describe what happened. He remembered his wife kissing his cheek, whispering in his ear that she loved him, and his children were sobbing in the background as he was expiring from cirrhosis.

That remembrance of love was the beginning of his healing. After implementing the God Spark exercise, he experienced a huge shift and was eager to return Home to be reunited with his family after being earthbound for more than 300 years. In my experience, souls that do not cross immediately tend to observe the process another time or two before coming back to accept the healing you offer, and eventually they will cross at a later session.

As I continue this journey, God has entrusted me with crossing over a larger number of earthbound souls. What started as one or two souls a month, has evolved to performing mass crossings for a minimum of over a thousand souls during my weekly session. I only directly communicate with those who have presented themselves to me through my clairs or physical phenomena during the week as they will be the souls requiring the most counseling and healing.

Some, however, do not require healing other than an increase in their God Spark. For example, some souls stay behind to be with their family. However, in my experience, earthbound souls cannot visit with the family that they left behind. Once these souls have been decreed to return Home, they can develop tunnel vision to that end.

Once, I had one Earthbound woman who cared naught for my boundaries, which had been repeated to her after she opened my bathroom door the first time. She still opened various doors in my home throughout the week, including one night while my husband and I were eating dinner. I heard a bedroom door unlatch in the hallway. When I went to investigate, two of my cats were sitting in front of the open door with a look upon their faces as if to ask, "What just happened?"

During my session, this woman indicated she had passed from a heart attack many decades ago leaving behind two young children. She stayed in this realm wanting to remain with them, but she could not. Her only focus was wanting to go Home as that was the only way she would be able to visit her children, who were now seniors but still living. It was also the only way to reunite with them upon their passing.

Most likely, however, apologies need to be made to alleviate the pain and anger that were brewing in life and fermenting in the darkness of the earthbound realm. Forgiveness needs to be given and received. Finally, they need to increase their God Spark within. As I begin to work with a specific person or group, all other souls present are encouraged to participate to receive the benefit of all counseling and healings so they may cross over. I say to them, as I would say to you, absorb and integrate what resonates, and leave all that does not.

I am providing below a basic list of steps that I take to prepare for and move through my crossing ceremony:

1. **Set your intention.** Begin by setting your specific intention to hold a crossing ceremony several days in advance, and to receive information to assist the Earthbound for the highest good of all. This puts

your Spirit Team, including your gatekeepers, the Higher Realms, and Departed on notice, and begins to set the boundaries and your expectations for the session.

2. **Clear yourself.** On the day of the ceremony, clear yourself, pendulum and board, crystals and/or other tools, and your sacred space with your tools of choice. I do this with reiki energy, singing bowls, white sage, and palo santo.

3. **Ground yourself.** Ground yourself through your usual grounding techniques.

4. **Restate your specific intentions for the session.** This helps to forge a better connection and reinforces your boundaries and expectations. It is at this time I bring in Source light to strengthen my pillar of light and increase my vibration so that I may connect with my Team.

5. **Ask the Departed why they have come.** When communicating with an Earthbound, I ask them why they have come. Some say that they have come to instill fear. If that is the case, disarm the Departed by showing that you are unafraid and command them to unmask. They may then say that God has decreed that they cross over. This is where you inquire as to why they stayed earthbound. In my experience, there is always a reason souls decide to

stay earthbound. Find out what that reason is and follow the breadcrumbs to get the information needed to understand the root cause and core issues of the Departed's actions and misdeeds during their life as that is where healing is required.

The Earthbound can only cross once all issues are resolved. That is when I implement the exercise for increasing their heart light, or God Spark. To do this, I ask them to close their eyes and place their hands over their heart space. I then ask God to bestow upon them His gift of an increase in their heart light so that they may feel His love and forgiveness and know that He is fulfilling His promise to them by blessing them with the gift of going Home to be reunited with their loved ones awaiting them on the Other Side. It is at this time that I tell the Departed that I will call forward their loved ones and ancestors on the Other Side to greet them upon their crossing.

6. **Open the door to Heaven.** There is a specific area in my sacred space where I burn a white candle and visualize opening a door of Divine Light to the

7. **Other Side.** The Departed will be eager to go Home as soon as the door is open. After a few

moments, you may confirm with your Team that all souls have crossed.

8. **Close the door to Heaven.** I then close the door to the Other Side by simply saying the following intention, "Now that all Departed have gone Home to be with their loved ones and ancestors in the Light, I close the door to Heaven, and so it is done."

9. **Close the ceremony.** When setting your intention to close communication for the entire ceremony as well, be certain to give thanks to God, your Team, and the Higher Realms for their presence and assistance. State your intention to close communication for the entire ceremony and end your intention with "and so it is."

10. **Clear, Ground, Protect.** Once the door of Divine Light and communication for the ceremony are closed, use the method of choice to clear yourself, your various tools, and sacred space. Ground and protect.

Now that so many earthbound souls are coming in for mass crossing, I have created what I call a "Safe House" and "Healing House," etheric abodes where the Earthbounds can go, depending upon their level of darkness, to wait for crossing so that they are not in my home.

At the end of my sessions, I set the intention for my gatekeepers to escort new arrivals to the "House" most appropriate for them. For``` the darkest Earthbound, I set the intention for Archangel Michael to escort them back to the earthbound realm until I hold my next crossing ceremony. The Departed still come in to make themselves known through my clairs on occasion, but after instituting both Houses, the physical activity in my home has become minimal.

While it is ultimately each soul's decision whether to cross or not, I would be remiss if I did not mention that you bear some God-given responsibility in their decision-making process. That responsibility should not be taken lightly as you are impacting each soul's journey and evolution that is brought to you to jump start the healing process and assist in crossing into the Light.

In closing, I would like to leave you with a message from my Spirit Team, which has reinforced to me the importance of why I – and many other mediums – may as well, assist the Earthbound in choosing love over fear, Light over darkness, and affording them another chance at life on the Other Side as God intended for them from the beginning: "You are God's feet on the ground loosening the grip of darkness on humanity."

If you take nothing else from this chapter and decide not to perform spirit rescue, please still take a moment to ponder the importance of that statement and consider your role - not just in your own ascension journey, but in that of humanity, and Gaia as well.

We are all one.

About the Author

Tami Roach is a lifelong resident of the rural Catskill Mountains of New York and the youngest of seven girls. She is an Empath, Certified Reiki Master, Akashic Records reader, Dragon Protocol Practitioner, Starseed, and Spirit Rescuer.

Wait! What is a Spirit Rescuer? She is a medium who communicates with, begins the healing process for, and crosses over earthbound souls who have existed in the darkness and pervasive fear of the earthbound realm anywhere from a few years to a few thousand years.

She helps earthbound souls to cross over to the Other Side so that they may continue their souls' journey in the Light and love of Home as Creator/God/Source always intended. As she does so, she lightens up Heaven and Earth as loved ones are reunited, which simultaneously assists humanity and Gaia in their own ascension.

Connect with Tami below:

spiritrescuer12758@gmail.com

ABOUT SOULFUL VALLEY PUBLISHING

Katie Carey, created the Soulful Valley Publishing House in May 2021. International Best-Selling Author Katie is the host of the Soulful Valley Podcast ranking globally in the Top 0.5%. Katie uses both the podcast and the multi-author books as a platform to help metaphysical coaches, energy healers, authors, and creative business owners to elevate their work, so that the people they are here to serve can find them.

Formerly the founder of STAGES, an alternative mental health charity for seven years, Katie is an advocate for Mental Health and Emotional Wellbeing, particularly since her own health was affected when she was ill-health retired due to disabilities at the Age of 48, with conditions brought about by trauma and a lifetime of toxic relationships.

Katie loves blending science and spirituality together and collaborates with people on the same wavelength in her multi-author books. Most authors have stories of synchronicities that led to them writing in books with Katie.

Katie's aim is to bring these concepts and ideas to more people who are seeking ways to support their own mental, spiritual, emotional, and physical wellbeing.

Katie has a history of working in TV, Radio, and Theatre as an Actress and Singer, which she manifested into her life in her teens. Katie lives in a Northamptonshire Village in the UK, where she is a Mum to three adult children and "Nanny Katie" to her grandchildren. Katie has made it her life's work to educate people to find healthier solutions and break free from ancestral, toxic, and generational patterns of lack and trauma. Katie is passionate about raising consciousness and currently does this with her work as a Mentor, Coach, Podcaster, Author, Publisher, and through her songs and poetry.

If you would like to collaborate with Katie in one of her multi-author books or to write your own solo book…

Connect with Katie below:

- Website: https://www.soulfulvalley.com
- Email: soulfulvalleypodcast@gmail.com
  FB, Twitter, IG and LinkedIn @soulfulvalley
- Podcast: https://apple.co/3BkJdkn

ABOUT SOULFUL VALLEY PUBLISHING

Katie's Amazon Author Profile:

More books both solo and co-authored by Katie Carey Available on Amazon.

Soulful Poems: Heal the Heart and Soul

Evolving on Purpose: Mindful Ancestors Paving the Way for Future Generations

Intuitive: Knowing Her Truth

Soul Warrior: Accessing Realms Beyond the Veil

Entangled No More: Women Who Broke Free from Toxic Relationships Building Their Own Empires

www.ingramcontent.com/pod-product-compliance
Lightning Source LLC
Chambersburg PA
CBHW052028090426
42739CB00010B/1822